HUMAN RIGHTS U.S.STYLE

HUMAN RIGHTS U.S. STYLE

From Colonial Times through the New Deal

by Claude M. Lightfoot

INTERNATIONAL PUBLISHERS, New York

COPYRIGHT ACKNOWLEDGEMENTS

The Supreme Court by Patricia Acheson, 1961, Dodd, Mead & Co., Inc.; *The Sinews of American History: An Economic History* by Clark C. Spence, ©1964 by Clark C. Spence, reprinted by permission of the publishers, Farrar, Straus & Giroux, Inc.: *The Better Half* by Andrew Sinclair, ©1965, Harper & Row; *Century of Struggle* by Eleanor Flexner, ©1968, Harvard University Press; *One Continual Cry: David Walker's Appeal to the Colored Citizens of the World 1829-1830*, ed. by Herbert Aptheker, 1965, Humanities Press; *Before The Mayflower* by Lerone Bennett, Jr., ©1969, Johnson Publishing Co.; *History of the Supreme Court* by Gustavus Myers, ©1925, Charles Kerr and Co.; *The Negro In The Making Of America*, Rev. Edn., by Benjamin Quarles, ©1964, 1969 by Macmillan Publishing Co., Inc.; Reprinted from *The Abolitionists: The Growth Of A Dissenting Minority* by Merton L. Dillon, ©1974 by Northern Illinois University Press. By permission of the publisher; *The Crippled Giant* by William J. Fullbright, ©1972, Random House; *Democracy In America* by Alexis de Tocqueville, translated by Henry Reeve, revised by Francis Bower, and edited by Phillips Bradley, ©1945, Random House; *Slavery Two* by Milton Meltzer, ©1972, Contemporary Books, Inc.; Reprinted with the permission of Charles Scribner's Sons from *Dispossessing The American Indian* by Wilbur Jacobs, ©1971 Wilbur R. Jacobs; *Slavery* by Stanley M. Elkins, 1976, 3rd ed., The University of Chicago Press.

Library of Congress Cataloging in Publication Data

Lightfoot, Claude M   1910-
    Human rights U.S. style.

    Includes bibliographical references and index.
    1. Civil rights—United States—History. I. Title.
JC599.U5L49   323.4'0973   77-21113
ISBN 0-7178-0481-X
ISBN 0-7178-0477-1 pbk.

CONTENTS

To Louise and William L. Patterson

PREFACE

WHEN THE American revolutionaries struck a blow against their oppressors in 1776 their actions were hailed all over the world. The people of the world in general, and in Europe in particular, regarded it as a turning point in world development. They joined with Thomas Jefferson who proclaimed that the revolutionaries had acted on behalf of all mankind.

In 1787, when the Founding Fathers went to Philadelphia and produced a constitution to guide the newly born nation, once again peoples all over the world proclaimed their acts as beneficial to all mankind.

What were the sparks igniting the hopes and aspirations of the peoples of the world? They are to be found in the fact that the American Revolution and the U.S. Constitution symbolized a turning point in humanity's age-long struggles against tyrannical and oppressive societies of Europe, and offered an opportunity for the common people to come to America to seek a place of their own. It provided hope for peoples of other colonies who were oppressed by the European powers. While the American Revolution and the U.S. Constitution represented these things, at the same time the new society also gave birth to some of the worst pages in world history.

The colonies and then the nation were born with severe class, sexual and unprecedented racial oppression. Neither the Revolution nor the Constitution changed the character of this oppression. If anything, following both events, they were greatly aggravated. These elements in the nation's tradition have been ignored or greatly underplayed. Whatever discrepancies are noted have been played down in the name of the progress we have made. What most historians have done in this regard is one of the biggest cover-ups in history.

As a Black citizen of the United States, whose people have been subjected to some of the most brutal treatment known to history, I have never had illusions that the system we live under could be characterized as a people's democracy.

As a child I was never impressed with July 4th orations which proclaimed this government as the most democratic political structure in the world. I can recall in my grammar school classes, while others sang phrases such as: "My country 'tis of thee, sweet land of liberty," I paraphrased them and sang: "My country 'tis of thee, the land of 'lynching bee.'" To me the Statue of Liberty at New York was the shield behind which thousands of my Black mothers and fathers, brothers and sisters, had been burned alive on public squares in holiday style. I was all the more alienated when I learned that not a single white person was ever tried and convicted for a lynching. It was clear that the machinery of government did not operate to protect the constitutional rights of Black people.

With this background I asked, "What kind of a democracy can this be?" When I came to manhood and studied American history in more detail, I concluded that the government is democratic but for "whites only!" Later I joined the Communist Party and studied the works of Marx, Engels, Lenin, William Z. Foster and others, and answers to my questions began to fall in place. I learned that in a class-structured society absolute and full democracy is impossible, for white as well as Black people. The governmental apparatus, no matter what form it takes, will always act in the interest of the class that is in power.

In our time and at the birth of this nation, the government has always done what was in the best interest of Big Business, the monied class. This was true even when the people had wrested concessions of a democratic character from the ruling class.

It is true that the governmental system as operated by the bourgeoisie was more advanced and progressive than the feudal and kingly dynasties of the past. (We should also note, however, that capitalism has also given birth to the facist form of state which marks a repudiation of all democratic forms.) But even these facts do not make the point that the present system was ever in its basic content a real people's democracy. Because of the distortions and over-simplifications of our democratic heritage, because the Bicentennial celebration was used to take advantage of a progressive tradition to bolster up a corrupt and dying system, and because of our hypocritical stance in world affairs where we pose as champions of human rights, I decided to focus in on what some may view as a negative approach to our national tradition. Whatever the greatness of the revolutionary tradition of 1776, this nation was born on a class basis. And upon this train there was brought into existence a society based on a racist and sexist tradition that has dominated every feature of our life since. Class, racial and sexual oppression did not begin here in the United States. The European colonizers practiced them long before they came to these shores. The racist feature, though born elsewhere, reared its highest and most terrible development here in our country. It began with Native Americans and with the enslavement of Black people. Eventually it reached out and persecuted all non-white peoples.

In preparation for this book I have relied to a great degree on original forms of research done by historians of the latter part of the nineteenth and the beginning of the twentieth centuries. In the recent period a new group of sociologists, economists and historians has come on the scene, and they, too, have helped to lay a factual basis for the material with which I shall deal with in this book.

However, most historians while revealing weaknesses in this or that institution still do not relate them to the system of capitalism. And when this is done, we are told we are making progress and that under capitalism and the U.S. Constitution we have instruments for greater changes. In this context the world of capitalism is presented as the "free world" and the world of socialism as the "slave world." Moreover, most historians who have muckraked the system have done it against the backdrop of separate institutions of social problems. In this book I have attempted to bring all the problems into a central focus delineating the source of all of them and to show how the main preoccupation of the ruling class has been how to get richer and richer. In this connection I have endeavored to bring to the light of day the contributions made by the common people in all categories to the advancement of democracy in the United States. On the basis of lessons and experience from colonialism through the New Deal, I present what I believe to be some guidelines to meet the problems of today.

ACKNOWLEDGMENTS

I AM deeply indebted to a number of people who helped me in various ways to produce this book. It will not be possible to name all of them. I feel very grateful to the members of the staff at the public libraries in Gary, Indiana who went out of their way to assist me in the research I needed. And Nancy Cohen, Carole McGrady and Joyce Pope Lightfoot were always available when I needed their skills. In many ways their assistance was more than technical. There were many people who read the manuscript and made valuable suggestions. But I especially appreciate the assistance rendered by my attorney and friend of longstanding, John Abt, who filled me in on the role of the U.S. Supreme Court as well as Victoria Mercado who helped me on research dealing with the Mexican people in our history. My knowledge of the genocidal treatment of Native Americans was greatly enhanced by suggestions from Judith Le Blanc, a Native American whose ancestors were forced into the death march called "the trail of tears."

Finally, this book would not have been possible without the inspiration and guidance of my adopted father and teacher, William L. Patterson, who for over forty years kept before me the necessity to present a truer version, the whole truth, of U.S. history, especially as it related to class and racial development. Needless to say that I alone am responsible for both the content and form of this book.

HUMAN RIGHTS U.S. STYLE

PART I

CLASS ORIGIN AND DEVELOPMENT

1 • EUROPEAN BACKGROUND

THE UNITED States was born against the background of the profound upheavals and class changes that took place on the European continent from the sixteenth century onward.

Revolutionary change took place in transportation and commerce, and for the first time in history the whole world was brought together as a single unit. A new class, a new system, came to power, bringing with it a tremendous growth in technology, science and culture; but also some of the worst forms of human oppression the world had ever witnessed.

The changes in transportation and commerce brought about the decline of the old trading centers in Europe and the growth of a new group of European classes and powers.

In the centuries which followed the demise of the Roman Empire, contact and trade relations among Europe, Asia and Africa were maintained by the Italian cities of Venice and Genoa. These cities, unlike Rome, were not great conquering powers; they were great merchant states. Venice reaped tremendous profits by the process of passing products of the East to the West and vice versa. The main source of the contact was Africa. Products from south of the Sahara were traded via the Arab peoples of North Africa. Consequently, the European people knew practically nothing of the West and East Coasts of Africa and especially below the Sahara. Africans had direct trade relations with Asian peoples. Despite the lack of intimate contact between Asia and Africa and Europe, products flowed back and forth.

Venice imported pepper from Sumatra and Ceylon; ginger from Arabia, India and China; nutmeg, cloves and allspice from the Spice Islands; precious stones from Persia; indigo and sandalwood from India; and glass, silk, rugs, tapestries and porcelain from one or another of the countries of the artistic East. Europe in return sent woolen cloth, arsenic, antimony, quicksilver, tin, copper, lead, coral and specie. After products arrived in Venice, the main transmission belt to northern Europe was the Germanic people living in Central Europe.

There were other overland trade routes between Asia and Europe through what is known today as the Soviet Union. But these were of a limited character since predatory bands along the way made trading hazardous. The Germanic people in Central Europe had contact with both trade centers. In order to protect themselves from attack by robbers and pirates and from extortions by feudal lords, who demanded toll for the right to travel through their provinces, in the thirteenth century a number of German towns entered into a confederation—the Hanseatic League. The League maintained trading posts in the main Baltic and North Sea, and ports, including centers like London and Amsterdam. Thus, the Italian cities and the Hanseatic League, based on Germanic people, were the main trade centers of the Western world until the latter part of the fifteenth century.

What brought about a change? In what way did changes in commercial and economic relations impinge upon the founding of the United States as a nation?

MANY historians attribute the main reasons for the changes to the capture of Constantinople by the Turks in 1453. This development closed to the Western nations many of the routes that formerly were used to maintain trade with Asia. There are some historians who dispute this fact. For example, Harry W. Littlefield says:

Myths have crystallized about two dates often used as the dividing line between medieval and modern times. The dates often quoted are 1453, when Constantinople was captured by the Ottoman Turks, and 1492, when Columbus discovered the New World. Both of these events were important but the transition from medieval to modern times was an evolutionary historical process extending over centuries and was not dependent upon any single event or any single economic social or cultural force.[1]

Littlefield is correct in taking note of the evolutionary process long at work before those major events. But he is wrong in failing to understand that history has its catalytic agents, in which, in a single event or a series of events, historical change is affected not only by the evolutionary process, but by the revolutionary process as well.

The capture of Constantinople and the discovery of America were events that led to revolutionary changes for the whole world. There were many other things which contributed to the necessity for the discovery of the New World. But they have to be placed against the background of the above-mentioned factors.

Writing about what changed the relationship of Venice, Gerard Fiennes, in his book *Sea Power and Freedom*, states:

Partly, the change was due to the fostering care of her kings, partly it was due to the discovery of America and of the passage around the Cape. . . . But in addition to these political and external causes, it may be remembered that during the fourteenth century the population was reduced to one-half by the Black Death, the whole system of Villenage on which agriculture depended was overthrown and that large tracts of land went out of cultivation, while during almost the whole of the fifteenth century the land was distracted and recovery retarded by the troubles leading up to and ensuing upon the War of the Roses. These events upset the balance between town and country and compelled the importation of necessities.[2]

Thus, economic factors became a compelling reason for the European powers to seek new routes to Asia. In this connection, the development of sea power became a necessity. Yet it was precisely at this time that Venice took a different path. With the threat of Osmanic power becoming greater and greater every year, they allowed their fleet to decay and devoted themselves to conquest on the mainland of Italy.

During this period the Atlantic-based nations developed sea power and began the exploration of the New World. Between 1500 and 1550 a large number of explorers crossed the Atlantic and began the exploration of the two continents. Balboa discovered the Pacific Ocean in 1513; Cortez conquered Mexico in 1519 to 1521; Pizarro conquered Peru in 1531-1541; DeSoto penetrated the North American continent in 1539-1542. These explorers and many others turned this period into the age of the European discovery of a new world. In the initial stage the Portuguese and Spanish people led the way.

Vasco Da Gama's discovery of an all-water route to India opened up a period of Portuguese expansion. War fleets as well as merchant ships were sent to the East, and within a few years the Portuguese had made themselves masters of a number of important ports. They laid claim to Africa, Southern Asia and Brazil. In 1580 Spain annexed Portugal and many of the latter's colonies were lost to the Dutch.

All during the period of exploration social forces were gathering on the European continent which would determine the future direction of all humanity. Mercantilism, the rise of a merchant class, the forerunner of the modern bourgeoisie, which had been in evidence for several centuries in the Middle Ages, began to clash with the aristocratic feudal fiefdoms. Ironically, countries like Portugal and Spain, which came first to the New World, did not bring back the material out of which a new bourgeoisie would develop, but mainly the continuation of the tastes and life style of the old feudal system.

The Spanish conquistadores came to the New World in search of gold and other precious metals. And even in cases where plantation life was established, the Spanish settlers viewed their presence as temporary. With wealth extracted from the natives, they visualized returning home and living in an aristocratic style.

MEANWHILE, in Northern Europe, England, Holland and France in particular, the struggle against feudalism and the aristocracy was developing at a faster pace than in Southern Europe. As a result of a number of wars—the Netherlands breaking away from Spain, the war between England and Spain—Spain declined in power. And bourgeois development was accelerated in Holland, Britain and France.

In the sixteenth and seventeenth centuries, the Netherlands was the most powerful of the developing capitalist nations. The circumstance which led to the decline of Holland and France relative to that of Britain is explained by the Hammonds:

> The wars of economic nationalism which succeeded the Wars of Religion of the sixteenth century have to be considered in two aspects. In the first

place, they determined which of the states of Europe should be the predominant power in parts of the world which had great economic importance. They decided between England, France and Holland as competitors for ascending in India and North America. In the second place, the strains of these wars told more severely on industry and commerce in some countries than in others and thus affected their relative material progress. In both these respects England gained at the expense of her neighbors.[3]

Geographic conditions and economic necessities no doubt combined to make Britain seek larger and better ships, which enabled her to outstrip her rivals in making contact with the remote parts of the world.

When the eighteenth century opened, France surpassed England in population—20 million compared to roughly 5 million. But Britain as an island had advantages that counted still more in the long struggle with France. England could pursue her commerce with a single mind, whereas France, and a long land frontier, had to divide her interests and maintain a large land army as well as naval power.

The revolution in commerce, accelerated by these circumstances and events, propelled the merchant class forward. But the new class of merchants rising up in the womb of a feudal system found that system incompatible with its development. The feudal lords and aristocracy, almost an idle class, made the merchant class pay tribute to them in many forms. As a result, the clash between these classes assumed more and more revolutionary forms. The struggle was waged in all the institutions of society. The rising merchant class found the religious forms and concepts alien to its interests. Under feudalism the state and the church were as one—indeed, the church was one of the largest possessors of land.

Feudalism, the kings and the aristocracy constituted the most severe and parasitic form of class exploitation. Nevertheless, in many respects the ethics of the society were not as corrupt and immoral as that brought into the world by capitalism. Karl Marx, while paying tribute to the ability of the new system of capitalism to advance the means of production by science and technology, and to promote democratic reforms in government to hitherto unscaled heights, nonetheless also saw the immorality behind the new system.

In the *Communist Manifesto,* Marx and Frederick Engels wrote:

The bourgeoisie whenever it has gotten the upper hand has put an end to all feudal, patriarchal, idyllic relations. It has pitilessly torn asunder the motley feudal ties that bound man to his "natural superiors," and has left no other bond between man and man than naked self interest, than callous "cash payment." It has drowned the most heavenly ecstasies of religious fervor, of chivalrous enthusiasm, of philistine sentimentalism, in the icy waters of egotistical calculation. It has resolved personal wealth into exchange value. . . . In one word, for exploitation, veiled by religious and political illusions, it has substituted naked, shameless, direct, brutal exploitation.

The bourgeoisie has stripped of its halo every occupation hitherto honored and looked up to with reverent awe. It has converted the physician, the lawyer, the priest, the poet, the man of science, into its paid wage-laborers.

The bourgeoisie has torn away from the family its sentimental veil and reduced the family relation to a mere money relation.[4]

The bourgeoisie, coming to power, waged great ideological struggles and proclaimed great goals such as: "Liberty, Equality and Fraternity," in France; and in the United States, "All men [presumably not women—CML] are endowed by their Creator with the inalienable right to life, liberty and the pursuit of happiness." These were noble statements of purpose and aims but in the light of practice they underscore the hypocrisy of the modern bourgeoisie.

In the name of freedom and free trade, it conducted piracy on the high seas and the most predatory wars in history. When the word "freedom" was used it often meant the right of the big monied boys to rob, exploit, cheat and even murder other people.

The Hammonds observed:

Thus, economic individualism occupied an essential place in radical theory, and as the right of the capitalist was deduced from a theory, it was treated as the right that was absolute and independent of experience. It belonged for the English Radical as for French like the right to life. . . . It involved the right to take what interest and profit you could get; to buy and sell as you please, a right that had been controlled in the Middle Ages.[5]

Capitalism is the system that resulted in the exploitation of all the races that make up humanity. It was the system that gave birth to racism, the most dehumanizing ideology of all time. Obviously, such a system found itself incompatible with many of the teachings of the Bible. And so it set out to change the religious world into a form that would not conflict with its oppressive and unethical practices. Therefore, the church under the old system had to be changed since it was a co-partner in the state apparatus. It, too, owned the land and exploited the serfs; it, too, restricted the bourgeoisie from growing. It furnished the ideological foundation to maintain the rule of the kings and aristocracy.

In this context, the bourgeoisie had to wage a struggle inside the church for progressive purposes. But the bourgeoisie also waged the struggle in order to be free from all forms of moral restraints. They had to denounce many church preachments which clashed with the sordid practices required in profit-making. They had to "render unto Caesar the things that are Caesar's and to God the things that are God's."

No doubt there were many honest men and women who were interested in the moral values as expressed in religious terms. But those were not the main reasons that the bourgeoisie and its ideologists launched a tremendous struggle against the medieval forms of church and state relations.

Europe went through a long period of the most ruthless wars of a religious character. The period of the Reformation, led by Luther in Germany and Calvin in England, is hailed as a great period for the exercise of freedom of religion. The classic form of the bourgeoisie's contempt for the medieval style of church and state relations took place under the leadership of Calvin. Calvinism differed radically from Lutherism. The latter, while challenging many tenets of the Holy Roman Empire, nonetheless did not depart basically from the feudal life style. Lutherism still saw economic relations as consisting of petty dealings of peasants and craftsmen in the small market town. Whenever Lutherism criticized economic relations it did so against what was considered a departure from the natural state of affairs. It was against the forms of greed of gain, the ruthless competition that disturbed the stability of the existing order.

Calvinism, on the other hand, reflected the growing aspirations of the rising bourgeoisie. The industrial and commercial classes were foremost in Calvin's thoughts. Early Calvinism did not abandon the claim of religion to endow economic life with morality. But the life which he and his followers were concerned with was taken for granted; they were the main features of a commercial civilization. They did not question the accumulation of riches or the methods through which they were obtained. Their main concern was the misuse of wealth for self-indulgence and ostentation. Tawney stated:

"Calvin. . . . set their [bourgeoisie] virtues at their best in sharp antithesis with the vices of the established order at its worst, taught them to feel that they were a chosen people, made them conscious of their great destiny in the providential plan."[5]

In other words, he showed the bourgeoisie how to rationalize some of the worst crimes in history. He made it appear as if they were God's will. He helped to prepare the way for the most hypocritical class in all the annals of humanity to come on the stage of history. The movement gained its greatest momentum in England and laid the foundation for the Puritan colonizers of the New World.

BOTH major and lesser powers participated in the colonization of North and South America. Colonization as begun, however, by Spain and Portugal in the South was carried out with the concepts of the old feudal society, which was still the dominant force. Colonization in North America began almost a hundred years later, and therefore reflected the mores and aspirations of the new class, the bourgeoisie. Colonization of the United States was carried out mainly by England, Holland and France, with England the dominant force.

The first settlers in the United States did not differ too much from the Spanish and Portuguese colonizers in Latin and South America. Most dreamed of gold and rubies and diamonds but actual experience in the New World soon punctured such dreams. Gradually a more realistic emphasis was placed on the possibilities of America as a source of raw materials and a market for manufactured goods, as well as a refuge for the many vagabonds and beggars set adrift in England by the breakdown of feudalism.

Thus, with England leading the way, the thirteen colonies were established against the background of the capitalist system in its most developed and worst form. The Hammonds describe what was happening in this most advanced capitalist power: "Thus England asked for profits and received profits. Everything turned to profits. The towns had their profitable dirt, their profitable smoke, their profitable slums, their profitable disorder, their profitable ignorance, their profitable despair. The curse of Midas was on this society."[7]

Such was the nature of the mother of the United States nation. We shall subsequently show that the offspring learned its lessons only too well.

As a consequence of these developments, our nation was born mainly on a capitalistic foundation. From the beginning it was free of almost all the hangovers of the old feudal system. The bourgeoisie in other major European countries still had to wage great ideological struggles against feudal concepts and in some instances, violent revolutionary struggle, such as the French Revolution in 1789. Nonetheless, the American nation was not entirely free from feudal hangovers. The two class forces that combined to build up the thirteen colonies were the trading companies and landed interests. The latter in both New Netherlands and the South reflected more of a feudal character. But the main colonizer was the merchant class. Even though initially the merchants lost money in their early colonizing efforts, great fortunes were built and the nation was born under the influence of these corrupted profit-seekers.

The discovery and the development of the colonies required massive labor power. The problem before the merchants was where the labor power was to come from. The Native American Indian peoples were not willing or able to transform themselves into this new breed.

Thus, in the pursuit of profits and labor power, the rising capitalist class reverted, in part, to forms of society that had long been obsolete.

Many centuries had passed since the great slave states had existed. Feudalism had come on the scene and had largely discarded slavery as a form of human relations. In the old slave states, more often than not the slaves were men and women who had been captured by other tribes or individuals. But the colonizers needed labor, and the first form it took was the enslavement of their own people. Due to the nature of the times, in which the bourgeoisie in its struggle against the aristocracy had to enlist the support of the serfs, peasants, artisans, etc., they could not make slavery a permanent form. Nonetheless, the conditions that the white slaves had to go through were dehumanizing. P. J. Dunning stated the nature of capitalism very well when he wrote:

With adequate capital, capital is very bold. A certain 10 percent will insure its employment anywhere; 20 percent certain to produce eagerness; 50 percent positive audacity; 100 percent will make it ready to trample on all human laws; 300 percent and there is not a crime at which it will scruple, nor a risk it will not run, even to the chance of its owner being hanged.[8]

The system that breeds the kind of mentality described by Dunning was at work in England in the sixteenth and seventeenth centuries. In England serfdom had practically disappeared in the last part of the fourteenth century. The great majority in the fifteenth century were free peasant proprietors. The wage laborers of agriculture consisted of peasants who used their leisure time working on the large estates. In addition to receiving wages, they were allotted arable land of four or more acres and a cottage.

Generally it had been the practice of the rising bourgeois class to call for the breakup of the big landed estates of the feudal lords. Such was the case in France where the bourgeois revolution was considered the means for serfs to obtain land ownership on a capitalist basis. But this was not the case in England. The prelude of the revolution that laid the foundation of capitalism there was in the last half of the fifteenth and the first decade of the sixteenth century. The poor, free peasants were ousted from the land and forced into the cities. The rapid rise of Flemish wool manufacturers and the rise in the price of wool in England accelerated this development. But the manufacturers could not absorb all the people thrown off the land. And many of these people, dragged from their mode of life, could not adapt to the new conditions. They became beggars, robbers, and vagabonds.

The most stringent laws were adopted to deal with the situation. In England, under the regime of Henry VIII, a law provided that beggars, old and unable to work, required beggars' licenses. Whipping and imprisonment was a steady diet for vagabonds. They were whipped until blood streamed from their bodies. Then they were forced to swear an oath to go back to their birthplace or to where they formerly lived and go to work. Imagine such a law! These people were forced to go back to the places where they were deprived of all their property and work possibilities. Later on this law was made worse. On the second arrest for vagabondage, the whipping was to be repeated and half on one ear sliced off. And for a third offense, the offender was to be executed as a hardened criminal.

In 1547, during the reign of Edward VI, a statute was adopted which transferred displaced people into a state of slavery. The law provided that "if anyone refuses to work, no matter what wage is offered, he shall be condemned as a slave to the person who has denounced him as an idler. The master shall feed his slave on bread and water, weak broth and such refuse meat as he thinks fit. He has the right to force him to do any work no matter how disgusting with ship and chains. If the slave is absent a fortnight, he is condemned to slavery for life and is to be branded on forehead or back with the letter 'S.' If he runs away thrice he is to be executed as a felon. The master can sell him, bequeath him, let him on hire as a slave, just as any other personal chattel or cattle. If the slaves attempt anything against the masters they are also to be executed. If it happens that a vagabond has been idling about three days he is to be taken to his birthplace, branded with a red hot iron with the letter 'V' on the breast and be set to work in chains, in the streets or at some other labor. If the vagabond gives a false birthplace he is then to become the slave for life of this place of its inhabitants or its corporation and to be branded with an 'S.' All persons have the right to take away the children of the vagabonds and to keep them as apprentices, the young men until the 24th year and the girls until the 20th. If they run away they are to become up to this age the slaves of their masters, who can put them in irons, whip them, if they like; every master may put an iron ring around the neck, arms and legs of his slave by which to know him more easily."

These laws provided a form of slavery for those who would not willingly fit into the factory system. This was the forerunner of those so-called white indentured servants. It was out of this background that the first significant labor power was obtained to colonize the United States.

THE conditions described in England were no exception. Hundreds of thousands of people all over Europe were on the point of starvation. They roamed from place to place seeking shelter and food. The religious wars in Germany, which lasted for decades, left the workers destitute. The wars between France and Holland laid waste to large areas and wiped out the belongings of many people. The English textile masters closed their mills in Ireland in order to avoid competition; and in 1740 a famine forced many Irish people to flee to other countries in search of bread. In France conditions were no better. It is estimated that in 1715 about one-third of the people of France, six million in all, starved to death.

These circumstances in England and Europe made it easy for the colonizers to enlist people as temporary slaves for the American economy. Anthony Bimba describes the situation in these words: "The colonizers were the same commercial adventurers, capitalists, exploiters, wealth-seekers, privileged masters of Europe. The government gave them great tracts of land in America and said in effect: 'take these wretches out of the cities and villages, transport them to America and exploit them to your hearts' content.' "[9]

Many free workers willingly signed away their freedom for a period of time to get transportation to the new land of "opportunity." But for most indentured servants there was only death and destruction. The hardships these white slaves had to undergo were terrific. Often, while enroute to the United States, more than half of them suffocated and were thrown overboard.

One ship sailing in 1730 with 150 immigrants had only 15 survivors. Another sailed in 1745 with 400 Germans of whom only 50 lived to see America; still another bearing 1,500 lost 1,100 dead on the voyage. Children seldom survived the journey. Often parents were compelled to see their children die of hunger, thirst or sickness and then see them cast into the water. Many a mother was cast into the water with her child.

Geiger, in his book *Redemptioners,* describes a situation, so horrible that it is almost unbelievable, of a ship sailing from Holland:

The hunger was so great on board that all the bones about the ship . . . were pounded with a hammer and eaten; and what is more lamentable, some of the deceased persons not many hours before their death crawled on their hands and feet to the captain, and begged him for God's sake to give them a mouthful of bread or a drop of water to keep them from perishing. But their supplications were in vain. . . . Sometimes whole families died in quick succession.[10]

Colonial agents in England seduced many people into signing up as indentured servants with glowing promises. But as time went by many relied more on fraud and more drastic measures. How many women and children were kidnapped and sold it is impossible to say.

The enslavement of women was a major feature of securing labor power. They were brought to America and sold for tobacco or for gold and silver. Oneal says that the shipping companies were not contented to deal with adults only.

The London Company of adventurers who settled Virginia were eager to employ child labor in the development of the resources of the colony. In 1619 its records acknowledge the arrival of 100 children "save such as dyed on the waie," and another 100, 12-year old or over, is asked for. In 1627 many ships arrived, bringing 1,400 and 1,500 children kidnapped by "spirits" in European ports.[11]

Finally the prisons of England were emptied and the inmates came as indentured servants.

Such was the condition of the white slaves. England organized this traffic in slaves from Anglo-Saxon people at a time when slavery had become obsolete. In so doing it wrote some of the worst pages in human history. Yet the colonizers based on this class foundation became even more inhumane; later Indian peoples were destroyed like wild beasts in a jungle, and Black people were subjected to the worst forms of slavery in history. These inhuman practices were born out of the system of capitalism and are directly related to the social forces which gave birth to the nation.

2 • THE STRUGGLE FOR A DEMOCRATIC CONSTITUTION

WITHOUT A single exception, none of the revolutions of the seventeenth, eighteenth, and nineteenth centuries, which were mainly bourgeois in character, carried out their promises of liberty, equality and justice. In England, after the "Glorious Revolution" of 1678, it took almost a hundred years for the working class to achieve electoral status; and in regards to women, they did not achieve the franchise until almost three hundred years later. In the United States, after the Declaration of Independence which proclaimed that "all men are created equal," Blacks remained slaves until about 80 years later, women did not receive the right to vote until 112 years later and the working class did not get the legal right to organize and collectively bargain until 150 years later.

Under the circumstances of the times, the capitalist ruling class had to grant some democratic reforms in contrast to what existed under the feudal system. But even the most limited reforms were made only after the people waged the sharpest forms of struggle. Nowhere is this truth more in evidence than in the two hundred year history of the United States.

No sooner had the last shot been fired in the Revolutionary War of 1776 when forces came into motion to wipe out the idealism contained in the Declaration of Independence, to destroy the more advanced form of democracy which existed under the Articles of Confederation and to establish a more suitable form of government for capitalist development.

What preceded and followed the Constitutional Convention in Philadelphia in 1789 verifies how difficult it is to establish even the mildest forms of democracy under this system. During the Revolutionary War the Continental Congress adopted articles which were to guide the newly established nation. These in large part were modeled after the Iroquois Indian tribal confederation which some have described as one of the finest forms of democracy to have ever existed. But such a confederation was feasible and possible in a classless society. It was totally inadequate in a class structured society. The constant rivalries among various elements of the monied class and the fear of the lower classes could not be handled in such a decentralized society. The anarchy which existed during this period had a profound effect upon the economy as a whole. Cynicism regarding the confederation was expressed by John Adams: "In every society where property exists there will be a struggle between rich and poor . . . mixed in one assembly equal laws can never be expected; they will either be made by members to plunder the few who are rich or by influence to fleece the poor."[1]

During this period the country went into a sharp economic crisis. Overdue on the national debt accumulated, continental securities fell sharply, and army officers had to sell at a huge loss the scripts they had received in lieu of pay.

In these circumstances it was the poor farmers who suffered the most. Their conditions were terrible and they did not possess political power to get relief. The situation evoked a tremendous mass upheaval. All through the summer of 1786 community and town meetings were held all over the country demanding reforms in favor of the people. One petition read:

We beg to informe your Honours that unless something takes place more favorable to the people, in a little time att least, one half of our inhabitants in our opinion will become bankrupt—sutes att law are very numerous and the attorneys in our opinion are very extravigent and oppressive in their demands, and when we compute the taxes laid upon us for the five preceding years . . . the amount is equil to what our farms will rent for. Sirs, in this situation what have we to live on—no money to be had; our estates dayly posted and sold as afore described . . . surely your honours are not strangers to the distressed of the people, but does know that many of our good inhabitants are now confined in fail for det and for taxes; many have fled, others wishing to flee.[2]

No relief came from this petition and Samuel Adams, one of the "sainted Founding Fathers" denounced these poverty stricken farmers as "wicked and unprincipled men."[3]

Finding no response to their grievances, as did the colonists from King George at an earlier date, the farmers took the path of struggle.

In September 1786 the farmers, under the leadership of Daniel Shays, with some 600 strong, tried to prevent the seating of the Supreme Judicial Court of Springfield, Massachusetts. The object of the action appears to have been to prevent further judgments for debts pending the next state election. The uprising was defeated, but it had a profound effect on the whole future of American history. The legislature eventually was compelled to take some action to provide relief. Samuel Eliot Morison sums up the results: "So ended Shays Rebellion. Its effects went deeper than any event since the Boston Tea Party . . . But how narrow had been the escape from civil war, if indeed it were an escape."[4] Washington, he further points out, "was alarmed and wrote: 'There are combustibles in every state which a spark might set fire to . . . I feel infinitely more than I can express for the disorders which have arisen. Good God! Who besides a Tory could have foreseen or a Briton have predicted them?'"[5]

DISSATISFACTION with a loose confederation form of government in general and fear of future revolts such as the Shays Rebellion were the backdrop for the convening of the Constitutional Convention in Philadelphia in September 1787. There have been arguments pro and con as to what motivated the Founding Fathers at Philadelphia. But almost without exception, most historians admit that the Shays Rebellion was in the background of their minds. Thus, when we honor our national heroes who helped to make America great, the name of Daniel Shays should be very high. Regardless of the outcome of the Constitutional Convention, positive or negative, it was certainly from the American people that our nation was started on the road to some forms of progress and the Shays Rebellion was the first major development after the Revolution.

The motivations of the convenors of the Convention have been discussed from every possible angle. But it is difficult to understand how anyone this late in history can deny that class motivations were not the central feature of what took place. The convenors themselves made no bones about what they wanted to achieve. First of all, take a look at the composition of those involved and the secrecy in which they met. The facts are so overwhelming that nobody denies the composition of those who gathered there. What is denied by most historians is their class outlook.

Donald Childsey in his book, *The Birth of the Constitution,* places the problem exactly like it was.

They had a great deal to talk about, for they had a great deal in common, being all of the same general class, men of property, men of business affairs, or legal lights. This was no more than natural. Who else could have afforded it? There were no representatives of day workers in the country. The farmers too, were not represented. Though there were six southern planters, including George Washington.[6]

The delegates were well educated. They brought with them the wisdom of England's greatest theorists, not to speak of the democratic theorists of France and more ancient times. They brought with them a background of government from England and the various colonies which had been set up as states. The state governments which had been enacted before Philadelphia formed the basis for the discussion at the Convention. Most of the delegates came to the Convention with a plan from their respective states. The mood and practice in the state governments are described by Esmond Wright in his book, *Fabric of Freedom, "The right to acquire and possess property without restriction was indeed as important a civil right as free speech, and to most people in the 18th century it meant more."* (Emphasis mine, C.L.)[7]

With few exceptions the right to vote and qualify for office required property or some form of monetary consideration. The situation varied from state to state. A poll tax was required in New Hampshire, North Carolina and Pennsylvania. In Virginia one had to own 25 acres of settled land or fifty unsettled. In Massachusetts the governor had to own one thousand pounds worth of freehold property. In South Carolina it was ten times that amount.

In spite of all denials to the contrary, the delegates in Philadelphia reflected the spirit and the mood of the ruling classes of that time. And the preservation of property was the prime motive behind all acts and proposals before that body. This is not to deny that here and there some delegate could not rise above monetary interest and approach a problem from an idealistic point of view. But even in most cases where this happened, when a showdown came, money triumphed over idealism. The Convention delegates in this connection based themselves more on John Locke who saw the primary purpose of government as the protection of private property. But they did not go along with Locke on government structure. Locke still saw the necessity of maintaining the monarchy, although in a limited capacity. The delegates in Philadelphia did not.

The most scholarly and theoretical-minded person at the Convention was James Madison. He had made an intensive study of the doctrines of most European writers. He was also the author of the Constitution. The various states presented plans that had some differences but, as Charles Beard characterized them, they were more about detail than substance. The compromises which were made represented essentially what Madison proposed, mainly a synthesis of Locke's views (without the monarchy), and some of Montesquieu's views which called for a separation of power in the various branches of government. In bringing together those two concepts, the United States set up one of the most autocratic forms of government that was erected by the modern bourgeoisie.

OUR government has been proclaimed the most democratic structure ever conceived in the minds of man. And on the surface, as far as capitalist democracy goes, this would appear to be the case. As far as the pronouncements by men of prominence at the Convention, this would appear to be the case. But when one studies more carefully the statements especially those made by the Federalists, men like Madison, Hamilton and Jay, men who dominated the Convention, the truth begins to fall into place. This is especially true when the structure of government is examined in some detail.

The so-called system of checks and balances in government, the theory of separate independent branches is one of the biggest ideological frauds ever drilled into the minds of man. As already stated, Montesquieu, an ideologist of the French Revolution was the author of this concept. However, the real motive behind this concept was as he expressed it: to prevent "the tyranny of the majority." The government established in Philadelphia was based on this concept and motive. Madison and others used the theory of "tyranny of the majority" quite openly, especially in the Federalist papers.

Our structure of government adds up to one of the cleverest forms used to conceal class dictatorship the world has ever known. Dictatorship is usually conceived of as the rule of a personal dictator in the form of king, emperor, etc. Sometimes it is expressed through a single personality surrounded by a small clique who possess some powers that even the dictator must reckon with. Such was the case under feudalism with the landed aristocracy. In any case, the power of any class-structured society, regardless of the form, expresses the basic and fundamental needs of the class that is in power. In the older forms of class rule the lower classes had no instruments in government to express their will at all. Later, as capitalism evolved in the womb of feudalism, sometimes concessions were made in which parliamentary forms were established which somewhat restricted the monarchy. But whatever was the case, the main reins of power remained in the hands of the class the king or queen represented. The circumstances under which the bourgeoisie came to power made it necessary for this class to exercise its rule in a different form and structure of government.

Many years ago as a child, and at that time certainly not a Communist, I heard a story which dramatized what the boys in Philadelphia were about. The story goes like this: An Egyptian Caliph on his death bed heard a mass of people outside the palace screaming "Death to the old tyrant." He called his eldest son, his heir, to his bed and asked him to go to the window and listen. The son heard how the people felt about his father and was greatly shaken by it. His father then explained to him the reason—he had not ruled the people wisely. He had taken everything openly and directly into his own hands; thus becoming a target for everything that went wrong. And he advised his son that when he would come to power, he should rule differently. "Go out among the people, choose the wisest ones among them," he said. "Keep the reins of power firmly in your hands. But do it in such a way that they will become the targets, not you."

The bourgeoisie must have heard this story long before me. When we are told why the government structure of checks and balances was established in the Constitution, it was in order to prevent any faction from taking complete power, and that this was the best way to preserve liberty for the people. But there were some among the delegates who told it like it was. For example, Amos Singletary declared:

These lawyers and men of learning and monied men that talk so finely, and gloss over matters so smoothly to make us poor, illiterate people swallow down the pill, expect to get into Congress themselves; they expect to be managers of this Constitution, and get all the power and all the money into their own hands, and then they will swallow up all us little folks like the great *Leviathan;* yes, just as the whale swallowed up *Jonah!*[8]

How prophetic! Two hundred years of experience has confirmed these observations.

In the debates that took place around the various branches of government, the greatest concern was how to keep Congress from exercising control over the executive and the judiciary. Up to this point, the greatest experimenters in democratic government forms were the British. After a long period of struggle, Parliament, the body of elected representatives, became the main power base. The monarchy, the executive and the judiciary were subordinate to this body, which was closest to the people. But even this structure did not prevent the bourgeoisie and the aristocracy from exercising its power over the people.

There were a number of reasons why this was possible in Britain. For one thing, the electoral process was so limited that the monied classes had no real fear about who would get elected. Electoral rights in Britain were far more restricted than in the colonies. In addition, Britain from the beginning, was a very small country and as its ruling class reached out to rule the world, they concentrated more on ideological means to maintain control than most countries.

Although property was the main basis for voting rights in the thirteen colonies, small property holders were very numerous and thus the trend was toward an enlargement of the franchise. Besides, when the delegates came together in Philadelphia they already had behind them some experience with more advanced democratic forms in several states.

Prior to the Constitutional Convention all of the states had adopted constitutions and as previously indicated, they varied in form. Several had adopted constitutions with relatively more advanced democratic forms. One of these states was Pennsylvania. It had adopted a different type of constitution which reflected the interests of the artisans, the Scotch-Irish frontiersmen and the German-speaking farmers. It was one of the most democratic of American revolutionary constitutions. Every male taxpayer and his adult sons could vote. Rotation in office was enjoined; none could serve as representative for more than four years in every seven. A single chamber legislature was set up, the only qualification for membership being that one must be a Christian. Membership was apportioned according to population. Instead of a single governor, this constitution provided an elective executive council with rotation of office to prevent "danger of establishing dictatorship." The president of the council, chosen annually by joint ballot of a council and the assembly, acted as chief executive. Another feature of the Pennsylvania constitution was the election every seven years of a council whose duty was to inquire whether the constitution had been preserved inviolate in every part, to order impeachments and to summon a constitutional convention if necessary.

"A Pennsylvanian wrote to Thomas Jefferson, 'You would execrate this state if you were in it . . . the supporters of this government are a set of workmen without any weight of character.'"[9] Morison says that Pennsylvania "Established the nearest thing to a dictatorship of the proletariat that we have had in North America."[10]

The Pennsylvania constitution was hailed by many in Europe as almost perfect. States other than Pennsylvania and Vermont adopted less democratic constitutions. Wright observes: "Only in Pennsylvania, North Carolina and Georgia could the new constitutions be said to be really democratic documents."[11] No doubt Wright dealt with Georgia and North Carolina in a relative manner. No slaveholding state can be characterized as a democratic state despite some features which may have been democratic for some people.

New Jersey also in some respects was an exception for it was the only state that gave voting rights to women. Whatever the variations in the few states cited, the character of most constitutions was based on methods for class control by the monied groups. And this was part of the background at Philadelphia for the adoption of a constitution that was considered by many as the most advanced document of its time, but which with the passage of time has proven to be among the least democratic.

The class nature of the document has been one of the best covered-up affairs in our history, and this includes most liberal historians. For example, Morison, in his work *The Growth of the American Republic,* after pointing out the defects in the document which reveal the class background of its framers, nevertheless argues that the "safeguarding of particular interests" was not the aim. It is true, according to Morison, that members "were conscious of these interests" but the main consideration "appears" to have been the need to set up a government that would be acceptable to the "popular prejudices for adoption."[12] Now it is quite possible that people with very special interests could work with those tactical views in mind.

But it is a misreading, deliberately or otherwise, to make the tactics the primary concern. Morison notes that almost all historians, whatever their school of thought, regard the delegates as inspired drafters of a "document of almost divine sanctions." This inspiration and divinity seems to have been so great that when the sesquicentennial of the Convention took place in 1937, the American people were assured that the architects of the Constitution had foreseen all future evils that might befall our country, such as "communism, radical labor and the New Deal," and took the necessary steps for protection.[13] Such clear-cut class interpretations reduce the speculation as to what motivated the Founding Fathers to nil. In any case, the records show what their motives were at the Convention by what they did even more than by what they said in debate. What is more, the records will show that whatever democratic progress we have made as a nation did not come from the hearts of the nation's founders, but through the struggles waged by the American people. The constitution that was adopted and the amendments that followed were a result of those struggles. And so unlike 1937 at the time of the sesquicentennial of the Federal Convention, the American people need to know the truth and place the real national heroes and heroines in their proper places. This would include all the people and leaders who forced through reforms against a money-hungry capitalist class, their agents and their apologists.

THE U.S. Constitution was born out of the same general circumstances that characterized those in England, France, Germany and other capitalist-led countries. Money making—profits were the motives behind the revolutions that overthrew the old feudal kingdoms. Those old governments were parasitical. They played little or no part in profit-making, but were always eager through taxes and other forms, to take a large share of the profits for the aristocracy. Under such circumstances, the system of capitalism was hindered in its growth. The bourgeoisie, therefore, waged great revolutions to rid itself of a parasitical aristocracy. And when it came to power, its chief concern was how to create conditions for a wide expansion of the new system. The feudal aristocracy, which continued to exist for a period of time, no longer was the major concern of the capitalist class. Its main thought now was how to construct governments that would provide protection against the lower classes which had taken seriously slogans such as "all men are created equal." The forms may have differed from country to country, but the content was the same.

The theme in Montesquieu, John Locke and the writings of others on how to prevent "the tyranny of the majority" was the guideline in the establishment of all bourgeois-led republics, including the United States. "The tyranny of the majority" could have many meanings. But for the bourgeoisie the slogan meant the ability to construct a government that would not interfere too much with the exploitative character of the profit system, would prevent those instruments of government closest to the people from having too much power to take control over their property in any circumstance. The slogan meant, as Adam Smith put it: "Civil government . . . instituted for the security of property is in reality instituted for the defense of the rich against the poor or of those who have some property against those who have none at all."[14]

Such was the meaning of "the tyranny of the majority." Such was the main concern of the "boys" who assembled at Philadelphia in 1789. How did they proceed?

The proposition advanced, of a federal government being based on three *independent and equal* branches of government—the legislative, executive and judicial—is a complete farce. Any examination of the structure of government will reveal that the legislative branch and especially the House of Representatives is the least equal to all other branches, including the Senate. The House is the body that is closest to the people. In the first place, each representative is elected by a relatively small and compact constituency. They are elected directly by the people every two years. Now, while the House holds the purse strings in its hand, and that is a certain form of power, by itself it cannot execute anything. Moreover, it cannot make laws without the participation of the Senate.

The Senate, which is the legislative body least responsive to the people, can cancel any proposal of the House. The Senate as first set up by the Founding Fathers was practically an appointed body. It was not based on any procedures which would allow the majority of the American people to decide its membership. Originally two senators were elected by the state legislature regardless of the size of the state. Later on, the people succeeded in changing this procedure. An amendment was passed and the Senate became a body elected by the voters.

Although this reform was carried out, the Senate still remained (and remains) the least responsive branch of Congress to the majority of the American people. It was elected for a period of six years as against two for the House of Representatives. It still represents two from each state, irrespective of size.

These mechanical differences between the bodies do speak to the differences in composition of the Senate as against the House. The House is often a training ground for those who want to become a senator. Also, from the standpoint of the possibility of getting elected, it is far more difficult to become a senator than a congressman. Much, much more money is required to wage a campaign on a statewide basis than in a local congressional district.

The House has very little say over the composition of the men who are appointed as administrators of the affairs of the nation, i.e. president's cabinet, etc. One could dissect differences which could add to the picture that the Senate is a "superior" body to that of the House; and that these differences are not accidental. Madison provided the rationale for the role of the Senate when in substance he said that our government ought to secure the permanent interests of the country against innovation. Landholders ought to have a share in the government to support these invaluable interests and to balance and check the other. They ought to be so constructed as to protect the minority of the opulent against the majority. The Senate, therefore, ought to be that body. John Dickinson hoped that the United States Senate would bear as strong a likeness to the British House of Lords as possible. But the Senate is a much more powerful chamber than the Lords by virtue of its co-legislative power with the House and its share in the presidential powers of appointments and treaty making.

Even on the matter of impeachments the Senate has more power. The House can vote to impeach, but the Senate is the body that makes the decision. Thus, at the legislative level the makers of the Constitution took out some insurance papers for the rich in the formation of the Senate.

In regards to executive power, the presidency holds greater power than the legislative branch. A graphic illustration of this power is revealed by former Senator Fullbright. In his book, *The Crippled Giant,* he states: "Perhaps the single most important difference between an American president and a Prime Minister in a Parliamentary system is that the latter is compelled to meet his critics face to face." Fullbright elaborates further:

The president, by contrast, is more nearly in the position of the British Monarch, except for the crucial fact that he has power and the queen does not . . . when the president speaks it is from a pedestal . . . congress is at a great disadvantage in discussing issues. Because the executive has a near monopoly on effective access to the public attention. The president can command a national television audience to hear his views on controversial matters at prime time, on short notice, at whatever length he chooses and at no expense to the federal government or to his party. Other constitutional office holders are compelled to rely on highly selective newspaper articles and television news spots which at most still convey bits or snatches of their points of view.[15]

In respect to the judiciary, this is the most powerful arm of government. And while it has no power to execute its decisions, it does have the power to cancel out whatever is done by both the legislative and executive branches. There is much controversy over whether the constitutional makers intended for it to have so much power. But one thing is certain—that when they made the tenure in office of Supreme Court justices permanent and not responsible to the electorate, the ground work for this great power was laid.

PERHAPS the greatest weakness and outstanding example about the "democratic" intentions of the Founding Fathers was the failure of the 1787 convention to provide a bill of rights which would provide some measure of security for the individual citizen. Its failure to do so brought the common people into motion. And just as the Shays Rebellion was in the background of the convening of the Constitutional Convention, it was the American people who forced through the addition of the Bill of Rights to the Constitution. Of all the miscalculations made by the Convention this was perhaps the worst of all. For even when the various states drafted constitutions, and while most were limited in democratic character, almost all wrote a bill of rights into them.

The State of Virginia led the way. At its convention on June 12, 1776, it adopted a declaration which has been hailed as one of the great liberty documents of all time. Morison says that it: " . . . parented not only other American bill of rights; but the French *Déclaration des droits de L'homme et du citogen* of 1789 and the Universal Declaration of Human Rights adopted in 1948 by the General Assembly of the United Nations."[17]

In some respects other states adopted stronger clauses than did Virginia. Pennsylvania had stronger statements than Virginia on religious liberty, added freedom of speech to Virginia's freedom of the press, and protected conscientious objectors to military service.

The foregoing should suffice to show that the federal government was structured in the interests of the rich. At the Convention's conclusion, the people went into motion and a great debate took place throughout the nation. David Loth in his book *Public Plunder,* states the attitude that followed the convention: "As it failed to satisfy any of the men who made it, so it aroused little affection in the country—more than one third of the limited voters—bothered to declare themselves on 'the greatest work ever struck off at a given time by the brains and purposes of man.' The preservation of property arouses fanatical support only among a small minority that possess enough property to worry about."[17]

But the people were not passive. Irving Brent in *The Bill of Rights, Its Origin and Meaning,* describes what happened:

When on September 17, 1787, the secrecy of the Convention was broken and the proposed plan was published, a tempest of public debate over its merits began to blow. Critics fell upon it with might and main. It was not a plan for a federal union, some said, but a dark plot to establish a centralized despotism and reduce the states to provinces. The president, others insisted, would become a monarch, perhaps worse than George III. It was a device radicals claimed, by which the rich and powerful would govern the country and oppress the plain people with armies, taxes and debts. It had no Bill of Rights, friends of liberty protested. In fact, scarcely a line of the Constitution escaped an attack, mild or passionate.[18]

The situation compelled widespread debate and the federalists, Hamilton, Madison and Jay produced over eighty-five papers to defend their position. But finally, they gave in and at the first Congress, held after ratification of the Constitution, James Madison arose and presented ten amendments that came to be known as the Bill of Rights.

Thus the American people, the farmers in particular, became the force that made the first real democratic advance in the nation.

3 • CONCENTRATION OF WEALTH

THE BEST example of what the intentions of the Founding Fathers were is how the structure of the government they created has been used to concentrate almost all the resources and wealth of the land into the hands of the few. Ferdinand Lundberg says: "It would be difficult in the 1960s for a large majority of Americans to show fewer significant possessions if the country had long labored under a grasping dictatorship. How has this process been contrived of stripping threadbare most of the population, which once at least owned small patches of virgin land?"[1] Lundberg raises a fundamental question about the concentration of wealth in the hands of the few and discusses many interesting answers. But what he fails to see is the basic reason—that we have had throughout our entire history "a grasping dictatorship" of the monied classes. And that the government has been used as one of the main vehicles to achieve their aims.

But its ways have been many and devious. The fact that the land and its resources are owned by a few has long been known. Many writers have done research and proved the case. But as time goes by, the concentration of wealth becomes greater and greater. There was a time when in the main, only the radicals and the radical press dealt with the growing concentration of wealth. Today this "seems" to be everybody's business. But for many of them, after they define the problem they leave the solution hanging in the air, or misdirected toward illusory solutions. Therefore it is no longer enough to say that in our two hundred year history we have witnessed a phenomena on a relative basis of the rich getting richer and the poor getting poorer. What is needed in the first place is clear knowledge of how this process has taken place, and the role of government in this process. There are some who still preach Horatio Alger's success stories, whereby hard work, thrift and intelligence were the way the rich went forward.

The ideology behind money-making was also said to be, in many respects, "God's will," "God's work." When these religious concepts became less believable, Social Darwinism, "the survival of the fittest" became the main theme. There is very little literature which ties in the concentration of wealth to what happened in Philadelphia at the Constitutional Convention in 1787. From time to time various branches of government have been unmasked and found to be full of graft and corruption. But in most cases, the centrality of the role of government as a whole, as a structure purposely designed to promote the fortunes of the rich, is hidden under the cover of corruption of this or that individual or govermental body or agency.

WHAT then was the role of government in making the rich richer? In what way can we today talk of dictatorship of a class within a democratic structure of government?

Since the founding of the nation, all three branches of government have been used as instruments to do the work for the rich. This has been true even when one or another branch has been more susceptible to making concessions to the people. Hard class decisions affecting the welfare of the rich have come from all of them. And when all the decisions of Congress, the House and the Senate, the executive and the judiciary are added up it can be proven that class dictatorship in this new form of democracy has been an even greater money maker for the class in power than in medieval times. The only difference is that the ability to do what had to be done required many different methods and institutions.

The nation at pre-birth, before the Revolution or the Constitutional Convention—the power of the King in England, mainly executive in form, together with colonial councils—combined to start the process of placing the land and its resources into the hands of the few. Gustavus Myers has documented this fact by research into original records from colonial times on. Each of the colonial states reflected the trend of the times Myers revealed: "In Maryland and Virginia great estates were secured by the influential few by the most fraudently methods; this was particularly so in Virginia."[2]

Even George Washington, who eventually became one of the richest men in the colony, secured his wealth as a result of grants of large numbers of acres of land. On February 19, 1754, on behalf of himself and other officers, a grant of 200,000 acres for their military services was secured.

What began in the colonies was carried out even more vigorously after the Revolution and the founding of the nation. One of the most outrageous acts of land grabbing was the contrast of what happened to the poor soldiers who underwent the most miserable conditions to make the Revolution and the leaders of the Revolution. At the beginning of the Revolution soldiers were given land as a means for recruitment. After the Revolution, "knowing the collective value of these military certificates, the speculators sent out their agents to trade upon the pressing needs of the soldiers for money to buy up these land warrants."[3] Afterwards Congress carried out the plan of buying back government securities at *full* value. It was this act which Charles Beard revealed when he pointed out that many of the delegates at the Constitutional Convention were holders of these securities.

An example of what followed was what took place in New York State. After the Revolution New York owned more than seven million acres of land that was regarded as wild. It was put on public sale and sold at such outrageously favorable terms to the monied groups that it "caused a considerable public scandal."

PERHAPS one of the largest foundations for the present-day wealth of the United States was the rapid industrial expansion that followed the Civil War. It was the period of great industrial advance, the Gilded Age. It was the time of the "Robber Barons" and the rise of the big trusts.

In this period an even more complex relationship developed within the capitalist class. Out of the landowners, slave owners and merchants of pre-Civil War days, there came to decisive power within the government a new grouping of capitalists in the form of industrialists and bankers. Competition was intensified. Wealth was concentrated into fewer hands, and the intra-class struggle sharpened, as well as struggles between classes. This situation laid the basis for one or another capitalist grouping to become a decisive force in all areas of government. The interchangeable nature of what grouping of capitalists was the key force in government at any given time helped to reinforce the idea that our government is a democracy. Also the fact that at no time has any single particular corporation (or conglomerate) fully dominated the affairs of government has given things the appearance of democratic control. It is only in the context of dealing with the class as a whole does the dictatorial character within our democracy unfold.

In the pre-Civil War period, the basic contradictions in the ruling classes were between the big manufacturing merchants and the big slave and land owners. The Civil War settled that matter; the bankers and industrialists came to be the dominant forces. The role played by munition makers in the Civil War, who sold all kinds of rotten equipment to the government, caused President Lincoln to write a letter to a friend; a letter which contained a prophetic vision of things to come. He wrote:

I see in the near future a crisis approaching that unnerves me and causes me to tremble for the safety of my country. As a result of the war, corporations have been enthroned and an era of corruption in high places will follow. The money power of the country will endeavor to prolong its reign by working upon the prejudices of the people until all wealth is aggregated in a few hands and the Republic is destroyed. I feel at this moment more anxiety for my country than ever before, even in the midst of war. God grant that my suspicions may prove groundless.[4]

Patricia Acheson describes what followed the war. She wrote:

Prior to the Civil War, Hamiltonian ideas of an America built on industry and commerce were more closely adhered to in the North, but the South and the West were made up generally of the farming class. The years following the Civil War, however witnessed the most amazing economic revolution in the nation's history ... The nation turned to the development of industry on a scale unprecedented anywhere.[5]

But what Acheson does not do was to describe the unprecedented ruthless exploitation that followed the coming to power of this section of the ruling class. There have been many descriptions of it but none compare with what William Z. Foster, one of the outstanding leaders of the Communist Party U.S.A. wrote:

The hundred and forty years between the War for Independence and World War I formed an unparalleled era of capitalist grabbing, robbery and exploitation in the United States. The world had never before seen the like. The capitalists were like ravenous wolves seizing and taking for their own the vast bulk of the country and its splendid resources.[6]

Foster then quotes Vernon L. Parrington's famous comment:

A huge barbecue was spread to which all presumably were invited. Not quite all, to be sure; inconspicuous persons, those who were at home on the farm, or at work in the mills and offices were overlooked; a good many indeed out of the total number of the American people. But all important persons, bankers and industrialists, received invitations. There wasn't room for everybody and these were presumed to represent the whole. It was a splendid feast.[7]

While these descriptions fit every phase of U.S. history, they are especially true of the Gilded Age, the rise of U.S. imperialism, and today.

THE locomotive pulling the train of history forward in this direction was land grabbing, especially for the railroads and oil industries. Following the Civil War, the main industrial focus was the building of the railroad industry from coast to coast. What happened in this connection set the stage for all other industries.

In 1860 the federal government still held title to more than half of the land area of the United States, roughly over a billion acres. Out of land in the public domain, and from that taken from small farmers, it is generally estimated that over 160 million acres were given free of charge to the robber barons connected with the railroad industry. These figures do not include what was given in the various states. This process began in 1862 when the first transcontinental railroad, the Union Pacific, was authorized and completed in 1869.

The Union Pacific and Central Pacific originally received ten sections of land for each track built. Later this amount was doubled. They also received government loans—$48,000 a mile in mountain territory, $32,000 in hilly and $16,000 in flat areas. Together with land grants, the states often paid expenses, provided tax exemptions and subscribed public money to railroad stocks. What was done in the states was supplemented by direct subsidies by the federal government.

After the Union Pacific was completed crossroad railroads were rapidly built. In some instances the government actually built the roads and turned them over to "private enterprises." The Pacific road received acreage about half the size of France.

The ability of the railroads to gain all these advantages was facilitated by bribery and corruption in all branches of government. This power was not always evenly distributed, and opposition was encountered along the way. It happened first in the states. The railroad companies not only were beneficiaries of land grants and various forms of subsidies, they also were able to exploit the farmers in the rates they charged for transportation of commodities. The exhorbitant rates aroused the wrath of the farmers as a whole, middle class and the poor. As a consequence, a movement developed in the Western and Southern states known as the Granger movement, and later the Populist. These movements succeeded in a number of states to force through some laws to regulate the rates charged by companies. A legal situation developed which tells a lot about the nature of the structure of government created by the Founding Fathers. The battle went on in government—on the state level, in the national legislative branches and eventually culminated in the U.S. Supreme Court. The railroads did not have a smooth road to power.

Its corrupt practices had to undergo struggle in all branches of government. The main instrument of government which determined the outcome of these struggles was the U.S. Supreme Court.

In the period prior to the Civil War, the Court under Chief Justice Taney was controlled mainly by the landed aristocracy. After the Civil War and the program of industrialization which followed, the Court under Chief Justice Chase came under the domination of the bankers. It was during this period that a clash took place between the banking and railroad interests. Myers describes this struggle:

By the beginning of the Civil War, a total of 30,000 miles of railroad had been constructed. During the next decade—at least before 1873—36,000 more miles of railroad were built constituting a greater extension than the entire mileage of the preceeding 34 years. . . . The promoters of those railroads had bribed act after act through Congress or state legislatures or both, and had corrupted county officials and municipalities to give them stupendous gifts of public lands, public funds . . . yet the construction necessities of actual cash were so great . . . that the railroads had to make out mortgages . . . Very little gold was in circulation. The receipts of the railroad companies were almost wholly in legal tender notes. If they were required to pay their fixed charges or contracts in gold, they would be completely at the mercy of the banks, that it would only be a short time before the banks would own outright virtually every railroad system. This was the . . . contest now underway between these two powerful interests. Which side would win? The Supreme Court of the United States would decide.[8]

A case came before the Court called the *Legal Tender*. It contained the aforementioned condition explained by Myers. The Court decided, by a majority of one, in favor of the bankers. The majority declared that all promises to pay in contracts had to be paid in gold. This decision which made gold the form of contractual payments aided the bankers because they had control of gold. The railroad interest did not accept this decision so they went to work to gain control over Congress and the Court.

Prior to this decision, based on bribery of the members of Congress, the railroad barons were the main capitalist grouping in power. According to the Report of the Public Land Commission of 1965, from 1850 to 1870 not less than 133 separate grants of public land had been made by Congress to a similar number of different railroad corporations. So Congress was not their problem; the problem was how to get control of the U.S. Supreme Court. This possibility came about with the election of President Grant. Vacancies on the Court permitted the executive and legislative branches of government to make new appointments that changed the composition of the Court in favor of the railroad interest. President Grant, on December 20, 1869, made two appointments of railroad lawyers to the Court, thus bringing this branch of government into line with the others to make the railroad interest the most powerful financial group in government. As a result of these developments, the railroads received many decisions which affected their welfare. Among the decisions of the Court were those which allowed them to keep all the land they had secured by fraud.

Among the cases was that of *Schulenberg* v. *Harriman*, which was decided by the Supreme Court in October 1874. This case arose out of an act by the Wisconsin legislature in 1856, which granted about 2,388,000 acres of public land for the purposes of railroad building. The act provided that the roads were to be built within ten years. The Wisconsin legislature made several such grants, all of which involved graft. This particular case involved a railroad which was to be built from Portage City to Lake St. Croix. The railroad was never built. Since this was the case, the state of Wisconsin claimed that the land should be returned. The Supreme Court denied the state the right to take back the land, and thereby legalized all previous acts of thievery and executed more corruption in the halls of Congress.

Another case which showed how the Court in this period was used by the railroads was the situation around the Credit Mobilier Company, which was constructed to build the Union Pacific Railroad. The public was so outraged by the grafting that had been done by this company that the U.S. Senate was forced to set up an investigating committee. The committee reported: That the total cost of building the railroad was $50,000,000, that the Credit Mobilier Company had charged $93,546,287.28, that from the stock, income bonds, and land grant bonds, the builders received in cash value $23,363,000 as profit, about eighty-five percent of the entire cost. The committee reported that the profits were immediately turned into stocks and divided by the capitalists involved. It was an act through which they gained complete control over an enterprise which was financed entirely by the public and the government.

In the process of various transactions, all kinds of looting of the public was revealed. A suit was therefore instituted to reclaim the land and money, but once again the Court ruled in favor of the railroad companies.

THE U.S. Supreme Court, whether under the influence of the bankers or the railroads or any other combination of capitalist interests during this entire period of the industrial revolution, was the main instrument to protect the interests of the class as a whole. Here and there one can find a few decisions which would indicate otherwise, but such instances are rare. In the struggles around the Bill of Rights it was shown that when the capitalist class was forced to make a concession it always endeavored to use the concession as a springboard to also protect the vital interests of the class.

This fact is further substantiated by what followed the Civil War. After that war, constitutional amendments were needed to establish, at least on paper, some means to protect the newly emancipated slaves. This was done with the passage of the Thirteenth, Fourteenth and Fifteenth Amendments. The Fourteenth Amendment was passed allegedly for the purpose of protecting the Black people's civil rights within the states. But this clause also contained a provision that provided protection for property rights. Even such a staunch defender of the system as Acheson admitted:

Able as these capitalists were they did not single-handed build their industrial or financial empires. Much of the early success of the rise of the corporation which permitted their fortunes was due, surprisingly to the fourteenth amendment and the interpretation of its wording by the Supreme Court. Although the primary intent of the amendment was to protect the Negro from the states interference with his civil rights, there was also another idea in the minds of its authors—to enable the federal judiciary to protect corporations from any local or state regulation by the due process clause in the first section. The authors of the amendment were Republicans and represented Northern business interests, and it is not surprising that they wrote into the civil rights amendment a way for courts to aid the corporations.[9]

How well the authors did their job was demonstrated in what followed. Between 1881 and 1918 there were over 700 cases in the Supreme Court dealing with corporate rights under the Fourteenth Amendment, whereas there were only 8 cases involving civil rights. One of the first cases that came before the Court, and which provided the opportunities for hundreds to follow, was the famous *Slaughter House Cases* in 1872. The decision in this case emerged from events in the post-Civil War Reconstruction period, when Congress established control over the Southern states. The Court was anxious to reestablish its control over what the states could or could not do to the business interest, so it took this case to establish the precedence.

The case arose when carpet baggers (agents of Northern big business), during the Reconstruction period granted a monopoly of the slaughtering industry in New Orleans to one corporation. By this act about 1,000 butchers were denied the right to work. Before the Fourteenth Amendment was enacted the butchers would have gone to the state courts, but now they went to the Supreme Court. The Court ruled against them, drawing a line between state and federal citizenship. The Fourteenth Amendment, it claimed, did not confer on citizens more rights than they possessed previously. The monopoly which caused the problem was therefore not struck down. The business community benefited from the decision because the people could not seek relief from state laws, which gave special privileges to big business.

The Court, in another case, *Chicago, Milwaukee and St. Paul Railway* v. *Minnesota,* strengthened the position of the railroads against the rate increases. This time it made a more specific ruling which made it clear that the states had no rights to restrict the railroads in profit-making. It declared the view that the state had no rights to fix rates, "that under the due process clause of the Fourteenth Amendment, only the courts could determine the reasonableness of the returns. With the law thus interpreted by the Supreme Court, corporations felt their power to be unimpeded; let legislatures respond to public indignation; the Court would protect corporate rights."[10]

Thus, once again, the power of the Supreme Court to annul laws by the legislative and executive branches was reinforced.

IT has been claimed that the Founding Fathers were men of genius, and this is true. The government they constructed provided for a division of labor between the various branches to protect the rich from "the tyranny of the majority." This was not only a matter for the Supreme Court; it was also provided for in the Senate and the presidency. These bodies were the sources to determine the composition of the various members of the executive and the judiciary. But even more importantly, between them they had the most power over the conduct of foreign policy and wars. In times of severe crisis, the president could do in the United States what was provided for in the martial law in Great Britain, the state of siege in France, and Article 14 in the Weimar Republic (the legal basis for Hitler's rise to power in Germany).

The president, as Commander in Chief of the armed forces, can use the armed forces to meet both domestic unrest as well as conduct wars. In connection with making war, certain powers are held by Congress, especially the budget. But as we have seen in the post-World War II years, we have fought several undeclared wars and Congress in the main was bypassed. The concentration of the wealth of the country, we have shown, is related to the role government has played. But another factor is how the government has been used to acquire riches through wars and foreign affairs. In this connection, wars have been big business's most profitable business. Nowhere has the parasitical nature of the machinery of capitalism been more revealed than by the conduct of foreign policy by the capitalist nations in the epoch of imperialism.

This is especially true in the United States which has become the topmost force in the world of capitalism. The rich have gotten richer and new forces have emerged rich in every war this nation has conducted, beginning with the destruction of the American Indian peoples and the Revolutionary War of 1776. It did not matter what the personal views of presidents were; they all conducted wars that mainly benefitted the rich.

This has been true of the so-called liberal as well as the conservative presidents. What was true in the birth and growth of the nation became "a thousand times" truer as we reached the end of the nineteenth century and in this century. The United States ruling class embarked upon the imperialist era under different circumstances than that of the European powers. And because of certain variations in situations, wars have been more profitable. The United States came onto the imperialist stage with the Spanish-American War in 1897, at a time when most of the world had already come under the control of Great Britain and the major European powers. Therefore expenditures by the United States for military conquest was less. The overhead required for assuming direct political control over governments which also required a permanent military force in the country was also less.

Victor Perlo, in his work *American Imperialism,* defined some of the differences of how imperialism developed in the United States and in Europe:

American Imperialism did not use colonial forms because the form of a nominally independent semi-colony proved more flexible and gave United States imperialism advantages over its European rivals . . . What were these conditions? Most of the European colonies were established in Africa and Asia, in places where fully developed nations did not exist, but merely a multiplicity of tribes and principalities. Most of the United States dependencies were established in Latin America where independent nations already existed . . . This made it more difficult to establish direct colonial rule. . . . Thus United States imperialism took place at a time when disguised forms of rule became more and more necessary in all parts of the world. . . . Finally, the Wall Street expansionists had to reckon with the democratic traditions of the people of the United States . . . During the final decades of the nineteenth century the farmers and urban middle class were resisting the domestic encroachments of the Wall Street monopolies. These currents merged in a political opposition to the most obvious forms of imperialist except the revolution of 1776 and the Civil War have been fought on expansion.[11]

Perhaps the most important factors were, 1) we possessed a country with a greater concentration of all the materials needed to build up and feed a multiplicity of industries; 2) we were geographically located so that this country was spared the destruction of domestic resources such as prevailed in Europe in the two world wars, which were the most destructive in history; 3) our manpower was mainly devoted to production in the factories, mills, mines and workshops; 4) we entered both wars only after Britain and the European powers had become exhausted; 5) and because of a relatively sharper period of direct involvement when factories were equipped to supply many of the needs of both the imperialist powers and the vast colonial world. Finally, all the wars in our history, except the revolution of 1776 and the Civil War have been fought on other peoples soil. Where we had to act alone all we needed was a small, well trained elite. Thus the Marine Corps became our main offensive weapon in this hemisphere. The corps' major purpose is contained in the oft quoted remarks of General Smedley Butler. Looking back in disgust with the role he had played, he stated:

I spent thirty three years and four months in active service as a member of our country's most agile military force, the Marine Corps. . . . I spent most of my time being a high class muscleman for Big Business, for Wall Street and for the bankers. In short, I was a racketeer for capitalism. . . . I helped make Haiti and Cuba a decent place for the National City Banks boys to collect revenues . . . looking back at it I feel I might have given Al Capone a few hints.[12]

ALL liberal presidents, in one way or another, participated in the imperialist expansion of the nation. In modern times, the period of the greatest expansion of big business and its influence over the government took place under men who were regarded as trust-busters and liberals. Both President Woodrow Wilson and President Franklin Delano Roosevelt are regarded as foremost liberal, anti-monopoly presidents in the nation's history. Yet the concentration of monopoly capital, its firm control over the economy and the government received its greatest impetus in World Wars I and II. Woodrow Wilson, before becoming president, joined with others in letting "the cat out of the bag" when he wrote:

The masters of the government of the United States are the combined capitalist and manufacturers of the United States. It is written over every page of the records of Congress, through the written conferences at the White House, that the suggestions of economic policy of our country have come from one source, not from many sources. . . . Suppose you go to Washington and try to get at your government. You will always find that you are politely listened to, but the men really consulted are the men who have the biggest stake—the big bankers, the big masters of commerce, the heads of the railroad corporations and of steamship corporations.[13]

When Wilson became president some liberal legislation of a reformist character was passed. In 1916 he pledged to keep the nation out of war. Later he put the nation in war. In the conduct of the war, his was the loudest voice proclaiming the aim to preserve the world for democracy. At the war's end, he went to Versailles with the slogan of the right of nations to self-determination. But during the war his administration made possible a tremendous advance in the economy and the enrichment of the few.

According to tax returns from 7,000 corporations, their net earnings in the prewar years 1911–13 averaged 11 percent on invested capital. Many industry's profits went up more than 100 percent. In 1914 there were 6,000 Americans with taxable incomes of between $30,000 and $40,000; by 1918 there were 15,460 people in this bracket. It is estimated that the war produced 42,000 millionaires. As a result of such trends, the United States came out of World War I the richest and most powerful capitalist nation in the world.

While this was the situation with the money boys at the top of the pyramid, it was not the case with the people. Just as the people suffered and made most of the sacrifices in the Revolutionary War of 1776, the same was true in World War I. The materials from which great profits were made by the millionaires, came from the people being forced to undergo huge shortages of the most elementary needs. In 1919 coal was rationed and the American people experienced 'gasless' Sundays, 'heatless' Mondays, and 'lightless' Tuesday and Thursday nights. Food was an even greater problem.

As is usually the case, in order to facilitate the mobilization of the nation's resources, the president surrounded himself with the monied men as advisors and administrators, thus creating a situation where decisions could be made with profits as the main motive. Congress handed over emergency powers, comparable to many dictators, to President Wilson. With power in his hands, he proceeded to set up agencies to coordinate and control the whole economy. The War Industries Board was one agency which facilitated control. This agency, in 1918, came under the grip of the millionaire Bernard W. Baruch, who was responsible only to the president. He controlled priorities of transportation, raw materials, fixed prices on finished goods, and regulated labor requirements. There were many other agencies which helped to control the economy.

What was done in World War I laid the basis for what happened in World War II, out of which emerged a number of billionaires and a largely expanded grouping of millionaires.

President Roosevelt came to office in 1933 as a liberal reformer. He carried through more reforms than any previous president. He surrounded himself in the prewar period with what was termed the "brain trust." In and outside his Cabinet he brought in men and women, largely from the academic community, mostly liberal reformers. Like Wilson before him, he declared that he would "chase the money changers out of the temple." Roosevelt also spoke out against the growth of monopoly capital. In 1932, at the height of the Big Depression and the year he was elected president, he declared:

> The unfeeling statistics of the past three decades show that the independent business man is running a losing race . . . Recently a careful study was made of the concentration of the business in the United States. It showed that our economic life was dominated by some six hundred odd corporations who controlled two-thirds of American industry. Ten million small businessmen divided the other third. More striking still, it appeared that if the process of concentration goes on at the same rate, at the end of another century we shall have all of American industry controlled by a dozen corporations and run by perhaps a hundred men. But plainly, we are steering a steady course toward economic oligarchy, if we are not already there.[14]

This anti-monopoly statement notwithstanding, when war came Roosevelt followed the same course as Wilson. He too, promised to keep the nation out of the war. But there came a moment when we entered, and the money changers were brought into the temple en masse. They came for "a dollar a year." But even before this process began, the key posts that related to the economy were held by Wall Street representatives.

Anna Rochester, in her classical work, *Rulers of America,* noted the contradictions:

> Roosevelt, having announced that he would drive the money changers from the temple, started with fewer obvious Wall Street appointees. But the Treasury was tied to Wall Street through the Secretary, William H. Woodin, a close friend of the Republican T. W. Lamont, and the Undersecretary, Dean Acheson, member of a Washington law firm, often consulted by Morgan's chief counsel. The Secretary of Commerce, Daniel C. Roper, was known as a faithful political servant of the cane sugar interest.[15]

Even in the period of the "brain trust," there were appointments coming directly from big business. Among them were S. Clay Williams, President of the R. J. Reynolds Tobacco Company, W. A. Harriman, banker and head of the Harriman interests in railroads and aviation and who held numerous posts throughout the whole period of Roosevelt's administration, Edward Stettinus Jr., son of a deceased Morgan partner and chairman of the Finance Committee of U.S. Steel Corporation. The Industrial Advisory Board within the

National Recovery Administration was made up of several corporation leaders which included Alfred P. Sloan Jr. of General Motors, Walter C. Teagle of Standard Oil, Gerard Swope of General Electric and Pierre DuPont.

But whatever happened in the early period of Roosevelt's administration was inconsequential as compared to what happened when we entered the war. Although World War II in the main was a progressive anti-fascist war, all Americans who participated in the war did not have the same aims. The big corporations were motivated by financial considerations. They took the opportunity to once again gain huge government subsidies with which to widen their productive bases.

The corporations, in addition to funds received with which to expand production, received tremendous finances from the government, directly and indirectly, for research, which facilitated the productive process.

The government offered many other incentives: a plan was used which could amortize the cost of expansion for five years, which deflated taxable income while inflating earning capacity. Excess profits taxes could be recovered if the business showed a loss after the war. An economist termed this arrangement as the "biggest and most resilient cushion in the history of public finance."

This whole program was in keeping with the cynical remarks of Henry R. Stimson who stated: "If you are going to try to go to war, or to prepare for war in a capitalist country, you have got to let business make money out of the process or business won't work."[16] In other words, while the working people and their children are to be slaughtered on battlefields, the rich stay at home and get richer. Such are the morals of capitalist society in wartime. And great liberal presidents like Wilson and Roosevelt, despite their democratic rhetoric, were partners to the schemes.

Throughout the war, big business realized its first aim, a broader concentration of wealth on the home front. But the tycoons of big business had more "fish to fry" than what was done at home. They set their sights on the postwar world. Dr. Virgil Jordan, president of the National Industrial Conference Board, together with Henry Luce, publisher, of *Time, Life* and *Fortune* magazines, popularized the true intentions of the Wall Street magnates with the slogan of "the next half of the twentieth century will be the American Century." In other words, the fat cats on Wall Street were fighting World War II for world domination. Dr. Jordan made this very clear when he declared, "We have in our hands almost alone the decisive instrument of overwhelming military and industrial strength. The American people must be prepared to use that strength to subdue the world or it will destroy them."[17]

Dr. Jordan's dream almost came true, except the alternative of ruling the world was not destruction of ourselves, as the history of the last thirty years has shown. Thus, the growth of capitalism, the monopoly by the rich over the resources of the land, came from concealed forms of class dictatorship, through control of all branches of government, and above all during war periods.

PART II

RACIAL OPPRESSION

4 • DESTRUCTION OF NATIVE AMERICANS

WHAT WAS done to white people at the birth and development of the United States as a capitalist society was relatively insignificant in comparison to the crimes committed against the colored races throughout the world as capitalism moved ruthlessly upon the stage of history.

Karl Marx quotes W. Howitt, a man who made a specialty of studying Christianity as follows: "The barbarites and desperate outrages of the so-called Christian race, throughout every region of the world, and upon every people they have been able to subdue, are not to be paralleled by those of any other race, however fierce, however untaught, and however reckless of mercy and of shame in any age of the earth."[1]

The crimes were committed on every continent of this earth. The foundation for what was done by the English, Anglo-Saxon people, to the non-white races all over the world was laid by the genocidal treatment of the American Indian peoples.

When the colonizers came to America a clash of cultures took place. For certain historic reasons, born out of natural and man-made causes, capitalism came first to Europe and especially in

45

England and Holland. The birth and growth of the new system advanced civilization to new and higher levels of development. But one of the greatest contradictions in history is that when mankind learned how to create and use a tool and developed its brain power, at each stage of this development the morality of the society and humanness of the people in power was circumvented by the drive for more wealth and power. Capitalism developed in an unprecedented manner: technology, science and culture. But at the same time the morality of society declined.

Frederick Engels described the process thusly

. . . civilization achieved things of which gentile was not even remotely capable. But it achieved them by setting into motion the lowest instincts and passions in man, and developing them at the expense of all his other abilities. From its first day to this, sheer greed was the driving spirit of civilization; wealth and again wealth and once more wealth. Wealth not of society but of the single scurvy individual—here was its one and final aim. If, at the same time, the progresseive development of science and a repeated flowering of repeated art dropped into its laps it was only because without them modern wealth could not have completely realized its achievements.[2]

The colonizers who laid the foundation of the U.S. nation reflected that which Engles wrote more than any people in history. The merchant class and landowners came to America at a time when this vast New World had opened up unprecedented opportunities for acquiring wealth. In the New World they would not be inhibited by social mores or values of previous societies. Before they came they had already adjusted their religious views to those deemed necessary to acquire riches quickly. Here they would not need to come in conflict with the old institutions of feudalism. Here they would not require extreme idealization of thinking but would be able to concentrate more on practical values. Here the development of capitalism could proceed in its purest forms and as a consequence in its worst form.

The desperate drive to get rich quick was not confined to the monied classes but also affected the lower classes, including former indentured servants. Broad masses became paupers as capitalism emerged in Europe. Dehumanization by poverty created desperate moods in the masses who were seeking any means to extricate themselves from the depths of despair. The merchant class, the traders and the land speculators conducted a propaganda campaign on how easy it was for anyone to go to the New World, and rise out of a low status and become rich. The idea cultivated was to get rich no matter what was required. Thus, many of these God-loving people were prepared to sell their souls to the devil, in the name of doing the Good Lord's work.

Among the colonizers, the worst came from Britain and Holland—the most advanced capitalist nations. Thus the history of our nation opens with a clash of cultures: one represented by the Indians at the most primitive stage and the other from the most advanced so-called civilization "capitalism." The morals and humane qualities of the Indians were on a much higher level than their "civilizers."

Lewis Henry Morgan, a noted anthropologist, made a detailed study of ancient societies, of the life style of the American Indians. He contrasted the morals of the Indians and the Europeans, concluding:

> Since the advent of civilization, the outgrowth of property has been so immense, its forms so diversified, its uses so expanding and its management so intelligent in the interest of its owners that it has become, on the part of the people *an unmanageable power. The human mind stands bewildered in the presence of its own creation.* The time will come, nevertheless, when human intelligence will rise to the mastery over property and define the relation of the state to the property it protects as well as the obligations and the limits of the rights of its owners. The interest of the society are paramount to individual interests and the two must be brought into just and harmonious relations.[3]

Will Durant, the author of *Our Oriental Heritage,* discussing various aspects of the development of civilization drove home the point made by Morgan and Engels when he wrote: "Dishonesty is not so ancient as greed, for hunger is older than property. The simplest 'savages' seem to be the most honest. 'Their word is sacred,' said Kolben about the Hottentots, they know 'nothing of the corruptness and faithless arts of Europe.... When property develops among primitive men, lying and stealing come in its train.'"[4] Based on these different sets of moral values a clash between the native Indians and the colonizers developed with ever increasing intensity.

When two cultures collide something is bound to happen. In ancient times the Romans conquered Greece, but they acknowledged the superiority of Greek culture. Basing themselves on what the Greeks had done, the Romans built a higher form of culture. In another time the Germanic peoples, representing a lower form of civilization conquered the Romans and extracted the best from their society. It has been this continuous cross fertilization of people of all colors in varying levels of social development, in various parts of the world, that has brought civilization to its present high level. It is conceivable that given a different approach the present level of technological and scientific progress made in the United States could have been accomplished without all the bloodshed and human cruelty that effected both the red and white races.

But the Indians were not treated by the colonizers as the Romans treated the Greeks, and the Germans the Romans. The colonists who came to America brought with them a new ideology. An ideology unknown in previous history: *Racism.* They regarded the Indians not as human beings but as wild animals whose destruction was a precondition for their self-aggrandizement and incidentally to "advance civilization." In destroying Indians they were doing "God's work."

Today there are many whites who are giving a different version of European-Indian relations. James Wharton, a white American who lived and studied with the Indians, concluded:

Ever since the white race has been in power on the American Continent it has regarded the Indian race . . . as its inferior in every regard. . . . Our national literature has become impregnated with the fiendish conception that the only good Indian is a dead Indian. The exploits of a certain class of scouts and Indian hunters have been lauded in numerous books so that even school boys are found each year running to the West with a belt of cartridges around his waist for the purpose of hunting Indians.[5]

One of the main problems between the colonizers and the Indians was the attitude toward the national resources and their usage. The Indians regarded themselves not as owners of the earth but part of it, as being part of the natural scheme. They did not believe in private ownership of the land, that rather that the land was for communal use and only the products it produced were to be taken from it. The colonizers had no such conception. To them the national resources were products to be exploited. Their program was to take, rape, and destroy in the pursuit of wealth. Behind both of these concepts were religious beliefs. The Indians believed that nature was God. But the colonizers placed no spiritual attachment to the land and natural resources and they could be exploited to one's heart content.

Arising out of a code of ethics of two different societies with one side viewing the other as "animals" there was written on these shores some of the greatest crimes in history. After more than four centuries of trying to destroy the spiritual beliefs of the Indians, little or no "progress" has been made despite these attempts. Why should Indians adopt Christianity when men calling themselves Christians have demonstrated that Christian concepts such as "Do unto others as you would have them do unto you" and "Thou art thy brother's keeper" indicate that the Christian credo has no influence on Christian actions? The Indians say that the white man talks with a forked tongue. He preaches goodness and practices evil.

Thus the clash between an ancient culture and modern civilization as expressed in the birth and development of the American nation has profound meaning for the present day world. In what way did the clash take place? What were the methods used to dispose of it?

THE classical examples of the brutal treatment of the Native American Indian people begins with the Pilgrim Fathers. The contrast between the professed religious character of the Pilgrims and the barbarism they displayed against the Indians opened up a chapter of hypocrisy which has continued throughout the entire history of this nation.

In March 1621, an Indian by the name of Samoset wandered into the new settlement at Plymouth Rock. Soon afterwards he returned with Squanto, an Indian who had spent some time in England, as his interpretor. Samoset was cautious about the intentions of the settlers but was anxious to assure them of his good feelings toward them. The Pilgrims were in no position to turn down a gesture of friendship and they proceeded to draft a treaty which outlined how they proposed to live together.

But the treaty was a masterpiece of deception—the colonists evaded their responsibility to keep the peace. All the provisions were mainly directed to the Indians as the possible peace breakers. And while peace lasted for several decades, it was the colonists who eventually broke the treaty and put the Indians on the defensive.

Meanwhile, the colonists were able to survive, thanks to Squanto who remained with them and taught them how to live in a set of conditions that the Pilgrims were not prepared for. He taught them how to set corn and fertilize its growth by placing a dead fish at the base of each hillock. He showed them where to catch fish and to procure other commodities. Many historians state that it is doubtful the colony would have survived without the all-round assistance of Squanto.

But notwithstanding such aid and assistance the settlers were suspicious of the Indians. Their prejudice was rooted in the assumption that the Indian was an obstacle to the progress of civilization. Indian generosity was explained as an act of God whose intervention had caused the Indians temporarily to behave in a benevolent fashion. In Puritan literature we find such statements as, "God caused the Indians to help us fish at very cheap rates. The Puritan fathers saw their life in the new world as part of God's plan and the Indians as mere agents to do their bidding or be destroyed."[6]

Peace reigned for a while between the colonists and the Indians. But eventually this gave way to strife and warfare as the Indians began to resent the enroachments upon their land by the Pilgrims.

The Puritans wrote page after page of cruelty and humiliation. The contempt with which the Puritans regarded Indians is revealed in this order from the general court of the colony of Massachusetts Bay in 1664: "It was ordered that noe Indian shall come at any towne or howse of the English (without leave) upon the lords day except to attend the publike meetings; neither shall they come att any English howse upon any other day in the weeke but first shall knocke att the doore and after leave given to come in (and not otherwise)."[7]

Eventually bloody war broke out, the first of the great Indian wars now known as King Phillip's War. Due to the traitors in his own ranks, the Indian King Phillip was eventually tracked down and killed. The colonist troops decapitated and quartered his body, and his head was taken back to Plymouth, stuck to a pole and put on public display for twenty-five years. Phillip's son was sold into slavery in the West Indies. This was the beginning of barbaric warfare that eventually culminated in the kind of acts perpetrated in Nazi concentration camps and the atrocities of U.S. troops in Vietnam.

The propaganda theme about the savage nature of the American Indians is the portrayal of them as scalpers. But scalping was not an Indian innovation. It was introduced by the governor of New Netherlands to facilitate collecting bounties on Indians. Once the Indians had assisted them in surviving the first few winters, the Dutch, hand-in-hand with the British, carried out a systematic program of genocide on all Eastern tribes.

The pious Pilgrims did their full share of scalping Indians. In this connection Karl Marx wrote:

Those sober virtuosi of Protestantism, the Puritans of New England, in 1703, by decrees of their assembly set a premium of £ 40 on every Indian scalp and every captured red skin; in 1720 a premium of £ 100 on every scalp; in 1744 after Massachusetts-Bay had proclaimed a certain tribe as rebels, the following prices: for a male scalp of twelve years and upwards £ 100, for a male prisoner £ 105, for women and children prisoners £ 50, for scalps of women and children £ 50. Some decades later, the colonial system took its revenge on the descendants of the pious Pilgrim fathers who had grown seditious. . . . At English instigation and for English pay they were tomahawked by red-skins. The British Parliament proclaimed blood-hounds and scalping as 'means that God and Nature had given into its hand.'[8]

Sweet civilization!

WHAT was done in the formative years of the colonies set the stage for dramatic episodes of even greater dehumanization of whites and genocide of Indians. The struggle for land was the key problem between the colonizers and the Indians. With few exceptions, the thirst and greed for the Indians' land swept throughout all the colonies. It mattered not what religion was involved.

Just as there were no scruples in the religious world on depriving the Indians of their lands, so it was in the political world. Thomas Jefferson, widely acclaimed as America's greatest champion of democracy, was the first president to call for the removal of the Indians from the East Coast into the West. However, this proposal was garbed in humane language such as: They were to be removed so that they could enjoy their culture without having to adjust to "civilized man."

So from 1802 onward, the problem of Indian removal was debated and eventually became the policy of government. In 1812 the Shawnees, like other tribes of the Midwest, were harassed, intimidated and "conned" into ceding their land. The government arbitrarily appointed several Indians as chiefs in land cession treaties. It is estimated that the Sac and Fox tribes lost 50 million acres of land, the Delaware tribe lost 3 million acres and were offered no more than $7,000. At times the government did not wait for treaties but by legislative actions annexed the Indian land. When Andrew Jackson became the president, Indian removal became the law of the land. Under the leadership of Jackson, who like Jefferson is widely acclaimed as a democrat, the removal of Indians became comparable to the removal of a herd of cattle. He denounced as an 'absurdity' and a 'farce' that the United States should bother even to negotiate treaties with Indians as if they were independent nations.

He exerted his influence upon Congress to pass a law that today under the Nuremberg Laws would be branded as genocide. Congress passed the Removal Act of 1830 which gave the president the right to drive out all Indians who had survived east of the Mississippi River. When the U.S. Supreme Court ruled against the law, Jackson is said to have remarked: "John Marshall has made his decision now let him enforce it." Notwithstanding the Marshall court ruling, in the next ten years almost all Indians were cleared out from the East, in most cases at the point of bayonets. It is generally estimated that close to 100,000 Indians were resettled west of the Mississippi. No figures exist as to the number massacred or losses due to disease and starvation on these 1,000 mile marches. This was the context in which the Cherokees were removed, which some writers describe as "one of the darkest chapters in American history." While Americans generally regard Jackson as a great democrat, Black people and Indians will say "for whites only" and only for "some whites." What he did in the removal of the Cherokees, the Seminoles, the Creeks and Choctaws by military methods will be forever associated with his name.

If there is anything that dramatizes the lie that the colonists sought to "civilize" the Indians, to make them embrace European culture, it is the removal of the Cherokee tribe from their natural habitat. For the Cherokees, more than any other tribe of Indians, tried to adopt some of the ways of the white invaders. They were doing what the Germanic people did when they were put under the heel of Caesar in the days of the Roman Empire, that is, attempting to accept the invaders' culture.

The Cherokee tribes, in their homelands in the mountains where Georgia, Tennessee and North Carolina meet, had made remarkable progress. Peter Farb in his book *Man's Rise to Civilization* makes this observation: "They established churches, mills, schools and well cultivated farms; judging from the description of that time the region was a paradise compared with the bleak landscape that the white successors have made of Appalachia today."[9]

In 1826 a Cherokee reported to a Presbyterian Church that his people possessed 22,000 cattle, 7,600 houses, 46,000 swine, 2,500 sheep, 762 looms, 1,488 spinning wheels, 2,948 plows, 10 saw mills, 31 grist mills, 162 blacksmith shops and 18 schools. In one district alone there were 1,000 volumes of books. And by 1828 the Cherokees were publishing their own newspaper and had adopted a written constitution providing for an executive, a bicameral legislature, a supreme court, and a code of laws.

Before the passages of the Removal Act of 1830, a group of Cherokee chiefs went to the Senate committee that was studying the legislation to report on what they had achieved in the space of forty years. They expressed the hope that they might continue to enjoy in peace their rightful heritage. Instead, they were subjected to brutalities and atrocities by white neighbors, harassed by the government of Georgia and denied the protection of the federal government.

After many threats, about 5,000 consented to march westward but about 15,000 decided to stay and General Winifred Scott (of Civil War fame) set out to exterminate the rebellious ones. Squads of soldiers descended upon isolated Cherokee farms and at bayonet points they were marched off to what would be called concentration camps today. No way existed for the Cherokee families to sell their property and possessions and the local whites took possession. Those that were rounded up were sent on a 1,000 mile march, a march that is called "The Trail of Tears." It was one of the most infamous death marches in history. A Frenchman, Alexis De Tocqueville, who came to the country to write a book about the new democracy, was shocked by what he saw being done to the Cherokee and Choctaw tribes. He was in Memphis at the time of the march and he wrote in his book *Democracy in America:*

It was in the middle of winter and the cold was unusually severe. . . . The Indians had their families with them and they brought in their train the wounded, the sick, with children newly born and old men on the verge of death. They possessed neither tents nor wagons but only their arms and some provisions. I saw them embark to pass the mighty river and never will that solemn spectacle fade from my remembrance. No cry, no sob was heard—all were silent. Their calamities were of ancient date and they knew them to be irremediable.[10]

The westward expansion following the Civil War, the development of the railroads, and the forced treaties deprived the Indians of all productive land and forced them to live on the deserts in reservations. In 1887 an act was passed called the Dawes Severity Act. At the time of the act, the Indian land base was 1.38 million acres. Between 1887 and 1934, 60 percent of land passed out of Indian hands. All kinds of treaties were violated and the federal government did nothing about the outright thefts. Up to 1868 nearly 400 treaties had been signed by the United States government and scarcely a one remained unbroken.

In regard to treaty making and its observance, once again the so-called savage Indian proved to be on a higher moral level than his barbaric civilizers. This fact was attested to by Atkins who had been a coordinator of English and Indian affairs and had negotiated many treaties. He wrote: "No people in the world understand and pursue their true national interest better than the Indians. . . . Yet in their public treaties no people on earth are more open, explicit and direct . . . nor are they (the Indians) excelled by any people in the observance of their treaties."[11]

At the close of World War II, when the horrible crimes in the concentration camps of Nazi Germany were revealed, the peope of the United States were shocked almost beyond belief. They were horrified when they learned what the Nazis did at Lidice, Czechoslovakia—the town was razed to the ground, and all its male inhabitants shot to death and all the women and children were sent to slave and starve in concentration camps. They were outraged when they learned that millions of inmates of these concentration camps were stripped of all personal items (including the gold in their teeth) and after being murdered their bodily remains were used as "natural resources," i.e., ashes and bones for roadbeds. In some instances, human skin was used to make lamp shades. Yet similar crimes were committed against the American Indians in the name of civilization (read capitalism). But most Americans did not cry out or become horrified at the inhuman treatment of the Indian people. It was a generally accepted fact that such treatment was necessary to advance civilization. Most people honestly believed that in dealing with Indians they were not dealing with human beings but with savages—in the words of President George Washington, "beast of prey, animals dressed up in human form."

The extermination of Indians by uniformed U.S. troops, by lawless bands of settlers and tradesmen who advocated extermination of the Indians as the simplest means by which they could confiscate land and other natural resources were regarded as acts of great heroics. Our history books have made heroes of some of the greatest crooks and dehumanized people the world has ever known. These so-called great men, most U.S. historians claim, cleared the forest, destroyed the Indian people, and laid the foundation for the great technological and scientific advances that we enjoy today. Such thoughts are fed to every generation of American children from the cradle upwards.

William Meyer, an Indian writer, tells the story of what happened in a raid led by a former minister, Colonel John M. Chivington, which attacked an Indian camp while its occupants were sleeping.

... on November 28, 1864, Sand Creek was the scene of a massacre of the Cheyennes by the Third Regiment of the Colorado Volunteers under Colonel Chivington. Chivington instructed his men: "Kill and scalp all, big and little; nits make lice." The butchery of the Chivington massacre at Sand Creek, though only one of many, many similar actions rarely recorded in genteel textbooks, was unequaled by Indian "savages" anywhere or any time during their resistance to the advance of white "civilization." Women were shot down while pleading for mercy. Other women were cut down with sabers and otherwise mutilated, to be left alive in lieu of more lively quarry. Children carrying white flags were slaughtered and pregnant women were cut open. The slaughter and mutilation continued into the late afternoon over many miles of the bleak prairie. Both male and female genitals were later exhibited by the victors as they marched into Denver, and some were made into tobacco pouches.

The camp had contained nearly 1,000 Indians. Though reports vary as to the number killed, the generally accepted figure of nearly 200 still stands, of whom about 150 were women and children. The Denver *News* reported that: "All (soldiers) acquitted themselves well.' Only three women and four children were taken prisoner and exhibited like caged animals in Denver. Great applause was given the men displaying their Indian 'scalps' between acts in Denver theatres."[12]

Crimes such as this could fill volumes. It was not U.S. fascists who clubbed infants to death in the arms of Indian mothers. It was not an acknowledged dictatorship which violated the Indian treaties and condoned the illegal expropriation of land. All this was done in democratic America.

These crimes were committed under the guise of advancing civilization. But then the question arises, were the Indian people capable of embracing the scientific and technological development of civilization? The evidence shows that they were as capable of social advancement as any other race of people on this earth.

5 • NOT A BACKWARD RACE

WHEN IT comes to discussing people who helped to make the United States great, the Native American Indian peoples are considered least of all. Almost all our literature and propaganda media portray them as savages incapable of development, indeed as obstacles to the advance of civilization. These lies are given as "justification" for their genocidal treatment. Some of the most sympathetic white writers dealing with the Indian experience and the rapacious and brutal colonizers of the United States have also placed limitations on the capacity of the Indian people to embrace higher forms of so-called civilization.

Simons, a socialist historian, made a contribution when he delineated the class forces at work which developed the United States as a nation, but he fell short in estimating the responsibility for the way U.S. history developed: "The Indian would die," said he, "but he would not serve. If the Indian had been more of a conformist, how different American history would have been."[1] In this context, he also placed the responsibility for Black enslavement on the Indians. For if they had responded and accepted oppression, enslavement of Blacks would not have been necessary.

De Tocqueville, who was horrified at the treatment of the Indians at the time of the great removal westward, and who predicted their demise also, could not free himself from the master race concepts. Wittingly or unwittingly, he too embraced the rationalizations for every rotten act perpetrated upon the Indian people. He wrote: "The Indians will never civilize themselves so that it may be too late when they may be inclined to make the experiment."[2] He gave their woodland existence and nomadic character as the reasons.

But were the Indian people a backward race incapable of

advancing to higher levels of social life? The contributions they made to the advancment of world culture even from the lowest level of human society gives a categoric answer to such slanderous concepts about them. What they developed here long before the ruthless capitalist colonizers came, helped to set the stage for the great achievements that came later.

The Indian people have a rich history of progressive development. When we take into consideration geographical and natural obstacles, they stand out second to no people in history. They have been characterized as savages, but such a characterization hides a multitude of sins. Durant, in his book, *Our Oriental Heritage,* placed this question correctly: "In one important sense the savage, too, is civilized for he carefully transmits to his children the heritage of the tribe—that complex of economic, political, mental and moral habits and institutions which it has developed in its efforts to maintain and enjoy itself on the earth. It is impossible to be scientific here; for in calling other human beings 'savages' or 'barbarians,' we may be expressing no objective fact but only our fierce fondness for ourselves and our timid shyness for alien ways."[3]

Durant was exceptionally observant when he wrote about the embellishments that the forward march of civilization has added to the foundations that most races acquired on their own. Almost all the races that comprise humanity had a more favorable base to add to their knowledge than did the American Indian.

THE growth and development of civilization was not the monopoly of any given race or people. It took place in direct proportion to causes produced by nature and the ability of one or another people to learn from previous civilizations.

Since the dawn of civilization, contact has existed among the peoples who inhabit Europe, Asia and Africa in one form or another. At one time or another, one or another people on these continents surpassed all others in the advancement of civilization. But this did not come about because of some superior traits that some people possessed. There were natural and social causes of an environmental nature that were the main determinant.

One of the yardsticks that can be used to measure the progress of a people is the form of contact they have or had with other people. The Chinese people at one time had a higher form of civilization than did most Europeans. As such, they made contributions to the advancement of mankind. European travelers, who had certain compelling reasons, visited ancient China and brought back many new methods of extracting from nature numerous products that sustained and developed human life and culture.

The Chinese conducted trade with European and African peoples, but at no time in their history did they leave their home base to take to the seas and come to Europe. Yet they could have done so. Basil Davidson, a noted historian and a specialist in African development, took note of the fact that the Chinese possessed ships more advanced than the ones used by Columbus to cross the Atlantic 106 years before. Yet, the Chinese never used their ships to come to Europe. Eventually, China barricaded herself behind a Great Wall and slowly began to retrogress.

There were great African civilizations south and west of the Sahara which traded with Africa and Europe. In the latter case, the trade was conducted through North Africa with the Arab peoples who had more direct contacts with the European nations. Most European people were unaware of these civilizations until the Portuguese, in the latter part of the fifteenth century, sailed around the African continent and discovered a civilization which they declared to be similar to their own.

The mode of transportation was an important element in the ability of one or another people to keep contact with other peoples and to learn from them. But the incentive to seek out means of transportation was facilitated by material needs. Contacts between African kingdoms and trade routes to Asia and North Africa were made with the usage of camels. It is estimated that at one time the Kingdom of Mali on the western coast of Africa had a caravan of over 20 thousand camels who criss-crossed the whole continent and transported products to and fro.

The internal relations in Europe were maintained by the usage of the horse. Later, as necessity dictated it, sea power became the main mode of transportation to keep contacts with the rest of the world.

IT IS against a background such as this that the relative lack of progress by the American Indian must be assessed. No people in history have been as isolated, internally and externally as the American Indians. And yet, in the face of such isolation, the progress that was made is almost miraculous.

No one can tell with certainty the origin of mankind on the continents of North and South America. Yet there are some facts that stand out and provide some possible clues. It is generally agreed that homo sapiens originated in Africa, near Tanzania and migrated to Central Asia, and from that point, spread out over the world. There are some historians and archeologists who have asserted the possibility at one time of a continent between Africa and South America. It is called the continent of Atlantis. But so far this possibility appears to be more a figment of the imagination than a realistic possibility. Others speculate that during the Ice Age, a bridge between Asia and North America existed across the Bering Straits and that Mongoloid people crossed it and came into North America and eventually migrated throughout both continents.

Of all the possibilities, this one seems to be the most plausible. The American Indian physical features are mainly Mongoloid, although within Indian culture, traces of other ethnic backgrounds have been ascertained. There is, no doubt, that at some point in history, due to some factors promoting travel not presently unraveled, other ethnic groups came to America.

We do know for a fact that the Vikings were here long before Columbus. Legend has it that in the early part of the thirteenth century, Musa, a king of ancient Mali, left the West Coast of Africa accompanied by a few thousand small ships, sailed into the Atlantic and never returned. His point of departure was from Dakar which, in relation to Brazil, is the shortest route across the Atlantic Ocean. It is conceivable that he came to the New World and was unable to return home.

But whatever the case, with the exception of Central and South Africa, the North and South American continents were the most isolated spots on the globe. Whoever and whenever people migrated to this part of the world, they were cut off from contact with the main centers of world culture. Therefore, life began here under the most difficult circumstances. Even the ability of the early European migrants to this country to survive was a mark of greatness. The European colonizers in Virginia and at Plymouth Rock were almost destroyed by the natural difficulties they encountered. In both cases, help rendered by the Indians was the difference between survival and destruction. In addition to the unusual terrain in the Americas and total isolation from the rest of the world, the Indian peoples who migrated here almost lost contact with each other as they spread across the two continents.

In this case, nature played an unusual role. For example, the mode of transportation was the decisive factor enabling people to maintain contact with other groups: transportation via waterways was facilitated by ships, and on land in Europe and Asia by horses, and in Africa by camels. The Indian people were not endowed by nature with any of these facilities. They built canoes to travel the rivers and lakes, which evoked great admiration; but they were not equipped for long travel or for rough waters. They cut trails through the wilderness and laid the foundation for lines of communication from coast to coast and continent to continent. However, most of the travel took place on foot because there was no beast of burden at that time. The Indian people had neither horses nor camels; the only domestic animal that could facilitate land travel was the dog. Although horses had existed in the New World for more than 60 million years, they became extinct after the Ice Age ended. And they did not return until the Europeans brought them over.

As a consequence of these factors, contacts between various Indian tribes and groups were limited. Tribes only a few hundred miles apart had very little contact. Yet, in the face of obstacles such as no other people in history have confronted, the Indian people at various points on the continent built magnificent civilizations and made outstanding contributions to the well-being of the whole human race.

Morison, in his work, *The Oxford History of America,* gives due recognition to the character of the American Indians:

There is no reason to regard the North American Indian as an inferior race. Backward in many respects he was, but he has proven to have every potentiality common to other human beings. Americans of European stock ... who have taken the trouble to live with the Indians and understand their ways, find them inferior to none and superior to many in firmness of character and integrity of character.[4]

Morison elaborates more concretely on Indian achievements:

There is no reason to deprive the American Indians of credit for developing their own civilization. There is no doubt that they themselves without external aid or example designed and built the marvelous pre-Columbian monuments and sculpture of Central America and produced the beautiful examples of goldsmith's work, pottery and implements which are now treasures in museums.[5]

The Indian people on the North, Central and South American continents, like the peoples of Europe, Asia and Africa, created civilizations of varying levels. The highest forms of civilization were found in Mexico and Peru. In these places, while retaining many of the features of primitive communal society, they had advanced to slave and semi-feudal societies before the European invaders came. In addition to these main centers of advanced Indian culture all through Central America, we are still discovering remnants of what was once advanced forms of social development. Anyone who thinks that all Indians had an inferior culture which had to be destroyed to advance civilization, is invited to visit the ruins of Petén in Guatemala, Copán in Honduras, Chichén Itzá and Uxmal in Yucatan, Teotihuacán in Mexico. In recent times, huge complexes have been discovered near Mexico City and replicas of them are on exhibition in many North American museums. There are white pyramids, comparable to the pyramids of ancient Egypt; astronomical observatories; royal palaces covered with exotic birds and human figures; and sculptered glyphs telling stories, only part of which has modern man been able to read. There are also statues of forgotten gods; jade carvings, and masks impressive as a Gothic cathedral or the Acropolis of Athens.

When these monuments and sculptures were first discovered, the people in the United States could not believe that they had been created by the Indian peoples, and they tried to explain them by all kinds of stories of Chinese or East Indian migrations. But it is absolutely certain that the three great civilizations of Central and South America created these things on their own. They, like all other advanced civilizations, arose after thousands of years of development.

In Mexico, the Aztec and the Tezcular Indian peoples reached a high degree of civilization. The historian William H. Prescott gave concentrated attention to the developments in both Mexico and Peru. He wrote: "The degrees of civilization which they had reached . . . may be considered . . . not much short of that enjoyed by our Saxon ancestors under Alfred."[6]

Zanta, a Spanish jurist who spent about nineteen years in Mexico, became indignant over the epithet of "barbarians" bestowed on the Aztecs, an epithet, he says, "which could come from no one who had personal knowledge of the capacity of the people or their institutions which in some respects is quite as well merited as in the European nations."[7]

In Mexico, before the arrival of the Spanish conquistadores, a class-structured society had been built. It was mainly in the stage of slavery. But even here, slavery existed in a more humane form. According to Prescott:

The slave was allowed to have his own family, to hold property . . . his children were free. No one could be born in slavery in Mexico . . . an honorable distinction not known, I believe, in any civilized community where slavery has been sanctioned. Slaves were not sold by their masters unless they were driven to it by poverty. They were often liberated by them at their death and sometimes . . . married to them. In ancient Egypt, the child of a slave was born free if the father was free. This code, though more liberal than most countries, fell short of the Mexican.[8]

In Peru, an even higher form of civilization had evolved. Here, the domestication of animals and a feudal form of society had been erected at the time of discovery. The employment of domestic animals distinguished the Peruvians from other peoples of the New World. The substitution of human labor by animals is an important element in the advancement of civilization, although, as previously indicated, the animals capable of bearing labor burdens on this continent, in contrast to others, did not exist.

The Spanish conquerors found a flock of domesticated animals when they arrived in Peru. There were several varieties of sheep—the llama, huanacos and the vicuna. It is estimated that the Peruvians at that point in history had a flock of 30 to 40 thousand sheep. All of them were used for wool and food. The llama, in the absence of horses, camels, etc., were used as beasts of burden, but there were great limitations. The llama was capable of carrying not more than 100 pounds.

The Peruvians produced many different articles from wool. Vicuna wool was woven into shawls, robes and other articles of dress, as well as into carpets, etc. The articles were finished on both sides alike and the smoothness of texture gave it the luster of silk, while the brilliance of the dyes excited the admiration of Europeans.

In Peru, society had advanced to a feudal state; but here again, as in Mexico, it came to feudalism in a more humane form. The land was divided into three categories, one for the sun, one for the nobles and one for the people. The land for the sun was comparable to land ownership by the church in medieval Europe. The land that was reserved for the nobles was comparable to the landed estates of the feudal lords. But in this instance, the land for the people was of a higher quality. The lands for the sun furnished the revenue for the temples and places of worship.

All the land was cultivated collectively by the people. The land reserved for the sun was cultivated first, then the land that sustained the old, the sick and the widowed. This humane aspect was carried over from the communal societies. Following this order, then the land of the nobles and that of the people in general was cultivated. The land allotted to the people was cultivated and divided into equal shares, with additional allowances for each child. Each year the land allotments were checked to make allowances for the increases in families.

The American Indian, mainly because of natural circumstances, as we have pointed out, lagged behind the European and other peoples in technological, scientific knowledge and in the domestication of animals, but not in regard to agriculture, in the cultivation of plants.

It is estimated that agriculture began in the Near East perhaps as far back as 11,000 years ago but did not begin in the New World until a few thousand years ago. Yet, in that relatively small space of time, they outstripped all other areas of the world in the variety of production.

Agriculture developed in the New World independently of the old. This was evidenced by the fact that wheat, barley and rye, which were the first plants cultivated in the Near East, did not exist in the New World. Conversely, there were many plants cultivated by the Indian people that did not exist in any other area of the earth. Agriculture in the New World was not only different from that in the Old World; in many ways it was superior as well. Indians cultivated a wider variety of plants than did the Europeans at the time of the discovery of North America, and they used methods that in many cases were more advanced.

The connection between the Indian people and domesticated plants is best revealed by the development of maize (corn). Wheat or rye can survive in the wild as a weed but no form of maize has ever been found growing wild; they must be planted and developed. Maize does not contain any way for its seeds and kernels to be dispersed and would become extinct if mankind didn't plant it.

Because maize was the foundation of all New World agriculture, anthropologists have labored long to find the basis for its growth. An answer was not found until 1960, in a number of caves outside Mexico City when archeologists discovered a record about 12,000 years old. According to some writers, no other region in the world has ever given a better picture of the step-by-step development of their civilization.

They uncovered evidence that up to 12,000 years ago, the caves were occupied by small bands of nomadic families, who were collectors of wild plants and hunters of small animals such as rabbits and birds. Later a shift took place. Plants were increasingly used as food. Between 7 to 8,000 years later, the people still relied upon wild varieties of chili peppers and beans. Later, about 7,000 years ago, maize appeared. Each ear was no larger than a thumbnail, but the Indians learned how to take the small cob and develop it into a plant, and began the cultivation of large cobs. The survival of the early colonists was largely based on maize. Edmund S. Morgan has documented the fact that as late as 1620-21, after fourteen years in the New World, the Jamestown settlers were still dependent upon the Indians for corn.

The discovery of how to develop corn has had a profound effect upon the dietary habits of the whole world. It was brought to Europe by the Spaniards in the 1570s, eventually reaching Ireland about 1606. (Records for production of world staple crops in 1966 show that two from the Indians of the Western Hemisphere—maize and potatoes: 531,641,000 metric tons, are second only to two crops from the Old World—wheat and rice: 562,185,000 metric tons.

The archeologists doing research in Mexico and Central America found not only when and how the Indians developed a seed for corn, but also many other products that are in wide usage today. A team of archeologists under the direction of Richard McLeish, threw new light on the subject of the rise of New World agriculture. Their studies revealed that upward of 5 to 6,000 years ago, a pod-type corn, cotton, squash and avocadoes appeared. In addition to these discoveries, the McLeish team uncovered many other developments which show that the American Indian was as progressive as any other race on the globe.

As a result of these developments, among the world's total food supply today, almost half the crops grown were first domesticated by

American Indians and became known to the European and other peoples only after 1492. In addition to corn and potatoes, two of the main staples, more than eighty other plants were domesticated. These include peanuts, squash, peppers, tomatoes, pumpkins, pineapples, advocadoes, cocoa (for chocolate), chicle (for chewing gum), various kinds of beans and vegetables and fruits. Cotton grown in the United States, in Egypt and in Africa were derived from species cultivated by the Indian peoples. Tobacco was first seen by Columbus in the form of cigars.

Without these developments, how different our eating habits would be today! When we take into account the fact that the Indians inhabited only a small portion of the whole world, and yet contributed over half of the world's agricultural products, their contributions are all the more amazing.

HOWEVER, the contributions of the Indians, though mainly in the area of agriculture, were not confined to food products. They learned how to take other products and produce many of the present-day necessities of life. Morison says:

From caoutchouc they fashioned elastic rubber balls which were used in a game similar to basketball. . . . and the latex they used for water-proofing bags, shoes and garments. Even the hunting tribes learned to fertilize their gardens with fish and wood ashes. Before Columbus arrived, Arawak already knew how to leach out the hydro-organic acid from the manioc or cassava plant, using the poison for arrows and the starchy substance for bread . . . they evaporated salt from saline lakes . . . and in dressing skins and preserving fur, they were equal to the best European tanners and furriers.[9]

Despite the limitations of chemical and tool knowledge, the American Indians, nonetheless, made discoveries that are used today in medical science. At least fifty-nine drugs came from them, including coca (for cocaine and novocaine), cascara sagrade (a laxative), datuna (a pain reliever), and ephedra (a nasal remedy).

Although many Indian medical cures and skills have been lost with the passage of time, they were very valuable to the early colonists who came without doctors and without any natural knowledge of how to use the tools and drugs given by nature. The Indians had a number of remedies for toothaches, gangrene, ulcers, backaches, rheumatism, and weak eyes. They were also able to perform some surgery and had advanced somewhat in the areas of psychiatry. The seneca snakeroot was valued as a cure for coughs and snake bites. Although this drug is not today recommended for snake bites, the *Pharmacopeia of the United States* reports that it is used as an expectorant, cough remedy and a stimulant.

The hemlock tree was used by Indians to cure scurvy among Jacques Cartier's men in 1535. A seventeenth century writer, John Josselyn, reported that the natives healed sores and swellings with the inner bark of a young hemlock. One tribe is reported to have pulverized the bark and swallowed it for diarrhea and made tea from its leaves to bring on perspiration to cure colds. Other tribes also used the bark to stop bleeding and to heal cuts. It is estimated that about 170 drugs listed in the *Pharmacopeia of the United States* were known to the Indians north of Mexico. Jacobs says: "Indian medicine shows that the historical arrogance white Americans have toward the Indian is misplaced because clearly, the Indians . . . were in certain areas of medical science far in advance of their European contemporaries."[10]

ANOTHER area of social development which shows the progressive nature of the Indian people is the science of linguistics. At one time, scholars who sought an explanation for the primitive beginnings of mankind's power of speech thought that a study of a primitive people like the Indians would give them a clue. But after studying various Indian languages, it was revealed that they were no more primitive than European languages; nor were they any more limited in their vocabularies.

It is generally estimated that a simple dictionary of the English language for use by those with an education beyond the high school level contains about 45,000 words. The King James version of the Bible used about 7,000. Yet it has been found that the number of words recorded in the Nahuatt language in Mexico is 27,000, in Maya 20,000 and in Dakota 19,000.

Although there were only two languages in written form in the New World, most Indian groups were able to communicate a rich unwritten tradition of poetry, oratory and drama. There were about 550 distinct languages and about 2,200 dialects.

The most advanced Indian civilizations were in Mexico, Central and South America. The Indian people in North America were at a lower stage of development. They lived mainly in the woodlands and subsisted by hunting, primitive methods of farming and the domestication of animals, although there were some tribes on the plains who lived in a more advanced stage of social development. But even those in the woodlands, before the European invaders came, were in a constant state of change.

Changes were resulting from the exchange of goods. Trade took place in copper, wampum, salt, tobacco and other items. As one tribe came to excel in the growing of tobacco, it began to trade off the surplus. Thus, surplus products were traded again and again throughout the Indian world. The influx of trade goods of hardwares, textiles and food from Europe accelerated the process of trade relations in the Indian world, even in the woodlands.

The woodland Indian tribes knew hundreds of years ago things that we are only beginning to learn. While they utilized all that nature had to offer, they also knew the meaning of what we today call ecology. The early pioneers, in their mad drive for wealth and power, ruthlessly destroyed both people and the products of nature. In both cases there is a law of "compensation." In the course of time, both people and nature will confront the exploiting forces. Historians have yet to show adequately the mentality that ignored the laws of nature and what it has produced in today's industrial world. There has been very little investigation of the effect of the free trade and the killing off of certain types of wild life. The colonizers who claimed a belief in an impersonal god in his treatment of nature operated as if they were God. To them, everything in nature existed for one purpose and one purpose only, namely, to be exploited to enrich the lives of the few.

In more recent times, as nature has begun to backfire and our cities are suffering from pollution, a more sober approach in some circles is being taken. It is now being recognized that the reckless exploitation of the Indian people along with minerals, waterways, soil, timber, etc., can no longer be sustained in the name of taming the wilderness. A modern-day progressive historian placed the problem in its proper perspective when he wrote:

Can modern America stand back and look at the historic west migration as a huge page in social history? Can we see how the white man's frontier advance is also the story of the looting and the misuse of the land? . . . Because of our exaggerated respect for the entrepreneur . . . we have failed in our histories to condemn this early rape of the land, . . . How can one assess the historical damage brought about by allowing commercial interests to override our true national interest?[11]

The despoilation of our natural resources, the increasing number of unsanitary waterways as industrial waste is allowed to enter into them, and the pollution of the air, have brought our civilization to the point where we must learn what the Indians knew several centuries ago. Indeed, Indian people are still pleading with the nation to learn from their experience. Vine Deloria, a Standing Rock Sioux, calls out:

American society could still save itself by listening to tribal people. While this would take a radical reorientation of concepts and values, it would be well worth the effort. The land-use philosophy of Indians is so utterly simple that it seems stupid to repeat it. Man must live with other forms of life and not destroy it . . . reorientation would mean that. The public interest, indeed the interest in the survival of humanity as a species must take precedence over special economic interests.[12]

There are some who are beginning to listen to the words and the contributions of the so-called savage woodland Indians. The former Secretary of the Interior, Steward L. Udall, in his book, *The Quiet Crisis,* wrote in 1963:

From this widsom we can learn how to conserve the best parts of our Continent. In recent decades we have slowly come back to some of the truths that the Indians knew from the beginning; that unborn generations have a claim equal to our own; that men need to learn from nature to keep an ear to the earth, and to replenish their spirits in frequent contact with animals and wild life. And most important of all, we are recovering a sense of reverence for the land.[13]

In other words, instead of "conquering" nature, some people are finding value in the Indian lesson of learning to utilize all that nature has to offer and not to abuse that privilege. There are additional developments which show that the Indian people on this continent, though backward in some things, were far in advance over the marauding "civilizers" from Europe. Among them is the art of government and the conditions out of which real freedom and real democracy can be obtained.

Frederick Engels, co-worker of Marx and a founder of a scientific theory for socialism, was so impressed by the Iroquois Federation that he wrote in glowing terms: "A wonderful constitution . . . no soldiers, no gendarmes or police, nobles, kings, regents or judges, no prisons, no law suits—and everything takes its orderly course. All quarrels and disputes are settled by the whole of the community affected by the gens or the tribe, or by the gentes among themselves."[14]

Some of the main features of the confederation were as follows:

1. A federation of five tribes with each having complete equality and independence in all internal matters.

2. The organ of the confederacy was a federal council of Sachems (leaders), all equal in rank and authority. The decisions of the council were final in all matters relating to the confederacy.

3. All decisions of the federal council have to be unanimous.

4. Voting was by tribes so that for a decision to be valid, every tribe and all members of the council had to agree.

5. Each of the five tribal councils could convene the federal council.

6. The meetings of the councils were held in the presence of the people. All could speak but the council alone decided.

Women were not elected to the council but had the right of recall of the men who were elected.

Some of the colonialists who observed this structure of government in practice were impressed, notably Benjamin Franklin. Some historians claim that the structure of the U.S. government was influenced by the Iroquoisian example. There is a great deal of similarity between it and the Articles of Confederation, the first form of government set up after the Revolution. However, such a loose confederation was inadequate to meet the needs of a class-structured society with its conflicting individual and class interests. In order to cope with such problems, a strong centralized and less democratic structure of government had to be established.

THERE is a point in understanding this past history. For what it tells us today is that if the same attitudes that led to the genocidal treatment of Indians prevail under present-day conditions, the future of the whole nation will be at stake.

Today many Indians are warning of this possibility. Among them is George Pierre, Chief of the Colville Confederated Tribes of Washington, who wrote a book about the present Indian crisis, and declared: ". . . it is not difficult to think of oneself as a God if one is strong, wealthy. . . . the white Gods never see their image, their weaknesses, their imperfections. . . . But the white man shall continue to falter until he realizes that every human being on this earth whether he be red, yellow, brown or black is his equal."[15]

The genocidal treatment of the Native Americans throughout our entire history, if for no other reason, places serious limitations upon the claims that this nation in its fundamental character is a democracy. The contributions the Indian people made to making America great must be the starting point in the evaluation of the great American tradition, for it is one of the most distorted aspects of that tradition.

The foregoing should suffice to show that the American Indians, though living in more primitive forms of social organization, made profound contributions to the advancement of civilization. They were not a static people and were subject to change. This in itself is evidence that the historic process did not require the genocidal treatment which was accorded them by their "Christian colonizers." Extended humane treatment, the American Indians could have become part of the further development of the nation. The policy of extermination of the Indians was not a basic necessary component for the development of the capitalist system in general. It was a super-imposed form which made the development of capitalism in the United States more painful for all people, including the ruthless colonizers.

Capitalism as it developed on a world scale had a number of basic characteristics shared in common. But these had more to do with content; the forms of capitalist development have varied from place to place. Capitalism as a system is ruthless, repressive and de-humanizing. In all instances of capitalist development, exploitative and super-exploitative qualities have been a basic necessity.

Throughout U.S. history, racial oppression as it applied to Blacks has been in sharp focus. But the genocidal treatment of Native Americans and the truth about what took place out on the western frontier has yet to be fully told. Moreover, this nation which is composed of many races and nationalities owes a tremendous debt to the original inhabitants of this land. And until Native Americans gain their full rights, no one in this land will ever enjoy full freedom.

6 • CAPITALISM AND THE SLAVE TRADE

THE SECOND aspect of racism in the development of the U.S. nation was the enslavement of Black people. Slavery in one form or another, at one time or another, has existed in all parts of the world. No race has been able to escape this horrible form of social development. But the form which the enslavement of Blacks took on with the emergence and growth of capitalism has no precedence in history.

When the continent of Africa was raped by the slave traders, slavery as a major aspect of society had passed; it had been supplanted by feudalism. But capitalism, a more advanced form of society, revived slavery under different conditions and in a worse form.

At this point in time, only the Black race was enslaved. As was mentioned in a previous chapter, whites in colonial America passed through a temporary form of slavery as indentured servants. But that did not last long. Also, here and there, efforts were made to enslave the Indian people both in North and South America. But for various reasons, those efforts failed. Therefore, for several centuries, the slaves were almost exclusively Black people.

Draining Africa of its labor power to build up civilization in other parts of the world left an effect that today challenges humanity to remedy. Slavery not only affected the Africans at home but also those who were dragged off to live a life worse than animals.

The crimes committed against Black people who were enslaved began off the West Coast of Africa and continued on the voyage to the New World, the horrors of which have been called "the Middle Passage," into North and South America. The peoples of Africa had long known slavery as a system of society. Various African tribes engaged in the practice. Slavery in those periods didn't exist on a racial basis. It resulted from one people conquering another and the conquered were forced to labor for the conqueror. But with the coming of capitalism, a new dimension was added to slavery, namely, racism. This was not true at the beginning of the slave traffic.

The first European nation to engage in slave traffic directly with Africans was Portugal. The Portuguese began as early as the first quarter of the fifteenth century to search out the African coast. By 1434 they rounded Cape Bojador, reaching Rio D'Oro in 1436. And with this as a springboard, they pushed along the coast to Sierra Leone, the Grain, Ivory and Gold Coasts to the mouth of the Niger. They finally reached the equator and opened up a slave trail in Africa of over four thousand miles from the Senegal River in the North to the southern part of Angola beyond the equator.

During this period, the traffic in slaves was not based on the European discovery of the New World, and consequently did not become a massive affair; nor as inhuman as it eventually developed.

For one thing, the Portuguese priests saw the slaves, who had been bartered for with European manufacturers, as captives with souls to save. An injunction was laid upon Prince Henry, the organizer of these expeditions, to bring true faith to these people. When slaves were uprooted in greater numbers, Portuguese convents received the orphans and gave them a Christian education; seminaries accepted Blacks as candidates for the priesthood and they were not recognized as beasts of burden but as men.

These approaches indicate that the history of the earliest slave trade, European directly with Africans, was not carried out on a racial basis. That came later. Zoe Marsh and G.W. Kingsnorth, in their work, *A History of East Africa* which examined early European contacts with Africans, took note of this fact. They wrote:

> When the Portuguese and others first made contact with the native states of West Africa, they found a culture there which they felt they could understand and appreciate. The feudal nature of the West African Kingdoms was enough like that of fifteenth-century Europe for the Europeans to recognize the system and to feel at home with it. True, they oversimplified the comparison and drew some unwarranted conclusions, but the important idea here is that they accepted the idea that native African states were on an equal footing with European ones. African and European kings considered themselves to be brother monarchs and addressed each other as such.[1]

This attitude existed when the slave traffic was between Africa and the Mediterranean Sea area of Europe. Capitalism had not developed to the point where labor power had become a necessity.

In 1492 Columbus discovered the New World, and in 1511 the first fifty slaves were brought from Africa to the Antilles. Frank Tannenbaum says that "by 1517 the trade had been so well established that a regular 'asiento' was given to the Governor of Bressa to introduce 4,000 blacks to America."[2]

IT WAS not long afterwards that a massive slave trade began. Initially, it was still the Portuguese who engaged in the traffic, but later, other European powers came into the act.

Spain alone, of all the Christian powers, considered the trade illegal; her ships never were allowed to engage in slaving, and the law was quite strictly enforced. There were two exceptions—Christopher Columbus's enslavement of Indians and the nineteenth century smugglers. The Portuguese, British, French and Dutch did the actual carrying of slaves from Africa to the New World.

While the Portuguese, Dutch and French built up the slave trade, eventually the British emerged as the greatest slave traders in the world, and possibly in history. In 1562, Hawkins, the son of a merchant, sailed to Sierra Leone and secured over 300 slaves and went with them to the Spanish colonies. This was the beginning of Britain's entrance in the slave trade. Queen Elizabeth, when she heard of his voyage, denounced it as a "detestable venture." But she cooled off when Hawkins disclosed his profits. She then helped to finance his next voyage. Eventually, Hawkins met with disaster and England's interest in slavery seemed to decline. About 100 years later, when the merchant class in Britain came into greater power, Britain, based now on a more solid capitalist foundation, entered into the slave trade seriously.

In 1672 Charles II chartered the Royal African Company. It dominated the English slave trade for over fifty years, during which time England became the world's greatest slave trader. Based on the enslavement of Black people, England built her commercial supremacy and helped to lay the basis for her emergence as the most powerful capitalist power of the times.

Competition developed among various British cities for a major share of the trade. Initially, London, the headquarters of the Royal African Company, was the chief port, but Bristol and Liverpool caught up and surpassed the capital. There were material reasons for this change: they were closer to the factories that supplied the goods for the Guinea trade; they also built longer, lower and faster ships, plus the docks to hold them, which made Liverpool the biggest port in the world.

Milton Meltzer says that:

By 1800 Liverpool was sending 120 ships a year to the African Coast, with a loading capacity of some 35 thousand slaves. The city carried about 90 percent of the slaves out of Africa. The average net profit of each voyage was 30 percent, and profits of 100 percent were not uncommon. The whole city, said a Liverpool Minister, "was built up by the blood of the poor Africans." Tailors, grocers, tallow-chandlers, attorneys—all had shares in fitting the slave ships. The trade used the labor of thousands of boat-builders, carpenters, coopers, riggers, sailmakers, glaciers, joiners, iron-mongers, gunsmiths, and carters. Just ten companies in the town controlled two-thirds of the slave trade. Production of the goods for the cargoes to Africa stimulated British industry, gave employment to her workers, and brought great profits to her businessmen. Much of that commercial capital helped launch the industrial revolution.[3]

Karl Marx, in his treatment of the basic forces behind the rise and growth of capitalism, took special note of the role of the slave trade. He wrote: "The turning of Africa into a warren for the commercial hunting of black skins signalized the rosy dawn of the era of capitalist production. These idyllic proceedings are the chief momenta of primitive accumulation."[4]

There were several factors which brought about the dominance of Britain in the enslavement of Black people, and laid the basis for the emergence of Britain as the foremost commercial and industrial power. Among these was the abstinence of Spain from the trade itself.

In 1713 Britain concluded a treaty with Spain which gave her a complete monopoly with the Spanish colonies. The treaty was known as the *asiento*. It provided for England to supply the Spanish colonies within a period of thirty years with at least 144,000 slaves at the rate of 4,800 per year. England also agreed to advance Spain 200,000 crowns and to pay a duty of 33 ½ crowns for each slave imported. The kings of Spain and England were to receive one-fourth of the profits. According to Dr. Du Bois, from 1730 to 1733, 15 thousand slaves were annually imported into America by the English, of whom from one-third to one-half went to the Spanish colonies.

In addition to the abstinence of Spain, the rise of industrial capital, which required sources for raw materials, set England apart from the other European powers. England established its own colonies where production of staple goods, such as sugar and tobacco, and later cotton, accelerated the need for labor power. While over 19 million British citizens migrated to the colonies either as indentured servants or on their own, this did not suffice to satisfy the thirst for profits which the New World offered.

The slave trade developed in the West Indies when it was discovered that sugar could be cultivated there, and that it brought great profits. In 1643 the sugar industry took root in Barbados. By the end of the seventeenth century, the exports of Barbados to Britain, which were composed almost entirely of sugar, were worth more than the exports of all the rest of Britain's colonies in America. In the eighteenth century, Jamaica became the greatest British sugar island, with a slave population of 300,000.

Finally, the colonization of North America, which at first was slow but as the plantation system based on sugar, tobacco and eventually cotton developed, gave the greatest impetus to the traffic in slaves. There are many estimates as to how many Africans were exported to North and South America. Estimates vary from 15 to 20 million. But whatever the case, it was one of the greatest migrations of people, forced or voluntary, in history.

IF, as has already been observed, the slave traffic was the basis for the commercial and industrial advancement of the modern world, what then was its effect upon Africa as a continent?

During the period of the most intensive development of the trade, voices were heard which could not reconcile the enslavement of Blacks and Christian principles, thus laying the foundation for theories of racial superiority and inferiority. The main argument for the enslavement of Blacks was that the white man was assuming a "burden"; that bringing them to the New World, even in the form of slavery, was a Christian act of civilizing a backward race.

But the results show just the opposite. In order to bring 20 million to the New World to work and slave for nothing, Dr. Du Bois estimates that between 60 and 80 million Africans died. Meltzer characterizes the so-called civilizers as follows: "The men who brought the black slaves from Africa to the new world were a mixed lot—cutthroats and Christian speculators and adventurers, gentlemen and pirates, seamen and surgeons."[5]

In regard to the level of civilization in Africa before the slave trade and colonization took place, many historians and anthropologists have discovered much evidence of highly developed African civilizations. As previously noted, one author wrote about the attitude of the Portuguese when they came to Africa.

The research of Dr. W. E. B. Du Bois more than three decades ago, much of which has been substantiated by many current historians, provides a masterful and scholarly answer to the racist ideologists of the theory of the inferiority of Black people. In one of his classical works, *The World and Africa,* he covers in detail various aspects of the effects of the slave trade and the colonization of Africa upon the people within continental Africa. In connection with the rape of Africa, Dr. Du Bois pointed out the background from which things began:

The rebirth of civilization in Europe began in the 15th century. At this time, African and Asian civilizations far outstripped that of Europe. . . . By any standard of measurement—homes, clothes, artistic creation and appreciation of political organization and religious consistency, throughout the whole of the Middle Ages, West Africa had a more solid politico-social organization, attained a greater degree of internal cohesion and was more conscious of the social function of science than Europe.[6]

The nature of the West Coast African societies and what led to their destruction was further described by Dr. Du Bois:

The greatest attempt in human history before the twentieth century to build a culture based on peace and beauty, to establish a communism of industry and of the distribution of goods and services according to human need . . . . What stopped and degraded this development? The slave trade; that modern change from regarding wealth as being for the benefit of human beings, to that of regarding human beings as wealth.[7]

There can be no doubt that the traffic in slaves was the main factor which retarded the development of civilization on the African continent. You cannot take a hundred million people off a continent, whether through slavery or the consequences of it, without leaving a vacuum for further growth and development, especially at a time in history when science and technology had not grown to what it is like in modern times.

In World Wars I and II, the European powers suffered over a hundred million casualties. But in most cases, in a period of fifty years, they have recuperated. Most of the capitalist powers could recuperate at the expense of other capitalist powers and intensified exploitation of other parts of the world, mainly the colonial peoples. The European powers also received massive aid from the United States, which suffered relatively little loss of lives during both wars and instead waxed fat and rich from the deaths of other peoples and the destruction of their resources.

This ability to rapidly recover was also enhanced by the growth of science and tools. Africans did not exploit any other continent, nor did they at any time have modern tools at their disposal. With the growth of imperialism, European and U.S. exploitation of African resources further contributed to the technological backwardness of the continent.

The whole world is in debt to Africa, and it behooves all humanity to share some responsibility to help bring the continent up to the level of others. There are those who will argue that some Africans were partners to the crime—that is, the slave traffic. This is true. But one must examine the main force involved, and the circumstances of the times. As was already indicated, slavery has existed among all the races of mankind. It has been a natural period in the evolvement of society. But slavery that existed in Africa was more in keeping with its ancient character, a more humane form. When African chiefs sold slaves off the West Coast, they could not know what the effect would be for the slaves abroad and for themselves at home.

It was the new form and character that slavery took under capitalism, and under colonialism and imperialism at a later date, that places the primary responsibility for the rape of Africa and its present-day backwardness upon the European imperialist powers and the United States.

THE new and most inhuman forms of slavery started with the movement of slaves from Africa to the Americas. In the mad drive for profits, we noted in a previous chapter what happened to the indentured slaves when they were transferred to the New World. But what happened to the Black slaves was on a scale much vaster and even more brutal. The "Middle Passage" has come to symbolize one of the most brutal pages in history.

How many slaves died in the Middle Passage is almost impossible to assess. But it can be generally estimated between 15 to 20 percent. The result indicates that several million slaves died on the high seas enroute to the Americas. The mortality rates varied considerably from voyage to voyage and year to year. This is reflected in a list of mortality rates among slaves traded between 1715 and 1775. The rate ranged from 5 to 9 percent in sixteen years; from 10 to 19 percent in twenty-two years; 20 to 29 percent in fourteen years; and was 34 percent in 1733. From 1715 to 1775, 237,025 slaves were shipped and 35,727 died, giving a mortality rate of 151 percent.

Tannenbaum estimates that it is difficult to calculate the loss in lives exacted by the slave trade; all figures are estimates. But it has been said that one-third of the Africans taken from their homes died on the way to the coast and that another third died crossing the ocean.

What were the causes for such a high rate of casualties? They came in the first place from the drive for profits, to squeeze the maximum amount from the situation. The thirst for profits has been one of the most dehumanizing factors of the forward march of civilization.

In a situation where the enslavers were white, and the enslaved Black, it was easier for a racial backdrop to develop. There can be no doubt, no matter what rationalizations developed later, that those who sent the slave ships off into the Atlantic did not regard their victims as human beings, but rather as wild animals. Mankind, in its struggle for survival, has learned to show no regret at the slaughter of animals in order to exist, and when people of certain races and color are needed for exploitative purposes, the consciences of the enslavers do not become involved; the process of dehumanization comes to affect perpetrators of the crimes as well as the victims.

Thus, the Middle Passage opened with Black slaves being herded together under conditions that in modern times would not be done to animals that we transport to kill and eat. There have been numerous books and accounts which have dealt with this matter in great detail. Presented here is a summarized version of some of the sordid deeds that took place.

The slaves, after their capture, were forced on long marches, sometimes hundreds of miles. They suffered from hunger, thirst and exhaustion. Consequently, many died enroute to the African slave market. On the coast, the slaves were forced to jump up and down, had fingers poked in their mouths, and their genital organs checked by a doctor. Those chosen by the slave traders were then branded. They were taken aboad ship naked and shackled together on bare wooden boards in the hold. They were packed together so closely that they could not sit upright. During the trip, which lasted from several weeks to three months, an almost unbelievable condition was created. The foul and poisonous air in the holds where the slaves were kept, caused many to die from suffocation; men and women were forced to lie for hours in their own defecation, with blood and mucus covering the floor, causing a great deal of sickness. It is estimated that the mortality rate from undernourishment and disease was about 16 percent.

Under such horrible conditions, many slaves went insane and others gave up the will to live. Many slaves committed suicide by drowning, or refusing food or medicine, rather than accept enslavement. The captain of a slave ship enroute to the West Indies describes one of the efforts of mass suicide as he came close to the islands. He asserted that he:

Thought all our troubles of this voyage were over; but on the contrary I might say that the dangers rest on the borders of security. On the 14th of March we found a great deal of discontent among the slaves, particularly the men, which continued till the 16th about 5 o'clock in the evening when to our great amazement about an hundred men slaves jump'd overboard, and it was with great difficulty we saved so many as we did.[8]

The horrible conditions in the holds of the ships have been described and verified by hundreds of records, testimonies before legal bodies, and in biographies of people who engaged in the practice. A religious leader in 1831 described what it was like in the hold. He wrote:

The height sometimes between decks was only 18 inches so that the unfortunate human beings could not turn around, or even on their sides, the elevation being less than the breadth of their shoulders; and here they are usually chained to the decks by the neck and legs. In such a place the sense of misery and suffocation is so great, that the Negroes like the English in the black hole of Calcutta are driven to frenzy.[9]

Not only did the slaves suffer terribly during the few months crossing the Atlantic, there were times when they had to stay pent up in the holes for as much as nine months. For example, there were times when a ship upon arrival to the African station found it had just been preceded by another ship and it had to dock and wait for more slaves to come. Meanwhile, the docked ship would be loaded up with what was available. It is a matter of record that some ships spent six months or more waiting to get a full load. And there were other cases where the slave ships upon arrival in the Americas found no buyers—and therefore sailed from on island to another until their cargoes were sold, whatever the circumstances of departure or arrival.

The main reason for the inhuman conditions on the ships was to transport as many slaves as possible on a given voyage, to make it more profitable; although it is evident from the casualties that, given a more humane approach, the profits would have been greater. In addition to profits, there was also another factor. The slavers lived in fear of slave revolts. And they had cause to fear. While most revolts took place at the point of debarkation before actual sailing time, nonetheless the records show that many uprisings also took place on the high seas.

If there has been any doubt about the immorality and cruelty that capitalism escalated in the modern world, the traffic in Black slaves should suffice to prove the point. As capitalism spread all over North and South America, it brought Black slaves to the auction block to start life anew under circumstances no people had ever suffered. Especially was this true as slavery developed in the United States, "the land of the free and the home of the brave."

Thus, the problems the slaves faced on ships were only the beginning of a lifetime of misery and degradation.

7 • SLAVERY: ITS WORST FORM

IN 1830 an ex-slave, David Walker, made a study of slavery in the United States and issued an appeal, a call to struggle to end it. He took his travel experience and Bible as his main source of material and declared:

Having travelled over a considerable portion of these United States, and having, in the course of my travels, taken the most accurate observation of things as they exist . . . has warranted the full unshaken conviction that we (Colored People of these United States) are the most degraded, wretched and abject set of beings that ever lived since the world began; and I pray God that none like us may live again till time shall be no more. They tell us of the Israelites in Egypt, the Helots in Sparta, and of the Roman slaves, which last were made up from almost every nation under heaven, whose sufferings under these ancient and heathen nations, were, in comparison with ours, under this enlightened and Christian nation no more than a cypher—or in other words, those nations of antiquity, had but little more among them than the name and form of slavery; while wretchedness and endless miseries were reserved . . . to be poured out upon our fathers, ourselves and our children . . .[1]

Since Walker made these observations and accusations, many historians have come on the scene and verified Walker's conclusions. But despite all the historical evidence, the period of slavery in the United States in most cases is played on a low key, while the greatness of our nation as a democracy is presented as the main theme. The two-faced hypocritical nature of part of our heritage was well understood by Walker:

I saw a paragraph a few years since in a South Carolina paper which, speaking of the barbarities of the Turks said, "The Turks are the most barbarous people in the world and they treat the Greeks more like brutes than human beings." And in the same paper was an advertisement which said, "Eight well built Negro fellows and four wenches will positively be sold this day to the highest bidder!" And what astonished me still more was to see in this same human paper!!! the cuts of three men with clubs and bludgeons on their backs and an advertisement for their apprehension . . . I declare it is really amazing to hear the Southerners and Easterners of this country talk about barbarity . . . It is positively enough to make a man smile.[2]

The hidious forms of U.S. slavery as delineated by Walker and many others did not come as a sudden development. The first slaves were brought here more in the form of indentured servants. At that time, there was no legal code which defined their status, as chattel or lifetime slaves. The institution of slavery also took on different forms in different colonies.

In New England, Black slaves were imported very early. In 1638 they came on the Salem ship named *Desire.* Massachusetts was the first colony to recognize the institution of slavery. The first slaves came as domestic servants, and others were treated as artisans. Slavery, while brutal in New England, was nothing like what subsequently developed in the South. In fact, Rhode Island, a colony founded on principles of religious freedom and freedom of dissent, denounced slavery as early as 1652. Liberty, they said, was not only for whites but for all mankind. The law, however, was not obeyed. The pressure of profits was too great. Still, slavery came very slow to New England.

In the eighteenth century, Blacks constituted only 3 percent of the population. Slavery did not take deeper roots because climate and soil made a plantation system impossible. History shows that during the Roman empire, plantation economy was the most favorable ground for massive enslavement as well as brutality. Because of geographical conditions standing in the way of a plantation economy, the New Englanders concentrated on the sea. It was in this context that mercantile capitalists began to flourish in this area more than in others; vast fortunes were built on commerce, with the slave traffic becoming a basic component of the economy. Thus, the pious Christian Puritans who came to the new land to worship God in their way became partners in the crimes of whatever happened on the high seas and in the plantation system of the South.

The Salem ship, *Desire,* started the traffic. The New Englanders built up the production of a commodity that became one of the central features of the slave trade, namely rum. The process went as follows:

The ships crafted from New England timber were small, ranging from 40 to 200 tons and manned by crews of about 18 men and a boy . . . They sailed out of port with cargos of beans, peas, corn, dairy products, fish, horses, hay, barrel stones, lumber, bricks, brass, lead, steel, iron, pewter, shoes, beads, candles, dry goods and muskets. They headed for the West Indies where they sold their cargos and took aboard rum. Sailing to Africa, they exchanged rum, trinkets and bar iron for slaves. Then they turned around and brought the slaves to the West Indies selling the Blacks for cocoa, sugar, molasses, rum and other tropical products. They returned at last to New England where the sugar, and molasses could be distilled into more rum.[3]

This process made rum and the traffic in slaves New England's largest businesses. Boston was New England's main slave port and some of her most prestigious citizens drew their wealth largely from slaving. Among them were the Cabots, the Belchers, the Waldos, the Faneuils. George Cabot was the ancestor of two U.S. Senators, Henry Cabot Lodge, father and son. Jonathan Belcher was a governor of Massachusetts. Samuel Waldo, an ancestor of Ralph Waldo Emerson owned the slave ship *Africa*. Peter Faneuil's gift of Faneuil Hall, called "the cradle of liberty," was made possible by profits from slavery.

These are facts that most historians choose to ignore when they write about the glorious men and women who made the American Revolution and soft peddle this aspect of the motivations of some of the revolutionaries.

Slavery as it developed in the New Netherlands under Dutch control was in a more humane form than in the British colonies of New England, especially the South. It is difficult to find an adequate explanation for the differences except in the general contrast between the hangovers of the feudal life-style and the capitalist mode of production. But whatever the reasons, the life of the slaves in New Netherlands was somewhat different.

When the Dutch colonized New Netherlands (New York State), they too needed labor power. The whites who came over soon stopped farming to get into the fur trade. Most of them, like conquistadores in Latin America, aimed at getting rich quick and planned to return to Holland to live a life of ease and comfort. Thus, by 1626, the Dutch West Indies Company began landing slaves on Manhattan Island to work on farms, public projects and forts.

Slavery, as it developed at that time, did not take on a racial character. In many instances, as in ancient slave times, masters and slaves worked at the same tasks and lived in the same houses. There were no laws to control the movement of slaves and an incentive system was worked out by the West India Company. It was a half-freedom system akin to the indentured servants, and serfdom in feudal times. As a reward to slaves with a long and meritorious service, a system was developed where such slaves held passes that certified their personal liberty. In return, the slaves gave an annual tribute to the company (a hog, for example) and a promise to perform labor at certain times. A possible explanation for this more humane approach is provided by Meltzer. He says:

The Dutch were not concerned about a rigid slave code. Perhaps because slavery had died out in Northern Europe when New Netherlands was founded. These settlers came to the colony without precedents to guide them, so they improvised as they went along. The courts gave the slaves the same rights as whites. The treatment accorded slaves was relatively humane, if the fact that no slave conspiracies or revolts occurred can be taken as evidence. Slaves even helped defend Dutch settlements against the Indians and were sometimes used . . . against rebellious white tenants.[4]

After the Dutch gave up their colony to the British, the conditions of slaves deteriorated. But still they were not as harsh and inhuman as what took place in the South at a later date. Slavery under British control of New York was greatly concentrated. The Royal African Company developed this new market into a very profitable venture. Laws were passed in 1665 making slavery a legal institution and the slave business became so profitable that some of the most prestigious families participated in the profit making. The merchant's coffee-house, the meat market and the flea market became the scene of auction blocks. In fact, New York became a headquarters for pirates and cut-throats. The notorious Captain Kidd, as well as other pirates, brought slaves there.

Even though the conditions of the slaves deteriorated under the British, some of the things that took place under the Dutch remained. Since the slave population was of a highly skilled character, which the slave master needed and force could not obtain, the slaves had some bargaining power. And this usually brought them adequate food, clothing and medical care. There were times when they could stop an auction by declaring that they would not work for any of the bidders. Some slaves were allowed to acquire private property and dispose of it as they chose. Some slaves were able to save enough money to buy their freedom.

But despite these relative better conditions than those in the South, slaves found means to register their dissatisfaction with their status. Slaves pretended sickness, loafed on the job, stole things to get what was owed them, and became drunk and disorderly.

The slave masters tried to curb these protests by more rigid codes. They ruled that slaves could not be on the streets after dark. Gambling in crowds or drinking in taverns were prohibited. While there were no slave rebellions under the Dutch, by 1712 conditions under British rule changed considerably and the slaves began to revolt. In 1741 an indentured servant charged three slaves with plotting to burn down the town, and kill all the whites; the city became hysterical. Mass trials took place and 101 Blacks were convicted, 18 hanged, 13 burned alive and 70 banished.

THE typical form which came to depict slavery in the United States, the worst in history, started in the colony of Virginia. But here too, it came as a process and was rooted in certain conditions. Slavery for Blacks began in Virginia in 1619, slowly trickling in. These first slaves also came as indentured servants. The records are not clear on all aspects of the slave status during this period; however, by 1660, hereditary and lifetime slavery had been made into law in Virginia and Maryland.

The lifetime status of Black slaves and the terrible treatment they received in Virginia and later in all southern states developed with the growth of plantation economy. It began with tobacco and sugar. But the real explosion came with the cultivation of cotton.

In Virginia and later throughout the South, legal codes were developed which defined the status of the slaves. Contrasting them with previous periods of history proves conclusively that slavery in the United States was unique, the most brutal, the most oppressive, with no precedence in history. In this regard, Kenneth Stampp who characterized slavery in the South as "a peculiar institution," says: "In its early stages the South's peculiar slavery grew slowly and uncertainly. The specific form it took in the eighteenth and nineteenth centuries was unknown to English law, and in some respects unlike the forms of servitude which had developed in other places."[5]

During the latter part of the eighteenth century, shortly before the American Revolution, and afterwards into the middle of the nineteenth century, more stringent laws were enacted all over the South. These laws came to be known as the Black Codes and they covered every aspect of a slave's life. They varied from state to state, but generally the content was the same. The main feature of all Black Codes was that a slave was not a person, but property. The laws were designed to protect the owners of the property. A slave had no legal rights whatsoever. His owner was empowered to do whatever he pleased with a slave, including murder. Murder was not specified as such, but the conditions placed under the law made murder a possibility, especially since no slaves could appear in court against a master. Even in self defense, a slave could not strike a master. A slave had no standing in court. He could not be a party to a suit at law. He could not offer testimony except against another slave or a free Black; he could make no contract, nor own property; although some states permitted certain forms of personal property.

The main content of the Black Codes was to insure maximum protection of the slave masters and to maintain discipline. Whenever there was a slave revolt or even rumors of one, new and more stringent laws were enacted. Slaves could not leave the plantation without authorization and any person finding a slave away without permission, could turn him over to public officials. The slaves could not own or possess firearms; they could not beat drums or blow horns. They were never allowed to assemble unless a white person was present. Machinery was also established to effectively enforce the codes. One of these devices was patrols which kept the plantations and the roadways under constant surveillance. In 1712 South Carolina passed an act to govern slaves that became a model for all the other states. It was so comprehensive that every aspect in the daily life of a slave was covered.

One of the most horrible and insane features of slavery U.S. style was the selling of one's own blood into slavery. There were many laws which prohibited social or sexual relations between the slaves and whites, both male and female. Maryland, in 1644, passed a law stipulating that a white woman who married a slave had to go into slavery. Virginia passed a similar law.

In most cases, sex relations which produced mulattoes did not come as a result of sex relations between a Black man and white woman; it was between a white man and a Black slave woman. In this regard what was done to the Black women also has no parallel in history. She was completely at the mercy of the slave master, his teenage boys, as well as overseers. They did not even have to ask.

They could enter the slave quarters, pick out a woman, go to bed with her while the Black husband and others helplessly looked on. Most states passed laws which declared that offspring coming from mixed relations would take on the status of the mother.

In Virginia, according to the Code of 1849, "every person who has one fourth part or more shall be deemed a Mulatto." Thus mulattoes as well as Blacks were consigned to slavery. In many instances, the mulattoes were given the status of house servants; but still they were slaves. Codes were also adopted to prevent Blacks from becoming educated, and laws were passed prohibiting the teaching of slaves to read and write.

IN the early nineteenth century the slave traffic was banned by the major European powers and this process began to end the institution of slavery. France, under the impact of the French Revolution and the slave rebellion on Haiti, ended slavery in its colonies. But it was precisely at the time when slavery was being eliminated that a process of acceleration began in the South. This shift took place with the rise of cotton as one of the main textile materials in the world.

Prior to this development, the area where most slaves were concentrated underwent a serious depression. The tobacco plantations along the Atlantic seacoast in general, Virginia, Maryland and the Carolinas in particular, were plagued with two problems, soil exhaustion and a glutted market. Rice and indigo brought little profit and the price of slaves was on the decline.

But the situation changed when cotton came on the agenda of history. Revolutionary changes took place in the textile industry in England. Inventions produced new spinning and weaving machinery, so that the manufacturing process was greatly cheapened. What was needed to complete the process was a machine that could more easily separate the cotton fiber from the seed. This problem was solved when Eli Whitney invented a cotton gin in 1792. With this development a trend of migration westward began in the South. A large number of planters from the Eastern states moved into the South Central areas and later, began the trek further west.

At the beginning of the nineteenth century, the Southeastern states had grown most of the cotton. But by 1821 the South Central states were producing about one-third of the cotton. By 1834 the coastal states produced only 160 million tons while Alabama,

Mississippi, Louisiana and others were producing 297 and one-half million tons. In 1832 the Lynchburg, Virginia newspaper complained that the constant immigration "to the great West" of the most substantial citizens was the daily subject of complaint among mercantile men.

The spread of the cotton plantations to the Southwest brought about a division of labor between the Eastern states and those in the Southwest. Ulrich B. Phillips says:

> With the increasing demand of the world for cotton, there was built up in the South perhaps the greatest staple monopoly the world had ever seen. The result was an enormous demand for slaves in the cotton belt. American ports, however, were now closed to the foreign slave trade. The number of slaves available in America was now fixed. The rate of increase was limited and the old tobacco South had a monopoly of the only supply which could meet the demand of the new cotton South.[6]

Almost every community in Maryland and Virginia had their agents who went to the countryside searching for slaves at the cheapest possible prices.

> The slave traders were a ubiquitous lot. They could be seen at the general stores, the taverns, the county fairs and on the plantations. Whenever they heard of the possibility of the sale of slaves they were there. When estates were to be probated or liquidated, they sought out the persons and pressed them for whatever slaves were involved. Few salesmen today have the dual talent of the anti-bellum period. They could convincingly argue that a Virginian no longer needed his slaves and with equal firmness could show a Mississippian where he needed at least ten new hands.[7]

Washington, Baltimore, Richmond, Norfolk and Charleston were the main cities in the older states engaged in the domestic trade. In the new South, Montgomery, Memphis and New Orleans were the main stations for the trade. While Washington was not the largest slave trading center, nonetheless, it was the most notorious. It was the center for interstate traders. It was a place where slaves could be shipped by land and sea: Foreign visitors to the nation's capitol were puzzled at the sight of slave auction blocks, slave jails and slave pens. Many of them as well as many Americans, such as John Randolph of Roanoke roundly condemned the practice of selling human beings in the capitol of the *"world's most democratic nation."*

THE contrast between how slavery developed in Latin America and in the United States further illuminates the depths to which the nation sunk.

While slavery in Latin and South America was brutal, oppressive and dehumanizing, it was nothing compared to how it developed in the area of North America, or in the English-led colonies. The differences within the institutions have been well documented by numerous authors. Stanley M. Elkins placed these differences in sharp focus when he observed:

> In the slave system of the United States—so finely circumscribed and so cleanly self contained—virtually all avenues of recourse for the slave, all lines of communication to society at large, originated and ended with the master . . . In the Spanish and Portuguese colonies we are essentially impressed by the comparative lack of precision and logic governing the institution of slavery there; we find an exasperating dimness of line between the slave and free portions of society, a multiplicity of points of contact between the two, a confusing promiscuity of color, such as would never have been thinkable in our own country.[8]

In the Spanish colonies, a set of legal codes, which mitigated somewhat against some of the excessive practices, was handed down from slavery as it had existed previously in Spain. Herbert Klein, in his contrast between slavery in Cuba and Virginia, delineates the nature of the Spanish Codes, showing that those in Cuba were of a more humane character. It is questionable whether the codes were carried into practice completely. Nonetheless, it is clear that they placed some restraint on the slave masters.

The codes which defined the nature of slavery in Cuba and other Spanish colonies were developed in medieval Spain at a time when slavery in general had become obsolete and represented a holdover in the feudal system which in large part had departed from direct slavery. For all the cruelty of this medieval society, the balance between property rights and human rights stood in a vastly different ratio.

The Spanish codification of slavery was called *Las Siete Partidas Del Rey Don Alfonso el Sabio*. These codes were established under Alfonso X between 1263 and 1265. They were the outgrowth of a relationship between the races that did not yet require racism as an ideology. They resulted from long and continuous contact between Castilian whites, Moors and Black Africans. The slaves in these conditions were mostly servants and not plantation hands. The mode of production had not reached the point where the mad drive for profits on big plantations had developed as the dominant feature of agriculture.

Thus, when plantation economy developed in the Spanish colonies, the slave owners had to confront a traditional background based on social mores and church edicts that could not be entirely ignored. In Cuba, the ancient slave codes were supplemented with additional codes which helped to provide a more humane form of treatment.

All of these codes while regarding slavery as "a necessary evil," provided some human rights. Under them, a slave possessed some legal rights. Legally, he was assured personal security and the right to some property. By his admittance to the Christian faith, he also enjoyed the sanctity of marriage and parenthood. Even after plantation economy was established, the Black slave was often employed in the skilled trades and small farm economy. He worked side-by-side with freedmen, white and Black. Also, under these codes and customs, it was much easier for a slave to win free status than in North America. In 1789 a new series of codes were adopted in Cuba which set controls over both the slaves and masters, and legislated on such matters as health standards, diets, working hours, clothing and even minimum housing standards.

One of the factors which shaped more humane treatment in Latin America than in North America was the role of the church. While the church sanctioned the institution of slavery, it also faced some moral contradictions for which it had to provide. In Latin America, the Catholic Church was part of the ruling hierarchy and its edicts carried legal weight. In North America the slave masters, while often supported or criticized by church forces, were under no obligation to conform to church edicts. In this case, the church and the state had been separated and slavery, unrestrained by legal or moral force, could be conducted as the slave masters chose so to do.

At the same time that the church was a restraining influence on the more brutal aspects of slavery, it could not afford to condemn slavery outright. For to have done so would have brought about a collapse of all of its moral doctrines and most probably would have hastened the demise of the whole system of which the church was such an integral part.

In Brazil, a Portuguese-led colony, the church did not play the same role as in Cuba and the Spanish colonies. Nonetheless, slavery in Brazil was in a more humane form than elsewhere. This was true in almost every respect.

The role of the slave in Brazilian society, unlike that in North America, was part and parcel of the totality of the society. Gilberto Freyre, a noted Brazilian anthropologist, explains the situation:

The slaves that came from the more advanced areas of Negro culture were an active, creative, and one might also add, a noble element in the colonization of Brazil; if they occupied a lower rung, it was due simply to their conditions as slaves. Far from having been merely draft animals and workers with the hoe in the service of agriculture, they fulfilled a civilizing function. They were the right hand in the formation of Brazilian agrarian society.[9]

In Brazil, it was easier for a slave to secure his freedom than elsewhere. There were laws which made this possible. A master, by law, was obliged to give liberty to his slaves on all Sundays and holidays, which came to about eighty-five days per year—almost one quarter of a year. During this time, a slave could work for himself and acquire money to purchase his freedom. Even slaves in rural areas could retain the produce from their gardens and sell them on the market.

It was also possible for a slave to purchase his freedom on "an installment plan." He would first have his price declared. If he and the master disagreed, the local courts would determine it. Whereupon, he made his first payment. After that point, the price could not be changed. It was also possible for slaves in the Spanish and Portuguese colonies to retain much of their African culture and background. And in Brazil, the slaves were permitted to learn how to read and write.

WHAT accounts for these variations in slavery in Latin America and the United States?

Some authors who have dealt with this problem have taken into account the nature of the social systems involved and what was required to feed them. Elkins in his treatment of the question pinpoints some related factors that were involved. He wrote:

Why should the status of slave have been elaborated in little more than two generations following its initial definition with such utter logic and completeness to make American slavery unique among all such systems known to civilization? Was it the motive of gain? Yes, but with a difference. [In] . . . the emergent agricultural capitalism of colonial Virginia, we may already make out a mode of economic organization which was taking on a purity of form never yet seen, and the difference lay in the fact that here a growing system of larger scale staple production for profit was free to develop in a society where no prior traditional institutions with competing claims of their own might interpose at any of a dozen points with sufficient power to retard or modify its progress.[10]

Thus, the initially unfettered capitalist mode of production was the main factor behind the differences, unhampered by hangovers from a previous system with its variation of circumstances. For example, the plantation mode of production, whether it was for sugar, tobacco or cotton, was the basis for mass slavery in the New World. But even when the plantation system developed in full force in Latin America, superstructural and traditional institutions came into play to differentiate between aspects of slavery in Latin America and the United States.

There were also other factors which made slavery worse in the United States. The invention of the cotton gin which sparked the growth of cotton textiles, required a massive expansion of slave labor. But this occurred at a time when slavery in the rest of the hemisphere had become obsolete, and the international traffic in slaves was coming to an end. It was also the period of the Haitian slave revolt and many domestic slave insurrections which injected fear into the slave master and evoked from them unprecedented repressive measures.

Perhaps the best example of the differences in slavery which developed between the United States and Latin America is the role of Portugal. Portugal in the sixteenth century was the least rural and most commercial country in Europe. Freyre says that the king of Portugal, in that century, was engaged in widespread commercial activities, bourgeois in character. But when Portugal came to Brazil to colonize and develop the plantation system, it did so in a different manner than the Spanish, Dutch, French or English. What accounts for this difference? On the one hand, Portugal was the main center for the exploration of Africa, developing the traffic in slaves and embarking upon the commercial stage of capitalism. And on the other hand, it developed slavery in its most humane form in modern times.

Some historians observe that the Portuguese colonial system was more fortunate than any other so far as the relations of the European with the colored races were concerned. They stress that such a system was the child of necessity rather than the result of any deliberate social or political orientation.[11]

George Kimble in *Tropical Africa 1960* provides a rational explanation for the peculiar Portuguese situation which dictated the necessity to approach the problem differently. He pointed out that Portugal in the early sixteenth century had a very small population, about a million at most, yet they managed to colonize Brazil, maintain establishments in India and off the coast of Africa from Tangier to Malinda. It did research in navigation, cartography and astronomy second to none, and traded with practically every country in the known world.

There can be no doubt that Portugal's small population was a big factor in her colonization policies. In this regard, she did not have some of the assets in manpower from the home country that Britain, Holland and even Spain possessed. They at least had indentured servants and a large white population to draw upon to go to the New World, even before slavery of Blacks became a massive affair. This was especially true of women. Very few women left Portugal to come to Brazil. Brazilian white colonizers therefore had to develop a family relationship with their Black slaves and native Americans. Thus, unlike the southern U.S. slave masters who stalked into the slave quarters, had relations with Black slave women, birthed children by them and had to hide the evidence from legal authorities as well as their wives, the Brazilians took their mulatto children right into the family. They could also live with the Black slave woman, for all practical purposes, as man and wife.

Another practical problem the Portuguese faced in Brazil was the fact that the white colonizers were only a small part of the total population, whereas in the United States, whites at all times outnumbered both the Indians and the Black slaves. This necessitated a Portuguese policy based more on incentive and coersion than just brute force.

While all the foregoing factors and many more that could be mentioned were in the picture, the central dynamic force at work was the relative lack of racist ideology of the Portuguese and Spanish, for that matter too, in contrast to the European peoples of central and northern Europe. This factor was borne out of tradition and historical development. The people of central and northern Europe down through the centuries had had little or no contact with Black Africans. Especially was this true in their homelands.

In the classical period of slavery in the days of the Roman Empire, white Anglo-Saxons were brought together with people of Semitic, Arabic and Black racial stocks as slaves. But in southern Europe, the nations on the Mediterranean Sea had throughout the centuries a continuous influx of Africans into their midst. While this was true of Spain and the Italian cities, it was especially true of Portugal which is only a stone's throw from Africa.

Freyre also took note of the hybrid character of the Portuguese background as a humanizing factor along racial lines. He wrote:

> The singular predisposition of the Portuguese to the hybrid, slave exploiting colonization of the tropics is to be explained in large part by the ethnic, or better, the cultural past of a people existing indeterminantly between Europe and Africa and belonging uncompromisingly to neither one nor the other of the two continents; with the African influence beneath the Europeans and giving a sharp relish to sexual life, to alimentation, and to religion; with Moorish or Negro blood running throughout.[12]

The history of Portugal is also rich in accomplishments by Black Africans and mulattoes who attained great heights in the cultural achievements of the nation. Thus, racism did not, nor could have played the same role in the life style of the Portuguese as it did in its northern European neighbors. In fact, it is almost impossible to develop racist ideology in the context of a people who at one time had been conquered by the so-called inferior race.

Of course, in spite of the variations of the levels to which racism was developed into human consciousness, it would be wrong to conclude that life for Black people in Brazil or elsewhere has been one of ease and comfort. And as the years rolled on while Brazil gained independence, and many chose racial miscegenation, in modern times Portugal, with its African colonies, became an increasingly ruthless exploiter and racist in outlook.

This was the background out of which slavery emerged in its worst form, and the United States became one of the most racist-led nations in world history.

8 • THE BATTLE TO END SLAVERY

THE SECOND major democratic advance after the founding of the nation was the elimination of slavery. And the long and difficult struggle waged by Black people and the white abolitionists, free-soilers and Marxist labor forces to end the system of chattel slavery represents one of the most heroic chapters in U.S. history. But at the same time *the necessity* for such a struggle after the Revolutionary War of 1776 represents some of the most shameful pages in our history.

The Civil War which eventually was required to put an end to the slave system was unique in modern history. With the exception of Haiti, a more rational approach was found to resolve the problem elsewhere. The failure to do what other colonialists did in the Western Hemisphere caused the American people to suffer unnecessary calamities.

Charles and Mary Beard in their book *The Rise of American Civilization*, showed how costly the institution of slavery was to the American people. They wrote:

When, at the close of the great tragedy, the statisticians came upon the scene to make their calculations, the world was astounded to read the record of the awful cost in blood and treasure. Comprehensive and accurate figures were not available and the most cautious estimates varied but there were gross totals that staggered the mind. On the northern side, the death roll contained the names of three hundred and sixty thousand men and the list of wounded who recovered two hundred and seventy five thousand more. On the southern side, about two hundred and seventy five thousand men had given their lives to the lost cause and an unknown number had been wounded. . . . In treasure the cost was not as easily appraised. The mere war expenses of the belligerents amounted to about five billion dollars in round numbers. The outlay for three years of reconstruction was placed at three billion more. In a strict sense the property destroyed in the struggle, the pensions paid to the surviving soldiers, the economic losses due to the immense diversions of energies were all a part of the price paid for the preservation of the Union.... one thing was certain, the monetary cost of the conflict far exceeded the value of the slaves.[1]

For various reasons, geographical, economic, and moral, the struggle began in the North to end slavery before the Revolution of 1776.

Although the economic factors were the dominant reasons for the demise of slavery in the North, the moral factor became a great issue. In fact, the nation underwent a moral crisis. The colonists who took the lead in the struggle for independence from Britain, unleashed an ideological campaign before revolutionary acts took place. They proclaimed the natural rights of men and highlighted the ideas of liberty and freedom. These concepts were eventually portrayed in the Declaration of Independence. There were many people both Black and white, who took such noble sentiments seriously.

The eminent Black historian Lenore Bennett tells a story which dramatizes how most Blacks felt.

There lived in Connecticut in the days preceeding the Revolution a patriotic preacher who was given to making pretty speeches about liberty or death. This preacher owned a slave named Jack. The preacher preached and Jack slaved and listened and wondered. One day Jack went to his master and said: "Master I observe you always keep preaching about liberty and praying for liberty, and I love to hear you sir, for liberty be a good thing. You preach well and you pray well, but one thing you remember Master—Poor Jack ain't free yet."[2]

The ideological campaign before and during the Revolution backfired in many ways. The contradictions between words and deeds were so great that many people spoke out, including a few revolutionary leaders. Once again Bennett put this problem in its proper focus.

Consider the background of that great event. A colony with a half-million slaves decides to go to war in support of the theory that all men are created equal and are 'endowed by their Creator with certain unalienable Rights, that among these are Life, Liberty and the pursuit of Happiness.' . . . Consider the climax. Black men, some of them slaves enter the lines and sign the Declaration of Independence with their blood.[3]

As a result of this contradictory situation many white people denounced the institution of slavery.

In reference to Blacks fighting in the Revolutionary War, Harriet Beecher Stowe, said, "not for their own land they fought, not even for a land which had adopted them, but for a land which had enslaved them, and whose laws, even in freedom, oftener oppressed than protected."[4]

Tom Paine, one of the main ideologists of the Revolution and one of its most sincere advocates of freedom, spoke out against not only British tyranny but also the tyranny of the slaveholders. James Otis, Thomas Jefferson, Abigail Adams and a few other leaders came out against slavery. But these were not the forces that took the initiative, under the hardships of an unpopular position, that brought about an end to the horrible institution of slavery.

However, the Black slaves did not stand alone in that great struggle. Herbert Aptheker, Marxist historian, says:

It is a great fact in American history that the Negro people found white allies. Those allies came in the main from among the poor, and throughout the history of the Abolitionist movement, the rich in it could be counted on the fingers of two hands. No, it was the "plain" man and woman, the artisan and mechanic, the factory worker, the yeoman and small farmer, the poor housewife who formed the bulk of the membership of the Abolitionist societies; who constituted the great audiences that filled the antislavery conventions, despite intimidations; who contributed the largest part of the pennies and dollars with which the Abolitionist movement printed and distributed the pamphlets, petitions and papers appealing for justice and condemning oppression.[5]

An eighteenth-century English writer, Dr. Samuel Johnson, took great delight in the contradictory situation of the revolutionaries. He asked: "How is it that we hear the loudest yelps for liberty among the drivers of the Negroes."[6] It was against this moral background, together with economic reasons, that even prior to the Revolution several Northern states had legislated against the slave trade. Benjamin Quarles says that fear of slave revolts was also a factor in what began to happen in the North. But whatever the totality of reasons, the ending of slavery was accomplished in the North without a war or massive violent struggle.

THE rise of capitalism in the world was accompanied by the slave trade. The trade in slaves and their labor on the plantations was the main basis for the merchant class to obtain capital upon which industrial capitalism emerged. This was especially true in Britain which was the first nation to carry out the Industrial Revolution. The slave trade was also fruitful in the North of the United States for the merchant class. But as industries began to grow, free labor proved more profitable than slave labor. It was against this background, and the steady increase of immigrants, that northern capital saw no need for a life and death battle to hold onto slavery in the North. And so during and after the Revolution slavery began to end in the North.

By 1820 slavery for all practical purposes had ended in the North. This progress toward freedom had implications for the entire nation. Due to economic factors, the North and South began to clash; and as the struggle went on, the main Northern forces thought that their interests would be protected through compromises.

While some Americans understood the self-interest involved in ending slavery, the Founding Fathers who assembled at Philadelphia in 1787 did not. They did not grasp the fact that to compromise on the problem would become the enabling act for the most violent war in our history.

There were some who recognized that industrial capitalism would increasingly come in conflict with the agricultural sector of the economy, but they believed that in time, slavery would gradually disappear from the scene without a sharp struggle.

This was in the background of the Constitutional Convention. The Convention reached a compromise on slavery. The Founding Fathers not only reached a compromise with the slaveholders, they helped to sustain the system by a number of provisions written into the Constitution. Among them was Article 1, Section 2: "No person held to service or labor in one state, under the laws there of escaping into another shall in consequence of any law or regulation therein be discharged from such labor, but shall be delivered up on claim of the party to whom such service or labor may be due." This clause laid the constitutional basis for the fugitive slave law of 1793 and the fugitive slave law of 1850.

In one provision of the Constitution dealing with the basis for political representation, the South was allowed to count slaves as a basis for congressional representation. At a later date, John Quincy Adams, the son of John Adams, and himself a former president, denounced what was done at the Constitutional Convention. He declared :

The extent of the sacrifice of principle made by the North in this compromise can be estimated only by its practical effects. The principle is that the House of Representatives is a representation only of the person and freedom of the North, and of the persons, property and slavery of the South. Its practical operation has been to give the balance of power in the House, and every department of the Government, into the minority of numbers. For practical results look to the present composition of your government in all its departments. The President of the United States, the President of the Senate, the Speaker of the House are all slaveholders. The Chief Justice and four out of the nine judges of the Supreme Court of the United States are slaveholders. The Commander-in-Chief of your army and the general next in command are slaveholders. A vast majority of all officers of your navy, from the highest to the lowest, are slaveholders. Of six heads of the executive departments, three are slaveholders; securing thus, with the President, a majority in all Cabinet consultations and executive councils . . . With such consequences staring us in the face, what are we to think when we are told that the Government of the United States is a democracy of numbers—a government by a majority of the people?[7]

What was revealed by John Quincy Adams was true most of the time between the period of the establishment of the government and the Civil War. During this entire period there were only three presidents that were not elected from the South.

The question arises: If there was opposition to slavery by some of the most outstanding personalities among the nation's founders, how could they have turned so much power over to slaveholders? There may be several answers, but the one of primary importance was racism. Even though some southerners, like Jefferson, owned slaves and spoke out against the system, basically they were as racist as any other slaveholder. It is a common thing for liberals and some radicals to quote Jefferson showing his opposition to slavery. But rarely is he quoted to prove how racist he really was.

In his notes on Virginia, Jefferson wrote some racist views that one would think came from the pen of Adolph Hitler in *Mein Kampf.* He wrote:

The real destination which nature has made, and many other circumstances, will divide us . . . and produce convulsions, which will probably never end but in the extermination of one or the other race. To these objections . . . may be others which are physical and moral. The first difference which strikes us is that of color. Whether the black of the Negro resides in the membrane between the skin and scarf skin, or in the scarf skin, whether it proceeds from the color of the blood, the color of the bile or that of some other secretion, the difference is fixed in nature and is as real as if its seat and cause were better known to us.[8]

These extracts of Jefferson's scientific version of Black people shows how deep-seated racist ideology can become. Jefferson called for the elimination of slavery, but he regarded Blacks as so "ugly, odorous, and reasonless" that he advocated a program to ship the slaves back to Africa. In this respect he was consistent with his proposals to uproot the Native Americans and ship them westward.

In fact, even though the North eliminated slavery without a war, and did it immediately following the Revolution, racist ideology was perhaps as strong in the North as in the South. This problem came up in the Dred Scott Case just before the Civil War. Chief Justice Taney reviewed the historical status of the Black population and he stated that only because of climate and slave labor being unprofitable did the northern states decide to abolish the institution. But this did not, he insisted, alter in any way their racial prejudices. As proof, he pointed to the character of oppression of Blacks that followed the freedmen in the various states. The freedmen were put in another form of bondage. "They had no rights that a white man was bound to respect."

Baron De Tocqueville made a keen observation about racism and the hypocrisy in the northern states, when he wrote:

I see that in a certain portion of the territory of the United States, at the present day, the legal barrier which separated the two races is falling away ... but the prejudice to which it has given birth is immovable ... who ever has inhabited the United States must have preceived that in those parts of the union in which Negroes are no longer slaves they have in no wise drawn nearer to the whites. On the contrary, the prejudice of race appears to be stronger in the states that have abolished slavery than in those where it still exists.[9]

In some respects, these are statements of the facts. One thing is clear—the ideologies which are ingrained in people will more often, in some form or another, linger on long after the base from which the problem arose has been overcome. Keeping this view in mind, we can see how some of the Founding Fathers wanted to eliminate the system of slavery, but because of their racist outlooks were prepared to make compromises with the slaveholders.

But as we have already indicated, social forces of an objective and subjective character were at work in both the North and South that could and did unite to destroy slavery in the South. What the Founding Fathers failed to do, the people did. And in the first place Black people themselves.

THE nation owes a debt of gratitude to Black Americans. The struggles they waged on their own behalf had a profound effect on the fight for democracy for all Americans. Black people throughout our history have always identified their struggle with that of the American people. They have done so under the most humiliating conditions. Never have a people given so much to a society and received so little in return. The variety of forms used in struggle against slavery by Black people in the United States have no parallel. And regardless of the forms the struggle took at various stages, they all helped to end the slave system and win an extension of democracy for the common people in general.

A good example of how well they understood the connecting links of their struggle with others was shown by how they viewed the War of Independence. They joined wholeheartedly in the struggle and at the same time voiced their sentiments for their own liberation. A Black writer dramatized this viewpoint in the *New London Gazette:*

Is not all oppression vile when you attempt your freedom to defend, is reason yours, and partially your friend? Be not deceiv'd ... for reason pleads for all who by invasion and oppression fall. I live a slave, and am inslav'd by those who yet pretend with reason to oppose all schemes oppressive; and the gods invoke to curse with thunders the invaders yolk. O Mighty God! Let conscience seize the mind of inconsistent men who wish to a partial God to vindicate their cause, and plead their freedom, while they break its laws.[10]

Notwithstanding the weakness of their oppressors on the home front, Blacks made the supreme sacrifice and put their lives on the line in the revolutionary cause against a foreign invader. It is generally estimated that over five thousand Blacks, slaves and freedmen, fought in the war of liberation. The first to shed blood was a Black man, Crispus Attucks. William Z. Foster says:

The Negro soldiers and sailors in the Revolutionary War acquited themselves bravely and with honor. They took part in numerous key struggles—Concord, Lexington, Bunker Hill, Brandywine, Ticonderoga, Boonesboro, Fort Griswold, Eutaw, Yorktown, Saratoga, Trenton, Princeton and many other places. They distinguished themselves especially in the battles of Long Island, Red Bank, Rhode Island, Savannah, and Monmouth.[11]

But despite their heroism, a process of exclusion began.

The act of exclusion was not well accepted by Blacks already in the army. They made their complaints known to headquarters. And George Washington recommended to Congress that those already in the army be allowed to re-enlist; Congress agreed and added a provision that no others would be allowed to enlist. Thus began a process of humiliation and discrimination for Blacks in and out of the army that has continued throughout our history.

There was the general feeling that the war would not last long. But as the war entered its third year—by the summer of 1777—a policy reversal was under way. The enlisting of Blacks met with decreasing opposition because it became difficult to raise volunteer forces. However, this decision to reverse discrimination against Blacks was also due to the activities of the British. The British realized that the institution of slavery was a major weakness of the continental forces, and endeavored to take advantage of the situation. In November 1775 Lord Dunmore, the royal governor of Virginia, issued a proclamation declaring that all slaves who joined his Majesty's troops would be freed.

The British proclamation had an electrifying effect on many Blacks. They began to desert en masse. They went on foot and by water. The desertions became so great that Thomas Jefferson declared that in the one year (1778) Virginia alone saw thirty thousand slaves flee from bondage, and we know that many more escaped both before and after that year. Georgians felt that 75-85 percent of their slaves (who numbered about fifteen thousand in 1774) fled; and South Carolina declared that of their total number of some one hundred and ten thousand slaves at the start of the Revolution, at least twenty-five thousand made good their escape.

The prolonged character of the war, insufficient volunteers, and desertions of slaves to the side of the British caused the revolutionaries to re-evaluate the enlistment of Black people into the army. Quarles, in his book, *The Negro in the Making of America,* says:

At the federal level there was little opposition to using Negro soldiers; in fact Congress by the spring of 1779 was ready to take the unprecedented step of recommending slave enlistment . . . Congress was forced into decisive action by the British occupation of Savannah and the opening of a second enemy campaign to subjugate the South. On March 29, 1779, Congress recommended to South Carolina and Georgia that they take measures immediately for raising three thousand able bodied Negroes. These would be formed into officers.[12]

Congress followed up its recommendation by sending a representative to South Carolina and Georgia. But after much sharp debate in the state legislatures of both states, the proposals were rejected. Thus, in the North Blacks were enlisted and fought in many major battles, but in the South the slaves were still rejected.

By the summer of 1778 the Continental Army was integrated and according to a report there were 750 men scattered over fourteen brigades. At that point Blacks showed unusual patience in fighting in what could be called a "white man's war." They were still the victims of the grossest forms of discrimination. The average Black soldier was a private; often he was nameless and referred to only as "a Negro man."

Ironically, while the state of Georgia refused to arm Black slaves, it was Blacks who prevented a rout of the revolutionary forces in the siege of Savannah in the autumn of 1779. Blacks came to Savannah as part of a French army. They came from Haiti and served under the command of the French officer, D'Estaings. When he landed on the coast of Georgia on September 11th there were 545 Blacks out of 3,600 men. Among them was Henri Cristophe, who later became king of Haiti. Perhaps these Blacks from Haiti who served in the American Revolution obtained military experience which stood them in good stead in the Haitian Revolution of 1804.

Although forced to fight under the conditions as outlined, the Black experience in the Revolutionary War was not all negative. Despite the fact that slavery remained intact in the South, slave participation in the army in the North led to an increased number of Black freedmen at the war's end. This increase provided Black people as a whole with a more favorable springboard from which the whole system of slavery could be more effectively fought. Black participation in the Revolutionary War was part of history's process, and it testifies to the fact that many Blacks, even in conditions of slavery, understood the workings of history and applied themselves with great skill.

PARTICIPATION in the Revolutionary War was only one aspect of a grand strategy that evolved as the fight went from one stage to another. Now it is clear that the employment of strategies and tactics more than often did not result from any high command alone. The slaves produced many outstanding leaders. But the brain power of the ordinary uneducated slaves produced many struggles which added to the totality of a grand strategy that eventually produced a great victory.

Another method of struggle the slaves adopted was armed insurrection. For a long time the slaves were portrayed as meek and humble creatures. To this day there are those who seek to convey this impression. Thanks largely to the scholarly work of Dr. Herbert Aptheker, a leading Communist theoretician, such lies have been nailed to the wall. In his research he uncovered many uprisings by slaves that had been previously unknown or undisclosed. From the very beginning, rebellious Blacks made slavery expensive and dangerous for the masters. The process began on the high seas and continued on the plantations.

One of the reasons why slavery assumed such a brutal character in the South was the deep fear the plantation bosses had of slaves. However, there was fear of slaves in the North as well. Although the major cases of revolt occurred in the South, there were numerous instances of violence and revolts in the North. Among them was a situation where over seventy Blacks were arrested and tried in court. Twenty-five were convicted and sentenced to death. The brutality displayed in putting them to death is almost unbelievable. In New York, an incident occurred where Blacks were burned at the stake, broken on the wheel, and gored alive while in chains.

What happened in terms of slaves resorting to violence against their oppressors in the North was minor compared to what happened in the South, from the beginning of the nineteenth century until slavery was ended. There were numerous slave revolts; most of them were sparked by the successful revolt of the slaves in Haiti in 1804, which had a tremendous effect on slavery everywhere.

The revolution in Haiti came after the French Revolution of 1789. The Haitian Blacks demanded that the slogans of that revolution— "Liberty, Equality and Fraternity"—apply to Haiti as well as France. And they waged one of the bloodiest wars in the history of the Western Hemisphere.

The heroism underlying that great revolution was also expressed by Wendell Phillips when he exclaimed: "Some doubt the courage of the Negro. Go to Haiti and stand on the graves of the best troops France ever had, and ask them what they think of the Negros sword. And if that does not satisfy you, go to France to the eight thousand graves of Frenchmen who sat at home under the British flag and ask them."[13]

Another important feature of the Haitian Revolution was the

brain power displayed by the slaves and their leaders. Toussaint L'Ouverture, as well as others, came out of obscure circumstances with no previous military training and defeated some of the best military minds of the times.

The impact of the revolution in Haiti was of worldwide significance, but its greatest effect was what happened in all the Americas, from Mexico to Chile. The slaves and colonies of France, Spain and Portugal went through revolutionary changes. The Haitian Revolution also had great repercussions in the United States and was a major influence in weakening slavery.

The morale of southern slaves was lifted and the slaveholders in the United States were frightened nearly to death. The slave masters of the South used every means to keep the news of the revolt from their slaves. For example, they tried to prevent Haitian Black sailors from coming ashore in the South. The fear engendered by the Haitian Revolution also had a great impact on the infamous slave trade. In fact Dr. Du Bois in his classical work, *The Suppression of the African Slave Trade to the United States,* credits it as the main factor for the enactment of a law in the United States in 1807 which prohibited the importation of slaves. He wrote: "The first great goal of antislavery efforts in the United States had been the suppression of the slave trade by national law. It would hardly be too much to say that the Haitian revolution, in addition to its influence in the years from 1791 to 1806, was one of the main causes that rendered the accomplishment of this aim possible. . . ."[14]

Despite the efforts of the planters to keep the news about developments in Haiti from their slaves, it seeped through and a revolutionary mood gripped southern slaves.

There were three outstanding figures that led revolts which struck fear into the hearts of slave masters—Gabriel Prosser, Nat Turner and Denmark Vesey. All three rebellions were defeated. Whatever the reasons for their defeats, however, they were of great importance in eventually putting an end to slavery.

OPEN rebellions were not the only weapons. Quarles, and many other historians, show a whole number of small, seemingly insignificant things, which also contributed to the final battle for freedom.

Quarles pointed out:

Slaves were careless about property, abusing the livestock and damaging the farm implements. They were so hard on hoes that it became necessary to construct, just for them, one that was especially heavy and strong. As a precaution, some masters required that every tool or implement be marked with the name or initial of the slave to whom it was given. But even if a slave did not manage to break the hoe, he might use it to cup up the crop, blaming his clumsiness if called down by the driver. In addition to destroying equipment they often resorted to fire. Fire insurance companies were sometimes reluctant to write policies for slaveholders.[15]

These and other techniques which destroyed property, plus feigning illness, contributed to lowering the productivity of the slaves. There are those who claim that at certain stages of the struggle, slavery became unprofitable for the slave masters. This is a much debated subject. But whatever the case, the slaves consciously *made* it less profitable.

Perhaps one of the most important acts which detracted from profits was the runaway of slaves. It is estimated that over a hundred thousand fled to the North, out of which 60,000 went to Canada.

The foregoing employment of strategy and tactics by Blacks speaks of a people, although in a strange land, separated from previous background, a minority in a majority society, who were as intelligent, resourceful and militant as any people who ever graced this earth.

But after 1830 and the defeat of the Turner revolt, even greater wisdom and flexibility came into play. This was highlighted by the free Blacks becoming organized in the North, and they began to launch an assault on slavery in the South. The spark that played a major part to ignite the struggle was the Walker Appeal issued in 1830. The period that followed the Appeal, and after the failure of the Turner Rebellion, was characterized by the intensification of struggles by Blacks themselves, but now more than ever with white allies. It is evident that Black leaders were convinced that, unlike Haiti Blacks, they could never achieve freedom without alliances with other forces.

This was the beginning of the period that produced the great Abolitionist movement. It was a movement of both Black and white, which sometimes was organizationally united, at other times split, but at all times conducting parallel actions. How Blacks worked with the Abolitionists, under the leadership of Frederick Douglass, represents a combination of strategy and tactics that was indeed profound.

On January 1, 1931, William Lloyd Garrison launched the publication, *The Liberator,* which agitated for immediate emancipation of the slaves without compensation. On January 6, 1832, twelve white men gathered in an African Baptist church and organized the New England Anti-Slavery Society. Garrison commenting on the significance of the meeting declared: "We have met tonight in this obscure school house . . . Our numbers are few and our influence limited; but mark my prediction, Faneuil Hall ere long echo with the principles we have set forth. We shall shape the nation by their mighty power."[16]

Garrison was undoubtedly inspired to take this initiative by his attendance at the first Black Peoples Convention in June 1831. In 1833 Garrison and other Abolitionists, Black and white, organized the American Anti-Slavery Society in Philadelphia. This organization became the main base of the white Abolitionists. But like so many other developments, the movement came into existence with many birth pains. There were many diverse opinions regarding tactics and strategy that it is a miracle it was able to survive. The movement was divided on questions such as women's rights, political action, religion, and above all, on the various manifestations of racism within the movement.

The Black Abolitionists were also divided on tactics. There were those who embraced the racist efforts to recolonize Blacks elsewhere. Martin Delaney was a foremost advocate of this policy. It was in this context that Frederick Douglass emerged and provided Blacks with the strategy and tactics that eventually proved to be successful. Douglass met the advocates of colonization, both Black and white, forcefully. In one of his lectures he exclaimed: "We are told to go to Haiti; to go to Africa. Neither Haiti nor Africa can save us from a common doom. Whether we are here or there we must rise or fall with the race."[17] The subsequent enslavement of the whole African continent by the imperialist powers and the control of Haiti by the United States proves how correct Douglass was. Moreover, these events showed how well he understood, at that time, the connecting links of Black oppression throughout the whole world.

The American Anti-Slavery Society was most seriously divided. The moral reformers and the anti-slavery politicians constantly quarrelled with each other and often exchanged vituperative comments. The moralists berated politicians for having descended from the lofty pinnacle of principle and for neglecting the interest of Blacks. The politicians accused the moralists of ignoring social realities and of antagonizing potential anti-slavery voters with disruptive tactics and radical theories. Time and experience has proven that there was truth on both sides of the question.

While the split on such issues was of great importance, the division between Black and white Abolitionists was of equal importance. The split between Black and white took place over issues which divided the moralists from the politicians. But the main cause was the recognition by Blacks, especially Frederick Douglass, for organization and instruments among Blacks themselves as an independent force. The conflict around this issue revealed serious racist positions by the moralist forces, who, in general, stood foremost in challenging racist ideology. There was much discussion in the movement about whether Blacks should participate with whites on an equal level, including social relations. The Philadelphia Anti-Slavery Society, one year after it was founded, spent five sessions discussing the question as to whether it was expedient for colored persons to join anti-slavery societies, or was it expedient for Abolitionists to encourage social intercourse between white and colored families?

In respect to both questions the convention went on record to declare: "Resolved that it is neither our object or duty to encourage social intercourse between colored and white families" but agreed, by a narrow margin, that it would be expedient to accept Negroes as members.[18]

Similar debates and discussions took place throughout the country on such questions. Blacks, undoubtedly repelled by such discussion, sought refuge in their own organizations. But when they moved to do so, they met the wrath of many white Abolitionists, especially Garrison. He went so far as to oppose the publication of Frederick Douglass's paper, *The North Star.* Later he called for banning it from the list of Abolitionist publications and declared Frederick Douglass as an enemy. Garrison confided to friends that he considered Douglass a malignant enemy "thoroughly base and selfish, destitute of every principle of honor, ungrateful to the last degree and malevolent in spirit and unworthy of respect, confidence or contenance."[19]

Douglass replied to his critics with equal bitterness: "They talk down there (Boston) just as if the anti-slavery cause belonged to them . . . and as if all anti-slavery ideas originated with them, and that no man has a right to peep or mutter on the subject who does not hold letters patent from them."[20]

Blacks, in the main, supported Douglass in this struggle and continued to pursue their independent activities. As time passed, Douglass more and more emerged as the outstanding theoretician, agitator, strategist and tactician of the battle to end slavery. He waged a determined but flexible struggle against wrong tendencies by both Black and white. Henry Winston, outstanding Black leader of the Communist Party of the United States, took note of these characteristics. In his polemic against separatist trends in the liberation movements of today, he used Douglass as an example. In his classical work, *Strategy for a Black Agenda,* he observed:

> For Douglass, self-union of the oppressed Black people—as the starting point of Black power—was fully consistent with *unity* with white Abolitionists and *coalition* with other white strata in order to advance liberation. He saw that Abolition could not be achieved if Blacks pursued a separatist policy.
>
> Douglass saw that all struggle, including that for self-organization, was a process. It would be self-defeating, he realized, for Black people to reject the strategy of coalition until some vague future date when they had achieved complete internal organization.
>
> Douglass did not waver in his conviction despite bitter attacks by Garrison and other sectarians in the Abolitionist movement who opposed a coalition strategy against the slave power. The passive acceptance of their views, he was convinced, would lead to the perpetuation of slavery for an indeterminate length of time.[21]

Under the wise and militant leadership of Douglass, Blacks kept their eyes on the ball and didn't allow secondary matters to cloud their judgement. Merton Dillon took note of this fact and wrote:

> Negroes frequently demonstrated their appreciation of the efforts and accomplishments of the anti-slavery societies, but they did not hesitate to criticize prejudice within the abolitionist movement. "Even our professed friends have not yet rid themselves of it," a Negro teacher lamented. To some of them, it clings like a dark mantle, obscuring their many virtues and choking up the avenues to higher and nobler sentiments.[22]

He cited many examples to show how the poison of racism was still manifested; for example: "In seeking to eradicate prejudice while at the same time accepting certain popular notions about the Negro . . . They might for example refer to their African brothers . . . as niggers or emphasize some alleged physical or mental characteristics."[23] In spite of these weaknesses and many others, as time went by the movements of both Black and white came closer together and continuously escalated the battle to end slavery to new and higher levels.

One of the best examples of this cooperation was the organization of the underground railway system which aided the runaway slaves. The successful flight of the slaves led to the enactment of an amendment to the Fugitive Slave Law of 1793. The law of 1850 now provided for severe penalties against people who aided slaves to escape. The new amendment evoked widespread support for the escaping slaves and the Abolitionist movement received a new impetus. Abolitionists formed vigilance committees to aid runaway slaves and to protect free Negroes from kidnappers.

AN INCREASINGLY new feature in the struggle was the merger of the self-interest of the whites with that of slaves. Southern slaveholders by their own inhuman actions, provided the background for this development.

The slaveholders evoked an unprecedented wave of terror against the Abolitionist movement. One victim of this terror was Rev. Elizah P. Lovejoy. His printing press was destroyed three times in Alton, Illinois. Finally on November 7, 1837, he was murdered in cold blood while trying to defend his press from a third attack. This brutal murder led to a revitalization of the anti-slavery movement. People now began to identify the problem of slavery with the freedom of the press.

Terror was employed in both the North and the South. Foster says Abolitionists were slugged and lynched. The slaveholders "offered rewards of $10,000, $50,000 and even $100,000 for the bodies or heads of prominent Abolitionists. On the New York Stock Exchange a southern sympathizer openly said that he would give $15,000 for the head of Arthur Tappan."[24] The wave of terror became so great that Congress, based on a recommendation by President Andrew Jackson, made it a federal crime to send Abolitionist literature through the mails. No doubt such tactics helped to advance the Abolitionist cause more rapidly.

It now became clear to many that slavery threatened to destroy the rights of whites as well as Blacks. Thus southern terror against whites added a new dimension to the struggle against slavery. The self-interest of whites merged with what was formerly one-sidedly viewed as a moral issue. As the struggle moved forward in the decades of the fifties and the sixties, the self-interest aspect increasingly became the dominant theme.

The various compromises made by the North to the South broadened the base for a firmer opposition to the slaveholders. The Abolitionists turned their attention to the political arena. First they organized the Liberty Party, but its base and program were too narrow to bring anti-slavery sentiment into the voting booths behind it. Later a merger took place between the Liberty Party and the Free Soil Party. The Free Soil Party represented the free small farmers, or people who wanted to expand free land as the nation moved westward. Its major preoccupation was with free land, not slavery as such. It was, however, opposed to the expansion of slavery. But even this merger of anti-slavery forces with Free Soilers was insufficient to gain a popular political base to wage a contest for power with the slaveholders. At the time these developments were taking place, a new trend was emerging in the country. A consensus was developing against further compromises with the South, a growing determination not to allow slavery to take place in the rapidly growing western states.

It was out of this development that the Republican Party was born in 1854, an amalgam of Free Soilers, anti-slavery Whigs, Democrats and Know Nothings. The Abolitionists, while not satisfied with its limited program, nonetheless began to support it as the best possible vehicle for implementing the anti-slavery struggle. Even Garrison, for all his dogmatic and sectarian views, welcomed the growth of the new party. While both the Abolitionists and Blacks supported the new party, they were very critical of it. They placed their faith in the party's potential for future accomplishment rather than its declarations of limted present intentions. Probably Samuel J. May voiced the expectations of most Abolitionists when he explained in 1856 that "the rank and file of the Republican Party are much more anti-slavery than many of their leaders and the tide is rising, and will rise to put these men into higher and truer positions than they now dare to take, or else put better men in their places."[25]

History confirmed the correctness of May's observations. The Civil War came and war's necessities forced a reluctant Lincoln to issue the Emancipation Proclamation. The Blacks therefore joined the Union Army and, as in the days of 1776, distinguished themselves in freedom's cause.

When the war first broke out there were illusions that it would be of short duration, as was the case in the earlier revolution. J. A. Rogers, a Black historian, describes the mood at the war's beginnings:

> So certain was the North of victory that the invasion turned into a picnic. Congressmen, their wives and society leaders followed the army in carriages with baskets of food, whiskey, champagne, and bands of music. . . . To the soldiers it was a sporting event. On to Richmond they shouted, singing and strumming guitars. In high glee, they tore down Confederate flags, looted southern homes, smashed pianos for wood to barbecue pigs.[26]

But these illusions were soon shattered as the northern forces suffered defeat after defeat.

After two years of defeats, Abraham Lincoln issued the Emancipation Proclamation with a statement, "I claim not to have controlled events, but confess plainly that events have controlled me."

At the war's end there were 149 Negro regiments, composed as follows: 120 infantry; 12 heavy artillery; 10 light artillery; and 7 cavalry. A total of 123,156 men. Killed in battle were 36,847. The Black troops made the difference between victory and defeat.

THE CIVIL War was followed by a brief period of the extension of democracy in the South. But it did not last long. In less than twenty years, the former slaves were deserted by their northern allies, and left to the tender mercies of the former slaveholders. Max Lerner describes what followed: "He had to pay a painful price for his freedom, grasping at it with unrealistic eagerness only to find that liberation could not liberate so long as the former oppressors kept their power. So he was hurtled from his dream of freedom back into the terror of the Reconstruction. He found that he had to achieve everything again from scratch."[27]

Observing these distressing developments, Frederick Douglass was not surprised and declared: "Liberty came to the freedmen of the United States not in mercy but in wrath, . . . not by moral choice but by military necessity. . . . Nothing was to have been expected other than what has happened."[28] It was a pathetic scene when John R.

Lynch, a Black congressman from Mississippi, arose to address the Republican Party convention in 1900 and cried out: "In his devotion to the cause of liberty and justice the Colored American has shown that he was not only willing and ready at any and all times to sacrifice his life on the altar of his own country . . . Must it now be said that in spite of all this, the Colored American finds himself without a home, without a country, without friends, and even without a Party? God forbid![29]

Lynch was correct. Black people, after fighting in two wars allegedly fought for democracy, still found themselves a long way from the "promised land." However as a result of both revolutions, some elements of democracy were won. If more was not gained, then the inability to obtain a peoples democracy in the framework of capitalism, a system where the pursuit of profits leads to dehumanization, comes sharper into focus.

The experience of both revolutions shows that it was not the ruling rich classes that advanced whatever democratic gains we have made, but it was the common people. The nation owes a debt of gratitude to the ex-slaves for what they did for the nation as a whole. The nation also owes a debt to the men and women who made up the Abolitionist and women's movement because the institution of chattel slavery could not have been destroyed without their initiatives and participation.

Thus ended one of the most eventful struggles in American history. Much was left undone. A new form of slavery evolved. But progress was made, despite zigs and zags in the struggle. The "promised land" for the Black people and all oppressed people is in sight. That is, providing the lessons of the struggle to end chattel slavery will be applied to the conditions of today.

9 • RACISM AND
THE EXPANSION WESTWARD

THE EXPANSION of the United States westward added a new dimension to racial development and strife. The addition of the Mexican and Asian peoples to racial subjugation brought together, for the first time, members of all the races within the United States.

At the same time that this was taking place, the major European capitalist powers expanded their empires by the subjugation of peoples of all non-white colors throughout the world. But this took the form of colonies in faraway places, whereas in the United States the oppressors and the oppressed coexisted and developed in the same geographical area. This was one of the main factors that led to the United States becoming the most racist-ridden nation in world history. Some may argue that because of the persecution of the Jewish people in Nazi Germany, Germany was the worst. It is true that what happenened in the concentration camps of Hitler Germany was one of the worst forms of genocidal treatments any people ever had to endure, but the time span and the number of people who suffered cannot compare with the 200 year history of the United States. And in this development all the races, not one or two, suffered various forms of genocidal treatment.

The fact that here in the United States all the races, Black, brown, red and Asian had to cohabitate with their white capitalist oppressors, brought into existence the most intensified forms of racist propaganda and persecution for a long period of time.

The ruling capitalist class from the day it was born has found it necessary to divide the ranks of the oppressed, mainly the working class. In those countries where the working class were mainly native or people of the same race, also, in some cases, of different national backgrounds, the ideology to divide could proceed along the lines of class and national chauvinism as the main weapons. But in a country such as the United States, racism had to constantly be used as one of the main weapons in the arsenal of the exploitative forces. The superexploitation of racial groups in these circumstances required not only a moral reason behind it, but this superexploitation was also used to bribe certain sections of the working class to participate in such oppression. Almost every struggle within the nation has had this character. The role racial persecution has played in the building of the nation has been one of the most distorted aspects of our historiography. Racial exploitation as a source of wealth in this society has been played down almost entirely.

In a previous chapter we pointed out how the government apparatus was used to concentrate most of the resources and the wealth in the hands of a few people. While surplus profits were made at the expense of all workers, the super profits obtained from Black, brown, red and Asian peoples helped to lay the foundation for the growth of this nation into one of the most highly developed industrial nations in world history. It is commonly admitted that the slave trade and the cotton plantations in the South provided what Karl Marx termed the primitive accumulation of capital, not only in this country but also in Great Britain.

What is not so well known is the role played by Mexican workers and farmers and Asian peoples in the building of the West. Young people in the United States have been, and are being, trained from the cradle upward by radio, television and the motion picture industry to believe that the West was won only by the hearty and resourceful white pioneers who left the big cities, rode wagon trains into the West, and overcame the treachery and terror of the marauding, heartless and scalping Indians.

Now it is certainly true that many of the white pioneers made great contributions in the buildup of the West. But what was extracted from Mexican and Asian peoples was of equal, if not greater, importance. Just as slavery in the South provided the primitive accumulation of capital required for industrialization, in the West the superexploitation of Mexican and other peoples laid the foundation for industrialization in the Southwest and Far West.

This process was also tied in with the institution of slavery, although capitalist economy in general became the main focus and beneficiary. Cotton was the main staple which advanced slavery in the South to a new and higher level. But its production rapidly exhausted the soil, thus making it necessary for a constant expansion of slave states.

DURING the decade of the 1840s a series of events took place which extended racial exploitation and persecution into the Southwest and the Far West. The state of Texas in the Southwest was a Mexican state. Under a liberal constitution granted by Spain in 1820, people who were citizens of the United States were given free land grants. Within twenty years, more than 20,000 U.S. citizens took up residence in Texas. Most of them were slaveholders. The white Texans repaid Mexican generosity by characterizing all Mexicans as "lazy, shiftless, cowardly, backward and immoral." They—the white Texans—regarded Mexican life as cheap. By 1834 U.S. whites outnumbered the Mexicans and a fierce struggle for the control of the state took place. White Americans began to struggle to separate Texas from Mexico and eventually to bring it into the United States.

Morison states that a major rationale for separation from Mexico was the "insecurity of slave property." The white Texans, who expressed a racist contempt for the Mexican people, were "impatient at the restrictions" which the government of Mexico imposed on the institution of slavery.[1] The Mexican government took a very strong stand against slavery. Not only that, but every effort was made to help destroy the system. Much has been written about the underground railroad system which aided the escape of slaves to Canada. But very little has been written about the role played by Mexicans in Texas, and across the border, to help Black slaves escape. There were a large number of slaves in that state. The British commission for the suppression of the slave trade reported that in 1837–1838, no less than 15,000 slaves from Africa were brought into Texas.[2]

As early as 1839, a large number of slaves had escaped from their Texas owners by crossing the Rio Grande. As a result, a sizable community of ex-slaves sprung up in Matamoros, Mexico. "The possession of slaves in western Texas," wrote Colonel Ford, "was rendered insecure owing to the contiguity of Mexico, to the efforts of the Mexicans to induce them to run away, they assisted them in every way they could."[3]

A slave insurrection in 1856 was uncovered in Colorado County. According to Texans, the slaves had planned to rebel, kill their

masters, and with the aid of Native American Indians, fight their way
to freedom across the border. Without exception, every Mexican in
the county was implicated. Over 200 slaves were arrested and beaten,
and many Mexicans were ordered to leave the county, and were
forbidden to travel the roads without passes. "Anti-Mexican sentiments," wrote a Dr. Taylor, "based upon the belief that the peons
imperiled the institution of slavery, broke out in meetings which in
Austin, Gonzales, and other towns passed resolutions protesting
against their employment."[4]

During this period, the most intense persecution of Mexican
nationals took place. Racist-minded Texans accused them of almost
every crime that took place in the Southwest. Eventually, former
U.S. immigrants entered into armed struggle to secede from Mexico,
with the aim of joining the United States. However the war
conducted in Texas met some opposition in the United States. For
example: An Abolitionist, Benjamin Lundy, brought out a pamphlet
called, *The War in Texas,* proving that the Texas revolution was a
conspiracy to open new slave markets and gain slave territory for
cotton. Lundy spoke with some authority, for he had been to Texas
where he had hoped to found an Abolitionist colony. His pamphlet,
depicting the Texans as a gang of horse thieves and land robbers,
"appealed to that widespread Northern sentiment opposed to the
political dominance of the South and the extension of slave
territory."[5]

Nonetheless, despite such opposition, the U.S. government aided
and abetted the movement for the secession of Texas and later
incorporated it into the United States. The climax came through a
war waged by the United States against Mexico in 1846. This war, the
first since independence, was also unpopular. Even Abraham
Lincoln opposed it as an unjust war. But President Polk, acting on
behalf of all the exploitive elements in the society, carried it out
regardless of opposition.

The annexation of Texas and the war of 1846 led to the signing of
the Treaty of Guadalupe Hidalgo. Mexico had no choice but to sign
the treaty for the United States was already in military control of the
Southwest. Under the terms of the Treaty of Guadalupe Hidalgo,
concluded on February 2, 1848, a vast territory including California,
Arizona, New Mexico, and Colorado were ceded to the United
States. The treaty also approved the prior annexation of Texas. The

lands which were greedily stolen by the United States were greater in extent than Germany and France combined.

All citizens of Mexico residing within the territories, if they failed to leave within one year after ratification of the treaty, were to become citizens of the United States. The overwhelming majority of the Mexican population became citizens by default. They would not allow the United States government to drive them off their land.

The treaty provided specific guarantees for the property and political rights of the Mexican population in a so-called attempt to safeguard cultural autonomy. Specific laws in the treaty insured that the language, religion, and culture of the Mexican people would be respected.

When the treaty of Guadalupe Hidalgo was signed, some 75,000 Spanish speaking people were living in the Southwest, approximately 7,500 in California, a thousand or so in Arizona, 60,000 in New Mexico and perhaps 5,000 in Texas.

In the Southwest, institutionalized racism was not yet an official law at the signing of the treaty, but it soon became so once the area was in the hands of the United States. With the passage of time this treaty, like hundreds of others made with the Native American Indian peoples, was violated.

The moment the war was over a struggle began to dispossess the Mexican people from their land. All kinds of devious schemes were devised to carry out this objective. Sam Houston, ex-president of the Texas republic, and who to this day is portrayed as a hero in the "winning of the West," brazenly declared: ". . . since Mexicans are no better than Indians, I see no reason why we should not go on the same course now and take their land."[6]

Military rule as well as unfamiliarity with the legal structure and land ownership in the capitalist system facilitated the take over of the land. Patricia Blawis, in her excellent book *Tijerina and the Land Grants,* presents a survey of the process that was used, especially in New Mexico.

The Mexican landowners had the mistaken confidence that their rights to the land were unquestioned. But a law was passed in 1862 which required fresh proof of ownership. Landowners were required to bear all expenses for investigation and survey. Many had no money and lost their land. Another method used to get land was to take advantage of the lack of knowledge of the tax system in the

United States in contrast to Mexico. Under Mexican and Spanish rule the land had never been taxed, only the products. After 1895, the Mexican people suddenly found their lands being seized for unpaid taxes that they had never heard of until auctioned off by a sheriff for little or nothing.

Under the Mexican system of land ownership, small families were given certain land for private concerns. But the bulk of the land was held for common usage. In violation of the treaty, a government official proceeded to assign all land held in common to the public domain, with government officials having the ability to dispose of the land almost at will. The surveyors and investigators were an unscrupulous lot.

Surveyor General H. M. Atkinson, for one, was openly in the cattle business with the notorious Thomas B. Catron, the First National Bank of Santa Fe, and other members of the Santa Fe Ring, which bilked Mexican farmers of thousands of acres. For years the Ring ruled imperiously. It elected legislators and delegates to Congress. It had the ear of the administration at Washington and could build up and pull down men at its pleasure. Whoever dared to oppose its purposes or methods, was purchased or intimidated into silence, or killed.

The head of the Ring was Catron, a speculator who became the largest landowner in the United States. He obtained possession of more than a million acres. He served for years as a U.S. attorney general and was the first U.S. senator when New Mexico became a state.

According to Ms. Blawis, Tijerina (who recently led a struggle to regain the stolen lands) frequently speaks of the "organized criminal conspiracy" of the Santa Fe Ring. He accuses the United States of complicity in the conspiracy, one element of which was the disappearance of titles proving land ownership. These documents had been burned or sold as "wrapping paper" by Governor Pile in 1870, and it was not until 1960 that some of the records were recovered from a Missouri book dealer, who had bought them from the family of Thomas B. Catron, attorney general of the territory at the time they vanished.

A Court of Private Land Claims was established in 1891, "made up of judges from the South who believed in slavery," states Tijerina. It was deliberately set up to reduce the acreage belonging to native New

Mexicans. More than two-thirds of the petitions that came before it were rejected, while many of those confirmed were reduced in size. "Legal-appearing devices were found whereby land grant heirs could be cheated, and by the time it had closed its books in 1904, the Federal Government had acquired control over 52 million acres of land in New Mexico."[7]

Stealing land was only one aspect of the savage and barbaric treatments of former Mexican nationals. The colonizers also took the land of the Native Indian peoples, but were unable to use them as their work horses.

But in the case of the Mexican people, they became "work horses." Like Blacks, they became one of the most dispossessed and superexploited people on the U.S. scene. It was their labor power and labor skills that helped to transform the Old West. They were the main workers in a number of industries, as well as in agriculture and cattle grazing.

BY 1860 Mexicans were a majority in the mines in the Southwest. They had great knowledge of the entire mining industry, and developed most of its modern equipment. One such discovery was the patio process for separating silver from ore by the use of quicksilver.

An example of the superexploitation is seen in the ratio of wages of white workers and Mexicans. White miners were paid five to seven dollars a day, while skilled Mexicans were paid two to three dollars a day. Mexicans performed the jobs of smelter men since whites did not know anything about this type of labor. Mexicans were forced to work in the unsafe underground of the mines. Since the life of a Mexican was viewed as cheap and worthless, he was forced to work under the most dangerous conditions. It is estimated that between 1858 and 1940, Arizona mines produced three billion dollars worth of metal.

Copper, which was discovered by the Indians in Santa Fita, increased from 800,000 pounds in the late nineteenth century to 830,628,411 pounds by the 1950s. It was the vast expansion in the electrical industry which enabled copper to dethrone its rival silver. Mexicans mined in the copper mines of Arizona, Utah, Nevada, and elsewhere. Thus they played an important role in making possible the illumination of the United States by electricity.

Just as the development of the mines was accredited to the white entrepreneurs, so was the sheep industry. But again, like the mining industry, sheep were developed and flourished because of the Mexican expertise in pastoral herding. Sheep were brought by the Spanish to New Mexico. From the founding of New Mexico until the Civil War, sheep fed, clothed and supported the colonies. The Spanish had accumulated 600 years of wealth and experience in pastoral herding.

New Mexico was the nursery whose herds produced the foundation stock for the entire West. Sheep were driven to California for food for the miners. They were also taken across to the Midwest where new flocks were nurtured. Wool production increased from five million pounds in 1862 to twenty-two million pounds in 1900. The increase of wool production in the West, greatly increased factory employment in the East.

With the establishment of the first western sugar beet factories, the modern era of lamb feeding came into its own. One reason for the rapid growth of the sugar beet industry in the West was the fact that sheep could be fed and fattened on the by-products of sugar beet production. Thus one industry supplemented the other.

Just as the white settlers knew little about mining, sheep or cattle, they were also unfamiliar with irrigation farming. The Pueblo Indians were irrigating between 15,000 and 25,000 acres in the valley when the Spaniards appeared on the scene. It is believed that the Indian irrigation systems of the Southwest are more than 900 years old. It was from Mexican and Indian experiences that white farmers learned how to irrigate.

THE massive immigration flow of Mexicans began around 1910 to 1930. It is not a coincidence that immigration increased threefold. For the 1910 revolution in Mexico, which smashed feudalism, left hundreds of thousands of Mexicans jobless and homeless. Between 1880 and 1910, 15,000 miles of railroad were constructed between Mexico and the United States which helped pave the way for Mexican immigration. In fact, the railroads gave free transportation to Mexicans, to be deducted from their future wages. This was also the period in which mining declined as the chief source of accumulating wealth for the few rich. The growing urbanism and the economy polarized around farming and the big ranchers needed cheap labor to superexploit in order to build their empires of capitalist wealth.

Thousands and thousands of immigrants came pouring to the Southwest with promises of jobs in agriculture. The white power structure was afraid that the revolutionary-inspired Mexicans would take over the region. Segregation was extremely prevalent. Mexicans were not allowed to eat in white restaurants, live in their part of town, or go to the same schools. If they did, they would be murdered or thrown into jail on some fradulent charge.

The period from 1908 to 1925 has been called, "open killing season on Mexicans." On November 18, 1922, *The New York Times* stated, "The killings of Mexicans without provocation is so common as to pass as almost unnoticed." The number of Mexicans murdered was more in this era of time than in Los Angeles in 1854, when a homicide a day was reported, with the overwhelming majority of the victims Mexicans and Indians. In the previous year, California had more murders than the rest of the states combined.

THERE is no precise figure of the number of immigrants that came here between 1910 and 1920, but it is generally agreed that it is well over one million people. Labor shortages and the quest for cheap labor accelerated, especially during World War I, the immigration of Mexican workers.

Three facts should be noted about this mass immigration period. One, Mexican immigration brought 10 percent of the total population of Mexico to the Southwest. Two, the overwhelming majority of Mexican immigrants were concentrated in the territory which they believed rightfully belonged to Mexico, the Southwest. Three, the mass migrations coincided with the birth of the Southwest as an economic empire, and in each instance Mexican immigrants labored in the building of industries in which there had been an earlier Spanish-Mexican cultural contribution and experience in working in that particular area. The industries in which Mexicans were concentrated, were those vital to the economic development of the Southwest, e.g., railroads, cotton, sugar beets, truck or farm produce.

In 1880, 70 percent of section crews and 90 percent of extra gangs on the principal western railroad lines, which regularly employed between 35,000 and 50,000, were Mexican.

In 1930 Santa Fe reported 14,000 Mexicans employed: 3,000 at Rock Island, 1,500 at Great Northern, 10,000 at Southern Pacific.

According to the 1930 census, 70,799 Mexicans were engaged in transportation and communication. Mexicans were mainly employed as common laborers, maintenance workers, and on street car systems. As early as 1928, boxcar labor camps of the railroads housed 469 Mexican men, 155 women and 372 children. In Kansas and Nebraska, Mexican settlements will be found to extend along the rail lines. The barrios of Kansas City and Chicago are outgrowths of Mexican railroad labor camps.

Large-scale importers of Mexican labor lent workers to other industries because railroads were seasonal work. Railroad employment stimulated farm work since the railroads provided transportation to various points of work. Mexicans made up two-thirds of the workers following the big swing in Texas. They traveled between 1,800 and 2,000 miles to get to each crop. Cotton farms in Arizona also imported Mexican nationals to work in the cotton harvest. By June 30, 1919, there were between 5,824 and 7,269 nationals imported specifically for the cotton harvest. This did not include Mexicans who came over illegally or without contracts.

All the workers who were shipped over here from Mexico were supposed to have their transportation costs deducted from their future wages. Some of these men never received a penny for their labor because the owners of the fields, mines, railroads, etc., would work them for two or three years stating that they hadn't yet paid off their transportation costs. This practice was common through the Southwest. In the winter of 1921, when the cotton boom exploded in Salt River Valley, Arizona, 10,000 Mexicans were deported back to Mexico because the U.S. government refused to give them public assistance.

In California, with 5,500 acres planted in cotton in 1920, the acreage in San Joaquin Valley increased to 172,400 in 1931. As cotton acreage expanded, more and more Mexicans were imported for the cotton harvest.

Commanding a premium price with a yield per acre nearly twice the national average, cotton became a $40,000,000 crop in California. Largely produced on high-priced irrigated lands, which had been capitalized on the basis of five decades of cheap labor, the expansion of cotton in California was promised upon the availability of a large supply of low cost labor exclusively earmarked for cotton growers.

Between 1919 and 1939, production of fresh market spinach, lettuce, cauliflower, snap beans and carrots increased five times or more, celery output tripled. There is not a single crop in production or harvesting that Mexicans have not played a role in its production. In production of truck crops, cotton, sugar beets, etc., where the least technological developments have been employed, cheap Mexican labor fits in "beautifully," Mexican labor was practically noncompetitive in the Southwest. Many Mexicans were also employed in Seattle to work in the Alaskan canneries.

Shipments of Mexican workers en route to employers were often kept locked up in barns, warehouses and corrals with armed guards to prevent their theft. For many growers would hire men to go recruit and steal Mexican laborers to be brought to work on their farms. Crews of imported Mexicans who attempted to break their contracts were marched through the streets of San Antonio under armed guard. Other Mexicans who attempted to break their contracts were chained to posts and guarded with shotguns.

In the sugar beet industry in 1927, out of 58,000 workers, 30,000 were Mexicans. (Today Mexicans comprise 75–90 percent of the total work force in sugar beets. Sugar beets are to be found in Ohio, Michigan, Minnesota, and North Dakota. Their average annual earning is between $500 and $600 per year.)

During the depression, many of the ranchers preferred Mexican labor over other types of labor and some of the companies attempted to recruit from Mexico. In an effort to prevent this practice, the governor in Colorado declared martial law and stationed national guardsmen along the border to turn back Mexican workers.

Around 1916, Mexican laborers began to appear in the industrial areas of Chicago, Gary, Indiana Harbor and Calumet and other cities in the Midwest. At first they were only hired as truck laborers; later they were employed in the steel mills, packing plants and canneries. From 1920 to 1930 the Mexican population in Chicago increased from 3,854 to 19,362.

In 1918 Mexican students were employed in Detroit auto plants. The Mexican population grew from 8,000 in 1918 to 15,000 in 1928. During the depression their numbers fell quite low because of the mass deportations.

In 1923, the National Tube Company, an affiliate of the United States Steel Corporation, brought 1,300 Mexican laborers from

Texas to work in Lorain, Ohio. The same year the Bethlehem Steel Company imported 1,000 nationals to work in its plant in Bethlehem, Pennsylvania.

Mexican labor did not reach large proportions in industrial labor in the Midwest for a number of reasons. The ranchers feared that if Mexican labor went and worked in new areas where they were not formerly employed, a quota system would be established.

Hence came the passage of the Texas immigrant law in 1929. The growers fought against Mexicans being allowed to work in other industries. They initiated a movement to stop importation of Mexican labor to the Midwest. The depression brought this movement to an end as over 65,000 Mexicans were deported and the Texas immigrant law was enforced.

Later, another method of getting Mexican labor was devised, called the Bracero Program. It was initiated because the growers stated that there were not enough domestic workers to pick their crops. During World War II the capitalists had to seek other means of securing cheap labor to work in the fields since a large part of the workforce was tied up in war industries. They turned to Mexico for their source of super cheap labor. The Bracero Program lasted from 1940 to 1960.

In the Rio Grande, Mexicans would be hired for fifteen cents a day, which was half the wage commonly demanded by the resident local laborers. Mr. Guiberson, representing the Agriculture Bureau of San Joaquin, best summed it up at a U.S. Senate hearing, "We are asking for labor only at certain times of the year . . . at the peak of our harvest and the class of labor we want is the kind we can send home when we get through with them."[8]

The U.S. capitalist class was able to make billions of dollars through racism under the Bracero Program, paying Mexican people a lower wage than that of white people. Article 15 of the 1951 bracero agreement stated, "The determination of the prevailing wage shall be made by the Secretary of Labor."[9]

On June 7, 1954, the Immigration Department decided to start enforcing the immigration laws, for there was already a surplus of Mexican labor in this country. They began their racist raids and witch hunts by preying on the churches, in parks, labor camps and even at grocery stores. They were deporting, on the average, 2,000 Mexicans a day for a period of months. During this period alone in

California, 84,000 Mexicans were deported. The Bracero Program came to a halt in 1963. But there were still thousands and thousands of green card Mexicans who were allowed to work here.

It is very difficult to determine the exact amount of profits the capitalist class made from the blood, sweat and work of Mexican workers. They would hire thousands of illegals and when it was time for them to get paid the growers would call the immigration authorities and the illegals would immediately be deported. Of course, without getting paid. That was one of the most common practices of the growers. Mr. Kelly, an official from the Immigration Service, stated, "We do not feel we have the authority to permit to remain in this country aliens who are here as agriculture workers, whether they are here legally or not."[10] In other words, they would be allowed to stay until it was time to receive their check.

We can conclude, that because of racism and the capitalist mode of production, **agri-business made** billions of dollars from Mexican labor. As pointed out previously, the profits made by these capitalists were used to build up the economy at the expense of the Mexican people.

EVEN after the United States annexed most of the Southwest from Mexico, it continued to interfere in the internal affairs of Mexico. At the beginning of this century, Mexico went through a number of revolutionary struggles, mainly of a democratic character, of the peasantry against the feudal landowners. Our government, at all stages of the struggles, sided with the most reactionary forces within Mexico and the rights of Mexico as a sovereign nation were constantly violated. Ironically, invasions occurred under President Woodrow Wilson, who after World War I won universal acclaim as the champion of "the rights of nations to self-determination." Yet this great apostle of self-determination had no hesitation to interfere in the internal affairs of Mexico.

In 1913, General V. Huerta, who had been aided by the U.S. government to overthrow the more liberal regime of Francisco Madero, didn't set well with President Wilson, and the United States refused to recognize the Huerta government which was closely connected to British oil interests. Wilson arrogantly declared: "I am going to teach the South American republics to elect good men."[11] In this same dictatorial spirit he stated: "If General Huerta does not retire by force of circumstances, it will become the duty of the United States to use less peaceful means to put him out."[12]

Based on these imperialist concepts, Wilson seized upon some minor incidents in 1914, invaded Mexico and captured Vera Cruz. Again in 1916, Wilson sent U.S. forces under General Pershing into Mexico to chase down Pancho Villa. Under Wilson's administration there was open talk of "taking over all of Mexico." Such was the racist role our government played "south of the border." And it represents some of the most shameful and hypocritical pages in our history. But racist acts in the West and south of the border were not confined to Mexicans, they were also applied with equal force to Asian people.

As time went by, subsequent changes in the direction of a more progressive Mexican government revealed why President Wilson and imperialist elements in the United States, among other reasons, were concerned about the nature of government south of our border.

In 1933, at the height of the great depression, a strike of berry pickers erupted in California. This strike brought about the direct intervention of the Mexican government against the slavelike conditions of their nationals in this country.

When the strike broke out, the matter was brought to the attention of the Mexican Minister of Foreign Affairs, Jose M. Puig Casaraurie, who had served as an ambassador to the United States, and was familiar with how Mexican Americans were treated. He immediately sent off a telegram to the consulate in Los Angeles in which he called for: "In strike movement originating in Venice render all assistance to Mexicans, taking all actions before authorities, social organizations, American federation of Labor etc., in order that this extremely just movement of Mexicans . . . may be successful."[13] The Mexican government brought pressure to bear upon the federal government and sent funds to aid the starving strikers.

General Calles, a former Mexican president, sent aid to the strikers and declared: "The importance of this movement is that our compatriots in a foreign land, when they have a just cause, may count upon the support of their brothers in Mexico."[14]

With this kind of unprecedented international pressure, the strike was won. When viewed in this context, the full meaning of President Wilson's concern about the kind of government in Mexico comes into even sharper focus. Unfortunately, the kind of government that existed at the time of the berry strike has not been a continuous feature of Mexican governments. Most of them have collaborated with the U.S. government and in this connection aided the horrible racist conditions imposed on Mexican workers, both citizens of the United States and non-citizens.

In more recent times, the Mexican workers, largely by their own efforts, have become a significant factor in the American labor movement. Their influence is far greater than their numbers and this argues well for the future of labor as a whole and for the entire American people.

As the nation expanded into the Far West, where sizable numbers of Asian peoples lived, continental United States now embraced peoples from all the races of humankind. And as with other peoples of color, racial oppression and superexploitation engulfed the Asians as well.

The migrations of Chinese and Japanese workers to the United States began during the period of the explosive growth in industry in the United States. It was the period which followed the 1849 gold rush to California and the enormous expansion of the railroad industry. The problem before the robber barons who controlled industry, was a broader base of cheap laobr. This was the context for the admittance of large numbers of Chinese and later Japanese workers.

The Chinese were brought in large numbers into the railroad industry. It is estimated that about 20,000 Chinese worked on the transcontinental railroad line and related construction jobs along the Pacific coast and in midwestern states. The workers employed on these lines were subjected to some of the most brutal treatment in U.S. labor history. In June 1867 over 2,000 Chinese railroad workers in the Sierras went on strike against the ten-hour day and against whippings which they were given to make them work faster. The strike was lost due to lack of support from the rest of labor. In fact, the employers were more successful in pitting native-born workers against Chinese and Japanese than any other category of immigrant workers throughout labor history.

Karl Yoneda, in "A Brief History of U.S. Asian Labor," documents this fact very well. A chronicle of events follow:

Labor unions were a prime source of massive anti-Chinese campaigns. In 1870 over 10,000 representing unions, "anti-coolie" clubs and other organizations met in San Francisco to organize the Anti-Chinese Convention of the State of California. The following year a white mob invaded the Los Angeles Chinatown, lynching 19 Chinese. In 1877, white hoodlums and unemployed workers attacked the San Francisco Chinatown for three days and nights, demolishing buildings, including 25 laundries. And a petty politician, D. Kearney, formed the misnamed Workingmen's Party of California based on the slogan "The Chinese Must Go."

In 1882 Congress passed the Chinese Exclusion Act, with a vigorous assist from one of the notorious racists of the day—Samuel Gompers, secretary of the Federation of Organized Trade Unions of the U.S.A. and Canada.

The exclusion law and other repressive state and local measures helped intensify persecution of Chinese. Many were expelled from California mining towns and attempts were made to remove them from all Pacific Coast states. In 1885 the Union Pacific Railway Company recruited 200 Chinese to work their Rock Springs, Wyoming, mine. This aroused strong opposition from union members. Irate white miners raided the Chinese camp, burning it down after wounding many and murdering twenty-six Chinese.

The first Japanese immigrants, about 26 men and women, were brought to Coloma, California, in 1869 under an eight-year contract to J. Shnell, a German adventurer, and were abandoned by him two years later.

From 1888 on, large numbers of Japanese began migrating to Hawaii and the mainland to work in industries where Chinese had formerly toiled. As their numbers increased, the racist cry of "yellow peril" grew louder.

The San Francisco AFL Labor Council called the first anti-Japanese mass meeting in 1900, where E. Ross, a Stanford professor, said in part: " . . . should the worst come to the worst it would be better for us to turn our guns on every vessel bringing Japanese to our shores rather than to permit them to land." (*San Francisco Call,* May 8, 1900)

It is significant to note that in California, as early as 1903 several hundred Mexican workers, suffering the same racism and exploitation, joined some 1,000 Japanese to form the Oxnard Sugar Beet and Field Laborers Union, electing K. Baba president and J. M. Larraras secretary. The union went on strike against low pay and unfair labor practices. Scabs, including Japanese, were brought in. A shooting took place in which a Mexican union member was killed and four were injured. Unity of the strikers was characterized in the local press: "There have been labor gatherings and parades during the past week. Dusky skinned Japs and Mexicans march through the streets headed by one or two former minor contractors and beet laborers four abrest and several hundred strong. They are a silent grim band of fellows, most of them young and belonging to the lower class of Japs and Mexicans." (*Oxnard Courier,* March 7, 1903)

When Larraras made application for a charter to AFL President Gompers, he was informed "the union must guarantee that it will under no circumstance accept membership of any Chinese or Japanese."

Gompers's vicious attacks on Asians continued. At his insistence, the 1904 AFL National Convention passed a resolution calling for the Chinese Exclusion Act to be amended to include Japanese and Koreans. Gompers's tirades were also heaped upon a Japanese socialist, Sen Katayama, who had first arrived to this country in 1884 to study theology. After returning to Japan he helped organize its first trade union. In 1904, he again came to these shores speaking against the Russo-Japan War and helped to establish Japanese socialist groups in Seattle, San Francisco and Los Angeles. In August, while attending the Sixth Congress of the Second International at Amsterdam, Katayama and Plekhanov, a Russian delegate, shook hands, pledging to fight against the war. These actions evoked Gompers to write in the AFL paper "this presumptuous Jap . . ."[15]

While these racist acts were carried out by the employers through the top labor hierarchy, there were other forces in the house of labor who joined with their Asian brothers and sisters to beat back both ruling class and racist practices. Again, Yoneda documents these facts:

The Industrial Workers of the World (IWW), formed in 1905 to fill the void left by the do-nothing policy of the AFL bureaucrats, issued a special appeal to foreign born workers, including Asians, to join them. One of its 1906 bulletins states: "We, the IWW, have organized the Japanese and Chinese in lumber camps, on the farms, mines and railroads, and the UMWA have organized Japanese in the coal fields of Wyoming. This is proof that they can be organized." The Wyoming Japanese referred to were the 500 who joined the Rock Springs UMWA local, of whom two were elected to serve on its negotiating committee. Upon learning this, Gompers instructed the local to exclude all Asians.

In 1906, S. Kotoku, well known Japanese anarchist, came to San Francisco, where he met with IWW and Socialist Party leaders. Greatly impressed by the IWW program, he helped form the Social Revolutionary Party with fifty Japanese. Several young Japanese socialists, Kotoku followers, formed the Fresno Labor League in 1908 to organize 4,000 Japanese grape pickers in the area. The IWW Italian Local actively aided this campaign.

In 1913, IWW Local 283 was established in a Ketchikan, Alaska, fish cannery with 100 Japanese workers among its members. That same year at the Wheatland, California, Durst Brothers Ranch, the IWW led a strike of 2,800 men, women and children hop pickers including Japanese, Hawaiians and East Indians. A confused fight ended with four killed and many wounded.[16]

Racism against Asians as described in this brief summary has existed since the first Chinese, Japanese and other Asians set foot on this soil. But during World War II, what was done to Japanese Americans reached an all time low.

In a war that was being fought against the menace of fascism, fascist methods were used against Japanese American citizens. Profascist forces in the United States launched a massive racist campaign against all people of Japanese ancestry. The Hearst and McClatcky Press, the American Legion and others who had sparked passage of the Japanese Exclusion Act of 1924 came into the forefront of the attack. Posters were put up proclaiming "Jap Hunting License Sold Here—Open Season Now No Limit." An illustrated article appeared in the December 22, 1941 issue of *Life* on "How to tell Japs from the Chinese." At the federal government level racist terms were frequently used by government officials, including President Roosevelt (our most liberal president).

Eventually the American version of a concentration camp took place. Not since the wars to drive the Indians westward and the traffic in slaves had the nation witnessed such a terrible treatment of a racial group as to what happened to all Japanese nationals. A partial chronology of what took place follows:

February 14th: General DeWitt sent a memorandum to the Secretary of War recommending evacuation of Japanese and other "subversive persons" from the West Coast.

February 19th: President Roosevelt signed executive order no. 9066 authorizing the Secretary of War or any military commander designated by the Secretary, to establish military areas and to exclude therefrom "any other persons."

February 20th: Secretary of War, Henry R. Stimson, wrote to General DeWitt designating him as a military commander empowered to carry out an evacuation within his command under terms of order 9066.

As a result of these orders, over 110,000 Japanese citizens were uprooted and put in American concentration camps. This included women and children. At the time this terrible racist crime was carried out, pro-Nazi Bundist groups were well organized and staging parades up and down the land, but were not molested.

Yoneda points out some of the probable reasons why such an evacuation did not take place in Hawaii, or to German and Italian citizens. He wrote: "In Hawaii, where the attack occurred, no mass evacuation took place. Why? Because there Japanese made up over a third of the population, held many elective offices and had become a major source of labor. Martial law was imposed to guarantee economic stability."

The question then is asked:

Why didn't West Coast Japanese Americans fight the evacuation order? Here, only a very small number of religious and other organizations such as the California CIO, through its then secretary Lou Goldblatt, spoke in opposition to the plight facing them. Also, it should be remembered Japanese workers on the mainland were mostly unorganized and not a major economic factor. The average Nisei age was 19, therefore not a voter threat, nor did they have an organization with political connections in Washington, D.C. as did those of German and Italian descent. Consequently, there was no mass evacuation even of aliens of German or Italian origin.

A handful of Nisei ignored or tested the evacuation order by various means but the courts ruled against them. Nisei Communists and progressives decided not to fight evacuation, though it was in violation of the most basic democratic rights—the rationale being all human rights would be lost if the Axis powers were victorious. Therefore the most immediate objective was to destroy fascism, and thus there was no choice but to "accept" the racist U.S. dictum at that time over Hitler's ovens and Japan's military rapists of Nanking.[17]

The foregoing should suffice to show that U.S. capitalism gave birth to a system that exploited and persecuted all the races of mankind. It also shows that "winning of the West" was accompanied by racist strategy and tactics which added to the inhumane treatment of people of Spanish and Asian descent to that of Native Americans and Black people make the United States one of the worst offenders of "human rights," the world has ever witnessed.

PART III
SEXUAL OPPRESSION

10 • BACKGROUND OF SEXUAL OPPRESSION

THE THIRD aspect of democratic limitations within bourgeois democracy at the birth and development of the United States was the oppression of women. While this problem is not the same as that of the Indian, Black, Mexican, and Asian peoples, nonetheless it constitutes a form of oppression of major proportion. This problem, like all others, was transplanted here by the money-hungry colonizers.

As already observed in previous chapters, the bourgeois democratic revolutions were preceded by intensive ideological struggles. These struggles were waged under the main theme of "the Natural Rights of Man." The ideologists of the rising capitalist system were quite deceptive about the limitations of democracy for the people in general, but not so in regard to women. They made it clear that women were subordinate to men. Sexual oppression did not originate with capitalism. It was born out of ancient slavery, continued under feudalism and given a new dimension under capitalism. Male supremacy like racism is an ideology designed to justify oppression. But while racism is a by-product of the capitalist system, the ideology of male supremacy is of longer vintage.

In times previous to capitalism, this ideology was mainly based on religious concepts and teachings. The primacy of man is established in the Christian doctrine with the birth of the human race. The Bible opens with man giving birth to woman, the story of Adam and Eve.

With the emergence of capitalism, the ideology behind the supremacy of man took on more of a "scientific" character. If man was endowed with certain inalienable and natural rights, among these were superior biological characteristics, which included mental qualities, over those of women. With few exceptions, most of the men who are honored today as great democratic theorists were among the foremost advocates of inequality for women. John Locke, in his second essay on civil government, placed women in a subordinate position when he wrote: "The husband and wife though they have but one common concern, yet having different understandings, will unavoidably sometimes have different wills too; it therefore being necessary that the last determination, i.e.,—the rule—should be placed somewhere, it naturally falls to the man's share, as the abler and stronger."[1]

Divorce laws in capitalist countries were man-made and stacked in favor of men over women. What was true in Britain in regards to women's role in society and the difficulty women encountered in ending a marriage was no less true in France after the great French Revolution of 1789. In fact, inequality for women was placed in the constitution of that time, in the 1804 Code Napoleon (the French Civil Code).

The first book of the Code deals with the enjoyment of civil rights, the protection of the personal domicile; guardianship, tutorship, relations of parents and children, marriage, personal relations of spouses and the dissolution of marriage. The Code states that the husband is the chief of the family and the wife owes him obedience. At the time of marriage, the property of both becomes common, but managed by the husband. The wife was viewed as incapable of any act in the economic sphere without the written consent of her husband. The Code limited considerably the grounds for divorce, especially by women.

Code Napoleon was revised on numerous occasions and the name changed, but the content remained basically the same. Code Napoleon was one of the most influential constitutional documents of all time. In one form or another, its content was adopted all over

Europe, in North Africa and South America, embracing over a hundred countries.

The male supremacist character of the Code was also based on the writing of Rousseau, who wrote: "The whole education of women ought to be relative to men. To please them, to be useful to them, to make themselves loved and honored by them, to educate them, when young to care for them, when grown to council them, to make life sweet and agreeable to them. These are the duties of women at all times and what should be taught them from their infancy."[2]

WHILE almost all bourgeois democratic philosophers and political scientists limited democratic concepts to the male sex, there were some exceptions. The most outstanding of these was John Stuart Mill. He wrote three essays titled "The Subjection of Women in 1869." These essays are by far the best bourgeois thought on the plight of women. Among other things, Mill wrote: "What is now called the nature of woman is an eminently artificial thing—the result of forced repression in some directions, unnatural stimulation in others."[3]

In this statement, Mill takes issue with the general view that women are endowed by nature with biological and mental differences which necessitate them being confined to certain roles in society and none other. Mill clearly shows the environmental causes of certain differences that were forced on women by men. The essays were especially written to counteract male supremacist views as expressed during the Victorian era in English history and especially as voiced by John Ruskin, who published a book in 1865 entitled *Of Queen's Gardens in Sesame and Lillies* in which he romanticized woman but consigned her to the home.

Ruskin warned women to stay away from accomplishment. "They might secure a smattering of information," he said, but they should "understand the meaning of the inevitableness of natural laws; and follow at least one of them as far as to the threshold of that bitter valley of humiliation into which only the wisest and bravest of men can descend."[4] In other words, women should understand their limitations and not seek higher education. In Mill's opinion, views like Ruskin's were nothing more than the most ingenious form of mental slavery in history.

However despite Mill's forceful advocacy of equal rights for women, he did not understand the source of women's inequality and what would be required to change her status. He did not understand, as did Frederick Engels, that the oppression of women was born on the day that society became divided into classes on an exploitative basis. And that the only way the problem of women's rights could be fully solved would be the total elimination of exploitation and oppression from society. This objective calls for the merger of the class and racially oppressed with those sexually oppressed against all forms of exploitation.

Thus, lacking such an understanding, Mill saw the solution solely in a legal sense in bourgeois society, in the struggle for the right to the ballot. As history unfolded since Mill's time, the limitations of women's rights under capitalism have been spelled out in concrete terms. We shall discuss this matter in a later chapter. The main thing, at this point, is to show that the inequality of women and the ideology of male supremacy continued with the birth and development of capitalism in general, and in the birth and development of the United States as a nation.

For more than a hundred years after the discovery of North America, the great majority of people who came to these shores were men. The early colonists reflected the same ideas as the Spanish *conquistadores* in Latin and South America. Both felt that their stay here would be transient. They would get rich through gold dust or tobacco planting and return home. But as time went on, the commercial revolution, the first phase of modern capitalism, was more and more transformed into industrial capitalism which required new sources of raw materials as well as commodity production in general. And it was in this context that women began to come to North America.

Some women came as wives and daughters of settlers. But that was not enough to guarantee the growth of communities and provide for more working hands for commodity production. Thus, despite male supremacist ideology which had consigned women to housekeepers and attendants, women were brought to the colonies by the exploiting classes for their labor power as well. Women, together with children, constituted a large part of the indentured servants. As such, they suffered almost unbelievable misery and exploitation.

Of course, these generalizations do not describe the conditions women faced in all places or in all aspects for the colonies varied from one to another. In a previous chapter, we took note of the treatment of the Native American Indians by the "God-fearing Pilgrims." But their ruthless treatment of Indians and Blacks was also present in their treatment of women. The early colonist fled from religious persecution, but what they did when they arrived on these shores leaves strong doubts in that respect. While some aspects of the church were different from that in the Old World, the women who came here were bound by the Old World tenets. The Presbyterians of New England did nothing to soften the teachings of John Knox, who wrote: "Woman, in her greatest perfection, was made to serve and obey man, not to rule and command him. Man is not of the woman, but the woman of the man."[5] In the church especially she should listen and obey: "Let woman keep silent in the congregation, for it is not permitted to them to speak but to be subject as the Law sayeth."[6]

It was therefore no accident that one of the first women's protests made in this country was for their rights in the church. It came with Anne Hutchinson who had fled from Lincolnshire, Britain, in 1633, seeking freedom of worship. When she came to Boston she began holding meetings and preaching the gospel.

John Winthrop, the governor of the colony, who had fled from the dictatorship of Archbishop Laud in England, became more dictatorial than the archbishop, especially as women became involved. He brought Anne Hutchinson to trial for violation of the tenets of the church, and she was sentenced as a "leper" and ordered to withdraw. Yet what happened to Anne Hutchinson was child's play compared to what happened later at Salem, Massachusetts. In 1692, in the hysteria of that year, nineteen people were put to death as witches. Most of the victims were aged and friendless old women. Thus, while capitalism gave a "scientific" basis to the inequality of women, the religious aspect still remained a potent force, especially at the birth of this nation.

THE tremendous suffering that women underwent to build this nation, and the heroic role they played in the American Revolution were completely ignored by the Founding Fathers after the Revolutionary War of 1776.

These men who are so widely acclaimed as great democrats and liberators, made it exceptionally clear that women in the new setup would not be considered citizens with equal rights, that women, unlike men, were not endowed with certain "inalienable rights." Some women sought to change this strange contradiction. Among them was Abigail Adams, wife of John Adams, second president of the United States. She engaged in extensive correspondence with him, pleading the case of women.

In 1776, when John Adams was in Philadelphia attending the Continental Congress, she wrote:

[To John Adams] May, 1776 I cannot say that you are very generous to the ladies; for whilst you are proclaiming peace and goodwill to men emancipating all nations, you insist upon retaining an absolute power over wives. But you must remember that arbitrary power is like most other things which are very hard, very likely to be broken; and not withstanding all your wise laws and maxims, we have it in our power not only to free ourselves, but to subdue our masters and without violence. Throw both your natural and legal authority at our feet.[7]

It is clear that Mrs. Adams did not realize what the source of women's oppression was and in what it would take and how long would be required to solve the problem. Nonetheless, she adds to the solution of the problem today, if for no other reason than to show the hypocritical role of the Founding Fathers.

The terrible conditions of women continued after the Revolution of 1776. And while some progress has been made, it has been slow and even to this day, women remain in a state of great inequality in our country.

As the nation developed, women remained devoid of legal rights, denied equal opportunities for education, and were the objects of special forms of exploitation, especially Black women.

The legal status of women in the early colonies was based on the English Common Law. Sir William Blackstone and his Commentaries formed the basis for most legal judgments. Even though some historians have pointed out that in the colonies the laws were applied less rigidly than in England, nonetheless women in America possessed very few rights. Their conditions were based on Blackstone's definition which placed married women completely under the domination of the husbands. Under this concept, if a wife was assaulted or raped, she could not prosecute her attacker unless her husband would bring suit.

It was in the marital contract that woman became almost a total slave to man. With few exceptions a woman had virtually no property rights. Upon marriage, her property and also her wages were merged with that of the husband. Upon his death she was only entitled to one-third of his estate. If she was childless she received one-half.

In cases where divorce or separation took place, the property could be divided. But this rarely took place on an equal basis. Unless a contract existed, the husband even had the rights of his wife's personal possessions "down to the dress on her back."

As time went by there were modifications made in the laws, mainly at the state level. New York State led the way and others followed. In 1848 New York State adopted a law called the Married Women's Property Act. The law grew out of a situation when a conservative judge, who had married a woman of property, wanted to secure that property from his creditors in case of financial disaster. Other legislators joined with him because they wanted to protect their daughter's property upon marriage. But even such a law, which was enacted for the selfish reasons of men, took twelve years before it was passed. It gave a wife full control over her real and personal property at the time of her marriage, and exempted it from her husband's debts. However, the wages earned by a wife were still the property of her husband. Ernestine Rose who campaigned for the law had no illusions about it. She viewed it as a legal advance for women, but not very much more, for at best, it favored the few and not the suffering many.

WITH the down-to-earth nature of the origins of the nation, the problems of U.S. education received very little concern from the ruling circles. It was regarded as a luxury for the rich, and the poor needed it only to the extent that it increased their physical labor. As for women, it was really not needed at all. It was even dangerous. A governor of Massachusetts commenting on what happened to the wife of the governor of Connecticut who lost her mind, attributed her misfortune to her "meddling": "In such things as are proper for men whose minds are stronger—she might have kept her wits and might have improved them usefully and honorably in the place God had set her."[8]

The growth of American cities and manufacturing towns demanded training in skills, and the demand for education grew even greater. In this context, women were advanced into the teaching staffs, but only on the lower levels. For a long time after the Revolution of 1776, women were excluded from higher education and from many professions. In 1771, in the state of Connecticut, girls were allowed to learn to read, write, spell and add. But this was done with discrimination; education for girls was separated from boys; and schools for girls were held between April and October, a time when boys were busy working on the farms.

In general, there was very little coeducation in the lower grades and none in the higher grades. Among the first schools to change this pattern was Oberlin College in Ohio which opened its doors to all sexes and colors in 1833. As a result of discrimination in education and exclusion from all institutions of higher learning, women lagged behind men in many essential areas of intellectual development.

A typical example of the hardships standing in the way of women entering the professions is the story of Elizabeth Blackwell. Ms. Blackwell rebelled against a life of social ease and passive study. She believed that women, because of their role as mothers, could play an important role in improving health and welfare. With this noble purpose in mind, she decided to enter the medical profession. The tremendous obstacles in her path added a new dimension to her desire.

In the pursuit of her goal, Ms. Blackwell spent two years in correspondence with and visits to doctors, some of whom helped her, while others condemned her efforts or ignored her. She applied to twenty-nine medical schools before she was finally admitted to Geneva College (later absorbed into the University of Syracuse) where she suffered a very painful experience. First of all, the faculty as a whole opposed her entry. They submitted the problem before the student body with the feeling that they would reject her. But the students surprised them by voting to admit her. Although admitted to the school, she was subjected to all kinds of hostility from students and townspeople alike.

But, notwithstanding such a nerve racking experience, she persevered and graduated at the head of her class. Nonetheless her problems did not end in school. Later Ms. Blackwell went to Europe to study and came back home to an even greater humiliation. She had great difficulties finding a place to stay or renting an office. Private patients did not come to her and she could not get access to the city hospitals. She was shunned by other doctors, and was also the victim of all kinds of foul gossip.

But Elizabeth Blackwell would not give up; she created her own opportunities to practice medicine. Eventually, she organized a hospital in New York City, the New York Infirmary, at 64 Bleeker Street and staffed it entirely with women. The establishment of this institution brought on additional problems. Before the hospital was opened a host of objections were raised by those whom the early friends of the institution attempted to interest in this effort: They were told that no one would let a house for the purpose; that female doctors would be looked upon with so much suspicion that the police would interfere; that if deaths occured their death certificates would not be recognized; that without men they would not be able to control the patients; that if an accident occurred, not only the medical profession but the public would blame the trustees for supporting such an undertaking.

On one occasion, a mob assaulted the hospital believing that a patient who had failed to recover, had been killed by the "Lady Doctors."

Women did not encounter the same kind of resistance in other fields as in medicine. But they did enounter resistance in their efforts to become lawyers, scientists, architects, etc. Those who aspired to become lawyers faced immeasurable difficulties. First of all, they had to apply to the Supreme Court of their state for a license.

The entrance of women into the educational and professional institutions varied from state to state, and from time to time, but whenever progress was made, it came from the sweat, tears and sorrows, in the first place, of the women themselves.

THE economic forms of the inequality of women have varied from time to time throughout U.S. history. But whatever the form, the content has remained the same. Women have been superexploited throughout our history. They are exploited as members of the working class, in addition to sexual exploitation.

The struggle to secure property rights in the main benefited upper-class women; it did not relate to the main problems facing working women. The theory of women's confinement to household duties, child bearing and raising, etc., did not hold as capitalism developed in the United States. From the earliest beginnings of the nation, women had to carry a double load.

The economic value of the women and children was borne out by the fact that women with a lot of children who became widows could find husbands with relative ease.

In the cities, with the development of the factory system, women and children were exploited in the most shameful manner. The ruling class of America had seen how developing capitalism in Britain had exploited women and children in the factories, mills, mines and workshops and they prepared to do likewise.

Thus, the textile industry in the United States as in Britain became the main industry to hire women. It also became the first sweat shop, grinding and draining the life blood of women and children through endless hours of toil. The terrible conditions of women were not confined to the textile industry as Mary Beard observes in her book, *A Short History of the Labor Movement.* In 1837 there were about 100 occupations in which women were engaged, usually for small wages and long hours. There were more than 15,000 women in the shoe industry of Massachusetts alone, hundreds of them earning only from 8 or 10 cents a day.

Anthony Bimba summed up the situation:

. . . it remained for the age of capitalism to enslave the body and soul of women and children . . . The capitalist system of production mercilessly dragged women and children from the fireside into the factories and made them wage slaves. . . . Capitalism has taken out of their homes children of five, six and seven years of age and made of them fodder for capitalist industry. The most horrible abuses of child labor in England were transplanted bodily to America as soon as the rise of industry and commerce made it possible to put the children of the poor at the machines.[9]

Such were the conditions as the United States began to arise as a manufacturing and commercial power.

After the Civil War and beginning of a revolution in industry, the terrible conditions of women and children spread. By being paid less wages for the same work as men, women were used to depress the wage level of the whole working class. In some instances they were used as strike breakers. A contributing factor to this situation has been the influence of male supremacy in the ranks of the working class. This ideology together with racism has been a major source of some of the conditions of the working class as a whole.

Toward the close of the nineteenth century, some reforms were effected in the conditions of women and children, which will be the subject of another chapter. But reforms notwithstanding, women are still exploited and in a certain sense, are third-class citizens.

The terrible conditions white women suffered as the nation developed on a capitalist base was a thousand-fold worse for Black women. History abounds with many examples of women as slaves, women who were raped, women who were murdered with babies in their arms like at My Lai in Vietnam, and crimes in the concentration camps of Nazi Germany. But Black women have been victims of the worst forms of human degradation longer than any other person in history. For more than four centuries she has been on the lowest level of this inhuman society known as capitalism.

The character of the oppression of the Black women is three-fold. It is sexual, class and racial. All three aspects are pervasive and are found in all the institutions of our society. Of late, there are those who claim that the Black male is the most victimized person. According to this theory the Black male was denied superior traits of the white male, namely the King Pin in his household, the protector of the weak female. While none can doubt that Black males suffered untold agony from this situation, their plight was nothing to compare with that of Black women.

Such was the background of sexual oppression in our national heritage. But women also have a background of struggle, without which this nation's record would be even more horrible. The women in our history made contributions not only to alleviate their own conditions but for the country as a whole. And despite her terrible oppression, the Black woman in her conduct through four centuries of oppression showed unusual strength and brain power to survive.

The role Black and white women have played in the development of American society, under unusually bad conditions, places women as a sex not only on an equal plane with males, but in many respects, on a superior level. Whatever democratic gains we have made as a nation have come in large part to the role women, Black and white, have played in American history. But their continued status as a special group for superexploitation and persecution provides a searchlight to show the democratic limitations within capitalism.

11 • WOMEN: SLAVERY AND SUFFRAGE

FOR MORE than two hundred years women in this country waged great struggles to put some substance and meaning into the word democracy, and for human rights. While the goal they sought—complete equality—has not been obtained, they have made some progress by their struggles. In so doing, they became one of the great social forces that have helped to introduce some humanity into an otherwise inhuman system. In every area of democratic advance, American women have left their mark. From colonial and revolutionary times until today great women have walked across the stage of American life. But like Black Americans, their contributions are largely an untold story.

The vast majority of women are unaware of the great feminist writings of the past. They are not acquainted with the struggles and achievements of the widespread women's movements in the nineteenth and twentieth centuries, and do not have access to scholarly studies (indeed how few exist which describe the part played by women in the French and American revolutions, the anti-slavery movement, and the development of organized labor). In short, women have been deprived of their history—thus their group identity.[1]

Charles Francis Adams, grandson of Abigail and John Adams, took note of the exclusion of women from the American Revolution when he wrote in the preface of his collection of the letters of his grandparents: "The heroism of the females of the Revolution has gone from memory with the generation that witnessed it, and nothing, absolutely nothing, remains upon the ear of the young of the present day but the faint echo of an expiring general tradition."[2]

The reason for this lack of awareness is not hard to find. Historians in the main have deliberately excluded the female just as they have excluded Blacks in order to foster the ideologies of racism

144

and male supremacy. Professor Arthur M. Schlesinger was one of the exceptions when over thirty-five years ago in his book *New Viewpoints in American History* he wrote:

An examination of the standard histories of the United States and of the history textbooks in use in our schools raises the pertinent question whether women have ever made any contributions to American National progress that are worthy of record. If the silence of the historians is to mean anything, it would appear that one-half of our population have been negligible factors in our country's history . . . And any considerations of women's part in American history must include the protracted struggle of the sex for larger rights and opportunities, a story that is in itself one of the noblest chapters in the history of American democracy.[3]

The story of the women's rights movement must be told over and over again, for in so doing our understanding of the forces that expanded democracy beyond what the Founding Fathers dreamed of, tells us something of what is required to put an end to exploitation and persecution in any form, whether it is class, racial, national or sexual.

MUCH could be written about the role of women in the American Revolution and in other areas of struggle. But for the purpose of this book, we shall concentrate on the role played by women in the anti-slavery and labor struggles; and in this connection, the struggles they waged on their own behalf. In all these areas the contributions made by women were decisive in moving the whole nation toward the goal of a people's democracy. The interrelationship of the most oppressed sectors of our society, the victims of racial, class and sexual oppression, was delineated very clearly by Andrew Sinclair in this book *The Better Half* when he observed:

Women however did not merely look for the freedom of their own sex. What I hope to make very clear is that reforms do not come singly; one leads to another, and the reformers are linked to place and time. There is both a society and a geography of reform. If a particular class or sex group is brought nearer to equality with those who are dominant, a third depressed section of the community will demand advance, for advance will have been proved to be possible. Agitation for one reform sparks off agitation for others.[4]

The whole history of the women's movement testifies to the correctness of Sinclair's observations.

It was in the struggle to end slavery by the Abolitionists that a women's movement was born. Prior to the anti-slavery struggle, women in various forms, as individuals as well as an organized force, made great struggles for their freedom. But out of these struggles an organized mass movement with a clear program did not evolve. In this connection, Eleanor Flexner says:

It was in the abolition movement that women first learned to organize, to hold public meetings, to conduct petition campaigns. As Abolitionists they first won the right to speak in public and began to evolve a philosophy of their place in society and of their basic rights. For a quarter of a century the two movements, to free the slaves and to liberate the women, nourished and strengthened one another.[5]

Kate Millet in *Sexual Politics* amplifies this point:

There is something logical in the fact that they should first band together for another cause than their own: it fulfills the "service ethic" in which they were indoctrinated. Slavery was probably the only circumstance in American life sufficiently glaring in its injustice and monumental evil to impel women to break that taboo of decorum which stifled and controlled them more efficiently than the coil of their legal, educational and financial disabilities.[6]

What should be emphasized is that a circumstance such as slavery was closer home. Because at the same time that slavery for Blacks was evil, what was happening to the Native Americans on the frontier was just as bad, and sometimes even worse.

In 1840 a worldwide anti-slavery convention was held in London. Lucretia Mott and a number of female delegates from the United States went to the convention but were not seated because they were women. A religious rationale was used for this crass act of sexual discrimination by those who were taking a stand against slavery. However, the women returned home determined to establish their own organization and to wage a struggle against the twin evils of slavery and sexual oppression. At that point the class roots and nature of the problem were not understood. In 1848 the first organized women's movement for freedom was organized in the United States, a move which greatly influenced European women.

Because of discrimination against women in the educational system, very few women had formal training. At the very first convention held in Seneca Falls, New York, it is claimed that no woman present felt competent to chair, and a man chaired the meeting. However, this circumstance soon changed, and women became among some of the most articulate orators, writers and organizers in both the Abolitionist and women's organizations. The Seneca Falls conference adopted a number of resolutions and a statement of sentiments which were a paraphrase of the Declaration of Independence.

The women were joined by a number of men who were Abolitionists. Foremost among them were Frederick Douglass and William Lloyd Garrison. Frederick Douglass argued at Seneca Falls for full political rights for women and frequently attended women's rights conventions. While most organs of public opinion ridiculed the movement founded at Seneca Falls, Frederick Douglass wrote in an editorial in his paper *The North Star* on July 28, 1848:

> Standing as we do upon the watch tower of human freedom, we cannot be deterred from an expression of our approbation of any movement, however humble, to improve and elevate the character of any members of the human family. While it is impossible for us to go into this subject at length and dispose of the various objections which are often urged against such a doctrine as that of female equality, we are free to say that in respect to political rights, we hold women to be justly entitled to all we claim for men.[7]

William Lloyd Garrison was no less ardent in the cause of women's rights than Frederick Douglass. In 1840 he travelled to London to participate in a world anti-slavery convention. Upon arrival he was shocked to learn that Lucretia Mott and other women had been barred from participation. He declined to participate in the meeting declaring: "After battling so many long years for the liberties of African slaves, I can take no part in a convention that strikes down the most sacred rights of all women."[8]

At a women's rights conference in 1853, the women were criticized from the audience by a male speaker because, in his opinion, the Seneca Falls Declaration of Sentiments unfairly blamed men for the condition of women. The allegation inflamed Garrison to the point where he arose and spontaneously exclaimed: "We must deal with conscience. The men of this nation and the men of all nations have no respect for woman ... Does not this nation know how great its guilt is in enslaving one-sixth of its people? Do not the men of this nation know ever since the landing of the Pilgrims, that they are wrong in making subject one-half of the people."[9]

Now it is true that the Declaration of Sentiments treated the source of the problem of women's oppression incorrectly, but at that time the class aspect of the problem had not come into focus sharply and so what was mainly dealt with was that which was visible to the naked eye. The fact was that the society almost as a whole engaged in sexual oppression. Beneath the surface, the system was promoted by people with a vested interest in the superexploitation of women. However most men without a vested interest had embraced the ideology of male supremacy. They had been trained that way, and even those who had no stake in the superexploitation of women, but who unwittingly embraced the ideology, had to some extent share guilt in the situation. With the passage of time this aspect of the problem became clearer.

The merger of the movement for an end to slavery and equal rights for women was accelerated by the role played by a Black woman, Sojourner Truth. The role she played has come down through history as a legend of great significance. She was born a slave and remained illiterate all her life. Her master disapproved of the man she loved and flogged her in his presence. She eventually married a man that he approved of and gave birth to thirteen children, most of whom were sold into slavery. In 1827 she secured her freedom when New York State, by law, freed its slaves. She became a domestic worker and later an Abolitionist.

At a women's rights conference in Akron, Ohio, in 1851 none of the women seemed able to answer an outbreak of heckling from males, and it looked as if their cause would be lost. Sojourner Truth came forward to speak. Many women, believing that the Abolitionist leader would harm their cause, sought to block her from speaking and begged Mrs. Gage not to give her the floor. But Mrs. Gage, who chaired the meeting, thought otherwise. Sojourner Truth moved slowly to the front, laid down her bonnett and began to speak.

Sojourner Truth then delivered a speech that electrified the audience and which demonstrated the great strength and vast creativity of the ex-slaves. Sojourner Truth proclaimed:

> The man over there says women need to be helped into carriages and lifted over ditches and to have the best places everywhere. Nobody ever helps me into carriages or over puddles, or gives me the best place—and ain't I a woman? Look at my arm! I have plowed and planted and gathered into barns, and no man could head me—and ain't I a woman? I could work as much and eat as much as a man—when I could get it—and bear the lash as well; and ain't I a woman? I have borne thirteen children, and seen most of them sold into slavery, and when I cried out with my mother's grief, none but Jesus heard me—and ain't I a woman?[10]

And then according to Mrs. Gage:

Amid roars of applause she returned to her corner leaving more than one of us with streaming eyes and hearts beating with gratitude. She had taken us up in her strong arms and carried us safely over the slough of difficulty, turning the whole tide in our favor. I have never in my life seen anything like the magical influence that subdued the snobbish spirit of the day and turned the sneers and jeers of an excited crowd into notes of respect and admiration.[11]

Mrs. Gage was so inspired by Sojourner Truth's speech that she arose and made her maiden speech which also speaks to the great courage and talents of people who are dedicated to a noble cause.

WOMEN in their endeavor to participate in the Abolitionist movement, had to endure elements of male supremacy as did Blacks who encountered many manifestations of racism. When the Abolitionists founded the American Anti-Slavery Society in Philadelphia in 1833 only a few women were allowed to attend. They were allowed to speak from the floor but not to join the society or to sign the declaration of purpose. Upon the adjournment of the convention about twenty women met and formed the Philadelphia Female Anti-slavery Society. Not long afterwards women organized for the same purpose in New York, Boston, and some New England towns. In 1837 the first female anti-slavery convention met in New York. There were eighty-one delegates from twelve states present. It is claimed that one of the delegates sent word to a prominent male abolitionist that when the women got together they found they had minds of their own, and could carry on the business without his direction. What the women did in this regard was similar to Blacks setting up their own organizations and newspapers.

In overstepping time-honored bounds, the women's movement aroused the wrath of pro-slavery forces in the North. "Mob violence was not unusual. In Boston in 1835 a mob swarmed into a building where Garrison was to address the Boston female antislavery society . . . Garrison was whisked out of a back door. He was later dragged through the streets at the end of a rope."[12]

The women's suffrage movement and the Abolitionists produced many great women leaders like the Grimke sisters, Sarah and Angelina, from South Carolina. They were daughters of a slaveholding family, yet from childhood they abhorred slavery. They fled from the South in order to fight the horrible peculiar institution and all it stood for. In 1836 they joined the Abolitionists and began a career of public speaking and writing that had a profound effect on both the movement for women's equality and against slavery. In fact, it was these southern-born sisters who opened the door for women to engage in public speaking. Angelina addressed an appeal to the Christian women of the South calling upon them to speak out against the slave system. At about the same time, the American Antislavery Society invited the sisters to speak at meetings in New York City. The first meeting had to be transferred to a small church because over three hundred people attended. No doubt the fact that the sisters came from the South and could speak about slavery from first-hand experience made them a greater attraction than most speakers. Before long the sisters were addressing mixed audiences, an uncommon thing to do in those days.

Angelina Grimke was the first woman to ever address a legislative body. In February 1838 a series of hearings on an anti-slavery petition was scheduled by the Massachusetts legislature. Henry E. Stranton suggested that she speak for the Abolitionists which she agreed to do.

Angelina Grimke later married Theodore Weld, one of the most outstanding leaders in the Abolitionist movement. Together, as man and wife they had a great impact on ridding the nation of some of the most heinous crimes known to humankind.

One of the most outstanding contributions women made to ending slavery was the underground railroad system. Through this system it is estimated that a hundred thousand slaves found their way to freedom. White women stood in the forefront of the system. They provided safe quarters for runaway slaves throughout the nation. But the main heroine of this system was a Black woman, Harriet Tubman. Like Sojourner Truth, Harriet Tubman is legendary, although most standard history textbooks, as is the case with Black history generally, overlook the tremendous contributions these women made to the extension of American democracy.

Harriet Tubman was still a young woman, about thirty, when she became a "conductor" on the underground railroad. It is estimated that in a period of ten years she made nineteen journeys into the South and rescued more than three hundred men, women and children. She was regarded among her people as "Moses." The slaveholders put a price tag on her head that eventually reached

$40,000. The miracle of all is that she was never caught, harmed or lost a passenger. Later, during the Civil War, she became a scout and a nurse in the Union army. As a "reward," at the age of eighty, Congress awarded her a pension of $20 a month. What a shame!

The role women played in the Civil War has also been hidden from view of the general public. This is true in all aspects of the war. When all things are added up, slavery could not have been ended without women playing the role they did. They not only served as nurses in army hospitals and went to work in sweatshops under horrible conditions, but they also contributed greatly to military successes as well as arousing the general public to the necessities of the war.

WOMEN were one of the most potent forces in the country in arousing the nation to understand the necessity to end slavery in the course of the war. The Emancipation Proclamation issued by President Lincoln in 1863 applied only to the states in rebellion. Legal sanction by Congress and a constitutional amendment were needed to put the the icing on the cake so to speak. The women's movement arose to the occasion and became a decisive force that helped to enact the Thirteenth Amendment to the Constitution.

Charles Sumner introduced into Congress the amendment to ban slavery forever. At that time it was uncertain as to whether a two-thirds majority could be won in both houses. In this connection, Stanton wrote to Susan B. Anthony: "The country was never so badly off as of this moment. . . . You have no idea how dark the cloud is which hangs over us . . . we Must not lay flattering unction to our souls that the Proclamation will be of any use if we are beaten."[13] In response to the urgency of the moment, Susan B. Anthony and Elizabeth Cady Stanton, another outstanding leader, came together for another major thrust. They sent out a call throughout the country to people who had been supporters of the women's movement. Among other things, the call was a summons to action. It declared: "Woman is equally interested and responsible with man in the final settlement of this probelm . . . Therefore let none stand as idle spectators now."[14]

Later a conference took place in a church in Union Square, New York. Hundreds of people came, among them the firey Angelina Grimke Weld, who came out of retirement. Out of the meeting the

National Women's Loyal League was formed; Mrs. Stanton was elected president and Miss Anthony secretary. The conference adopted resolutions pledging support to the government as long as it conducted a war for freedom. They also pledged to collect a million signatures to a petition urging Congress to pass the Thirteenth Amendment to the Constitution. An office was opened in Cooper Union (New York City) and a massive campaign to collect the signatures was launched.

The campaign was conducted for about a year and a half. It is estimated that over two thousand men, women and children participated. To collect a million signatures at that time was not a practical possibility. However, the forces behind the league did a yeoman's job in collecting about four hundred thousand signatures.

Even before they completed their work, they sent the first hundred thousand to Washington and placed them on the desk of Senator Sumner from Massachusetts, who offering them to the president, commented as follows:

Mr. President, I offer a petition which is now lying on the desk before me. It is too bulky for me to take up. I need not add that it is too bulky for any of the pages of this body to carry.... It will be perceived that the petition is in rolls. Each roll represents a state. For instance here is New York, with a list of seventeen thousand seven hundred and six names; Illinois with fifteen thousand, three hundred and twenty, and Massachusetts with eleven thousand six hundred and fifty one.... This petition is signed by 100,000 men and women who united in this unparalleled manner to support its prayer.[15]

As Sumner pointed out, a larger army was yet to come. It came with an additional three hundred thousand signatures, a historic achievement. But there was more to this campaign than collecting signatures. A tremendous propaganda campaign was required. At first the going was rough, but that soon evaporated under the impact of the work done by the league. They convinced large numbers of people in the North and West that an end to slavery would regenerate the whole society. Stanton and Anthony held in abeyance the problems of women and stressed the problems of the slaves. But they did so with the illusion that at war's end, women would also get their rights. They were correct in their assessment that the ending of slavery would add a new dimension towards a people's democracy. But they overestimated the tempo of the times, the level of social consciousness and, above all, the strategy of the ruling class.

Sinclair takes note of what was to come. He wrote;

Their effort to build up a fund of gratitude among anti-slavery reformers which would be repayable later was a failure. After the war each reform group returned to its own priority even at the expense of other reforms. When a reform nears legal success, its backers become politic, ready to sacrifice any helping cause that may lose support. Reforms may grow together but, short of a social, they are victorious alone.[16]

Sinclair raises a profound problem of the extension of the democracy in the framework of the capitalist system. The history of the battle for democracy shows that each time a reform is forced through, the ruling class provides insurance papers to prevent the particular reform from becoming a catalyst that could dig deeper into the system. We showed in a previous chapter how the protection of private property was added to the Bill of Rights which ostensibly was placed in the Constitution to protect the liberties of the American people.

In the aftermath that followed the Civl War, once again an amendment was added to make one reform. Insurance papers were taken out to contain the reform at that level and not to open the door so wide that the whole system could become jeopardized. The ruling classes in both the North and the South understood what was not understood by some of the main leaders of the women's movement. Nor did the leaders of the Abolitionist movement understand the full consequence of what was to follow. The ruling circles saw that the abolition of slavery had been linked with the fabric of the society: The freeing of the slave was only one freedom among many demands. And if "the rash call" for women's equality prevailed would that not be followed by the Irish immigrant wageslaves who would want their rights too? The ruling class saw that reforms did not come singly but in a group. And so they worked to prevent that from happening.

THE events that followed the Civil War and Reconstruction, while on one hand adding a new dimension to the word democracy, also portrayed some of the most tragic developments in our history. What a different path history would have taken if the leaders of the women's movement, the Abolitionists and Black peoples organizations had understood how Karl Marx from afar understood the Civil War and what could follow. It was during the Civil War that Marx issued his historic slogan, "Labor cannot emancipate itself in a white skin where in the black it is branded."[17] Conversely, Marx was also saying that labor in a black skin couldn't be free as long as it was branded in a white skin. Marx already understood the necessity for unity of all diverse forces and classes that were commonly oppressed under capitalism. And because there was no such understanding in the Civil War period, eventually all the oppressed forces in the society suffered a setback.

The problem began with the effort to enfranchise the ex-slaves. The slaves had been freed in the seceeding states by the issuance of the Emancipation Proclamation on January 1, 1863. But that still did not provide legal status, so Congress passed the Thirteenth Amendment to the Constitution and it was ratified on December 18, 1865. However, despite these measures, the status of the ex-slave as a citizen with full citizenship rights, the right to vote and hold public office still hung in the balance. This situation evoked a great debate in Congress.

As the debate developed with ever greater sharpness and differing opinions, word leaked out that the proposed Fourteenth Amendment would enfranchise Black males, but women would be excluded. Moreover, proposals were being made to include in the Constitution the word male so as to have no doubt about where the authors were coming from. Miss Anthony and Mrs. Stanton once again toured the nation urging protest petitions to be sent to congressmen urging them to vote against the inclusion of the word male in the amendment. As the resolutions and petitions poured into Congress, there was growing evidence that many of the male forces, who had for so long spoken out so forcefully for equal rights for women, were retreating.

Senator Charles Sumner, long an advocate of women's rights, made a speech in which he spoke about equal rights in general but said nothing about women in particular. Several days later, women were greatly alarmed when Sumner rejected a petition calling for the right of women to vote, characterizing it as "untimely and injudicious." That this long time defender of women's rights would repudiate the women's claims to translate theory into reality was an outcome no woman had suspected.

The women decided that they had to work harder to avert further defections. In May 1866 the first women's rights conference since

1860 was called in New York City. Resolutions were presented which were to plead with Congress to consider suffrage for women, and at least to withdraw the word male in defining electors. Miss Anthony's speech was adopted and later placed on the desk of every senator and representative.

Theodore Tilton, Henry Ward Beecher and Wendell Phillips were present at the conference. Beecher took his stand with Miss Anthony's position. He declared: "We are in the favored hour, I therefore say whatever truth is to be known for the next fifty years in this nation let it be spoken now . . . I therefore advocate no sectional rights, no class rights, no sex rights, but the most universal form of right for all that live and breathe on the continent . . . manhood and womanhood suffrage for all."[18]

The speech of Wendell Phillips was alarming. His had been one of the most uncompromising voices on women's behalf. But now his firmness was gone. Sumner and Phillips, both staunch fighters for the abolition of slavery and for women's rights, had begun to retreat on the latter question. A new problem now came into focus that was to divide the peoples movement for almost another century. On June 16, 1866, the Fourteenth Amendment was submitted to Congress containing the word male three times. Again there was a wave of protest, but now the situation was on a new level.

In the first phase of the struggle before Congress acted, it was one thing to oppose various propositions being proposed. But now that the amendment had passed through Congress and would go to the various states for referendum, the problem was whether to accept the amendment or to oppose its ratification by calling upon the electorate to delete the word male and add the vote for women.

Mrs. Stanton, Miss Anthony and many women suffragettes decided on the latter course. This decision widened the gap between the women's movement and the Abolitionists. The Abolitionists came into the open and waged a sharp ideological campaign against them under the slogan that it was the "Negro's hour." The Abolitionists, who had long championed the rights of Blacks and women, now gave priority to the problems of the ex-slaves. Their assessment of the situation was that it was impossible to win both reforms, and to concentrate on both would probably result in losing both. The advocates of women's suffrage were convinced that both could be won. Subsequent events proved them to be wrong, but in the final analysis both sides made some serious errors in the handling of the matter.

The question comes up, how could Mrs. Stanton, Miss Anthony and their followers go so far afield after such a valiant record in the Civil War? What mistakes did the Abolitionists make? First of all, the women suffragettes never fully understood the pernicious and pervasive nature of racism.They saw it really as a secondary feature of capitalist persecution. Of necessity they joined into the struggle to end slavery because at that point (before the Civil War) it was the dominant question before the nation. But more importantly, neither they nor the Abolitionists understood the class nature of sexual and racial oppression. Both forces had illusions about what constituted equality.

Both underestimated the class forces at work which would place limitations upon how much equality would be allowable under the system. The Abolitionists had illusions about what was called the "Negro's hour." In my view, they were correct in placing a priority on suffrage for the ex-slaves, but with a divided people's movement, they failed to understand that even "the Negro's hour" would not be sustained. The events that followed the latter part of the Reconstruction period showed this to be the case. Lastly, the women's movement did not correctly appraise the situation in the country; they overestimated the possibilities.

Flexner placed this situation in the proper context when she wrote:

From a historical vantage point, their optimism seems unfounded. Slavery and the condition of the Negro had been a boiling national issue for thirty years; a war had been fought over it. No such intensity existed yet regarding the status, even among the women themselves, excepting in a still relatively small group. Opinion in Congress and throughout the North was concerned with assuring the vote for the Negro; it was relatively uninterested in how such a controversial measure would effect women.[19]

Yet this appraisal, while outwardly true, misses the main target. The main reason for the drive to enfranchise Blacks came not only from zealous anti-slavery advocates, but also from a more powerful force, the northern bourgeoisie. This class of industrialists went into the Civil War primarily for money purposes. They were not swayed by moral sentiments about the rights and wrongs of slavery. When the Civil War ended, these people found that to give the vote to the ex-slaves was a class necessity for them, just as emancipating the slaves during the Civil War was a military necessity. The Republican Party, which represented this class, fought for the enfranchisement of Blacks in order to create a counterforce against the ex-slaveholders. They needed the Black vote to reorganize the South and guarantee the rule of the business forces. To these forces, "the Negro's hour" was to be a temporary affair. This fact is borne out by events that followed the enfranchisement of Blacks.

Carpetbaggers went South, reorganized the electorate, forged an alliance in government of Blacks and poor whites, and through them began to accelerate the conditions for capitalist control over the southern economy. When this had been achieved, and the ex-slaveholders came into line, the Blacks were deserted by the Republican Party and the "boys on Wall Street." This factor in the situation seemed to have been missed by both the feminists and the Abolitionists. Moreover, both of these forces seemed to have missed the efforts of the ruling class to divide the forces of the people at the same time they promoted the cause of the ex-slaves. There is a profound lesson in this phase of U.S. history for the problems of today. The splits between woman and woman, between Blacks and women, between male and female, build the foundation for prolonging the agony of all.

The lack of a class outlook caused the Abolitionist movement to leave the field of struggle after the reformist phase of Reconstruction. The women's movement for the right to vote went off on "its own thing." Thus, the eventual betrayal of Blacks by northern capitalist forces, left them facing a hostile and terroristic Southern ruling class without any significant allies. What was achieved in electoral status was rapidly cancelled out in the South without any significant protest.

What subsequently followed was a deterioration in both the Black freedom movement and the movement for women's suffrage. This condition continued until the end of the century. At the beginning of the twentieth century, with the birth of the National Association for the Advancement of Colored People (N.A.A.C.P.) the Black liberation movement was given a new impetus. A new category of white liberals became associated with the movement. In fact, it was a woman, Mary W. Ovington, together with several other liberals and Dr. W. E. B. Du Bois, who took the initiative to bring the organization into existence. Meanwhile, the movement for woman suffrage entered a new stage. The struggle of the right of women to vote was revived on a broader base. It received its new stimulus by successful campaigns in the West, out on the frontier. Beginning in the state of Wyoming, a number of states granted the right to vote to women.

Paradoxically, the growth of the movement for the right of women to vote was also facilitated by national chauvinism and racism. A big debate took place in the western states over the matter. The period had witnessed a tremendous growth in immigrant labor from Europe and Asia. There were those who stood against giving the vote to women, arguing that it would result in giving foreigners the right to vote, and they would overpower the so-called native-born Americans. Regarding this matter, Senator Borah, a Republican of the state of Idaho argued: "Mr. President we are not a homogeneous people yet by any means. We have the oriental question on the Pacific slope, . . . There are 10,000 Japanese and Chinese women in [the Pacific slope] states, and I have no particular desire to bestow suffrage upon them."[20]

Just the opposite point of view was expressed by Senator Newlands (D. Nev.). He voted for an amendment to enfranchise women, but he did so on racial grounds. He declared: "I stand, therefore, for the extension of suffrage to white women. [But] I stand for the denial of the right of the suffrage in this country to the people of any other race than the white race."[21]

Eventually, out of fear of the immigrants and out of the strong moral movement for reforms, a new base was created for woman suffrage. In the thirty years after the Civil War and Reconstruction, it was temperance that chiefly engaged the attention of progressive women in the small towns. The Women's Christian Temperance Union trained a generation of agitators who later entered the suffrage movement, exactly as the anti-slavery crusade had trained the first feminists. Gradually, the priority of educated western women changed from abolishing the saloon to getting the vote for themselves. Often their interest went hand in hand, for a woman's vote was presumed to be a dry vote.

Thus in 1919 women received the right to vote about the same time that prohibition was established in the Constitution. The conditions had become favorable. President Wilson was personally opposed to the crusade for women's right to vote, but eventually he gave in to the pressures.

With the United States at war and with a great increase in the number of women engaged in business and industry, it became clear in 1918 that the state of public morale dictated the wisdom of a constitutional amendment. Wilson therefore went before Congress in September 1918 and asked for passage of a suffrage amendment. Congress passed the amendment on June 4, 1919. It was ratified and went into effect on August 26, 1920.

The foregoing data reveals that the struggle for the right of women to vote was a long torturous affair. This most elementary democratic demand did not come as "manna from heaven," from the ruling class, but from the people in general and women in particular.

To get the word male in effect out of the Constitution cost the women of the country fifty-two years of pauseless campaign thereafter. During that time they were forced to conduct fifty-six campaigns of referenda to male voters; 480 campaigns to get legislators to submit suffrage amendments to voters; 47 campaigns to get state constitutional conventions to write woman suffrage into state constitutions; 277 campaigns to get state party conventions to include woman suffrage planks; 30 campaigns to get presidential party conventions to adopt woman suffrage planks in party platforms, and 19 campaigns with 19 successive Congresses. Millions of dollars were raised mainly in small sums, and expended with economic care. Hundreds of women gave the accumulated possibilities of an entire lifetime, thousands gave years of their lives, hundreds of thousands gave constant interest and such aid as they could. It was a continuous, seemingly endless chain of activity.[22]

Yet after all these years of tremendous efforts, women in the political arena still have little or no power, not to speak of economic power.

12 • WOMEN AND THE LABOR MOVEMENT

WOMEN MADE notable contributions in the advancement of the cause of labor in this country. Perhaps this is one of the best examples of the untold story of the women's movement. The militant struggles and achievements of working women are almost unknown.

The ideology of male supremacy, like racism and all exploitative theories, falls flat on the face of things when a survey is made of what transpired during the growth and development of the nation industrially. The theory has been long held that nature had made women the weaker sex. Therefore she had to be restricted from participation in the economic, political and social processes. Her duties were confined to labor around the household, raising children and chores which were backbreaking, nonetheless considered not requiring the strength of body and mind as that of the male. In the early stages of the struggle, this ideology had to be conquered as the main aspect of the struggle. It came up every time women stepped out of their so-called special role "nature had consigned them."

At one time, the right of women to offer a petition containing grievances was contested. A debate took place in Congress and John Quincy Adams, the son of Abigail and John Adams came to the defense of women. In a series of speeches in Congress, among other things he stated:

Why does it follow that women are fitted for nothing but the cares of domestic life, for bearing children and cooking the food of a family, devoting all their time to the domestic circle . . . to promoting the immediate personal comfort of their husbands, brothers and sons? The mere departure of women from the duties of the domestic circle, far from being a reproach to her, is a virtue of the highest order, when it is done from purity of motive, by appropriate means and the purpose good.[1]

160

Throughout the nineteenth century women were increasingly drawn into the work force and labored in the shops and factories, often under conditions worse than men. When they joined the labor force their oppression became twofold, as females and as workers. In addition to long hours of inhuman toil, the average working woman still had to carry on household burdens.

What are the factors which accelerated this trend? The "purity of motive, by appropriate means and the purpose good," which young Adams spoke of was in evidence nowhere in U.S. history.

The changes took place on the basis of struggle, but were mainly due to the needs of the evolving capitalist system and its central aim—profit making. It is true that the advancement of technology in certain industries facilitated the usage of women but that is not the whole story. This limited viewpoint was expressed by a Senate commission which was set up to investigate the conditions of women in industry. The commission reported: "Machinery, combined with division of labor and the substitution of water, steam and electric power for human muscles has certainly made it possible to employ the unskilled labor of women in occupations formerly carried on wholly by men."[2]

But the need of capitalism to draw women into the labor market was also facilitated by labor shortages from time to time, especially in wartime, by the desire and ability to get cheaper labor, by the creation of a reserve labor force for strikebreaking, as well as for depressing the wages of all workers.

FROM the very beginning the situation was viewed as a source of extra profits. The *Boston Courier* as early as 1829 wrote:

Custom and long habit have closed the doors of very many employments against the industry and perseverance of women. She has been taught to deem so many occupations masculine and made for men only that, excluded by a mistaken deference to the world's opinion from innumerable labors most happily adapted to her physical constitution, the competition for the few places left open to her has occasioned a reduction in the estimated value of her labor, until it has fallen below the minimum and is no longer adequate to present comfortable subsistence, much less to the necessary provision against age and infirmity, or the every day contingencies of mortality.[3]

Another newspaper estimated in 1833 that women earned only one-fourth of men's wages, while still another asserted that three-fourths of Philadelphia's working women "did not receive as much wages for an entire week's work of 13 to 14 hours per day as journeymen receive in the same branches for a single day of ten hours."[4] This situation of unequal pay for equal work for women has doggedly been maintained by the business interest from the very first day women began to enter the work force.

Grace Hutchins, using the 1950 census reports and figures from the Securities and Exchange Commission, calculates:

... that in 1950 manufacturing companies realized profits of $5.4 billion by paying women less per year than the wages paid to men for similar work. The extra profits . . . formed 23 percent of all company profits that year. The Wage and Hours Division of the Department of Labor has found that in April 1970, over 17 million dollars in underpayments were made to over 50,000 employees most of whom were women.[5]

The feminist movement makes it attack on men in general for the plight of women in general. And while the majority of men share some responsibility for the continuation of women's oppression, it is also necessary to understand the source from which the problem arises and who profits from it. When the economic nature of the problem is understood, then the source comes into closer view. Mrs. Amumdsen in her book *The Silent Majority* correctly observed this fact when she wrote:

But the common man does not of course have much to do with decisions to hire or fire, to raise wages, and to create benefits for workers, whether male or female. Sex prejudice is pervasive, yes, but that does not mean that every one is equally responsible for the sexist differentiations on the labor market. It is to those enpowered to make decisions we must look when we want change . . . and when we want to find out why it hasn't taken place.[6]

Hence, a different set of priorities and ideology developed among working women, based on a class base and class outlook.

A woman working a ten or twelve hour day whose earnings were almost half those of men, whose lines were often branded by the sweatshop and whose relation to their employer lacked any safeguards to personal dignity or job tenure, 'equal rights' was a question of more than education or getting the vote. For them equality also meant better pay for their labor, security from fire and machine hazards or the unwanted attentions of a foreman and a chance to get home to their domestic tasks before complete exhaustion had overtaken them. Until more of them could work for these goals through a trade union other issues were remote.[7]

No doubt this class approach which began to focus on the heart of the problem is one of the reasons why so little is known about working women in their struggles in contrast to what has been written about the women's suffrage movement.

FROM the earliest times, working women have built organizations and unions to protect their welfare. And in so doing they made contributions to the growth and development of the entire labor movement. But women who work have encountered male supremacy within the unions and found it necessary to struggle against efforts to exclude their full participation, just as the women's movement had to resist and fight male supremacy in the Abolitionist movement.

In the 1840s women in milltowns began to organize and strike. They founded an organization called the Female Labor Reform Association, and after a period of six years they secured the ten-hour work laws in New Jersey, New Hampshire, and Pennsylvania. The first known strike of women factory workers occurred at Pawtucket, Rhode Island in 1824. In the textile mills of Lowell, Massachusetts, women workers built up a stable organization called the Lowell Female Labor Reform Association. It was led by Sarah Bagley, perhaps the first woman trade unionist of note in the country. The Lowell Female Labor Reform Association became an auxiliary of the New England Working Men's Association. Because it became increasingly clear that women alone could not successfully confront the bosses and win, like all other oppressed forces, they, too, needed and sought allies. Even though some unions excluded women, such as the printers and cigar makers, (a situation that didn't change until after the Civil War), women made vigorous efforts to join the mainstream of labor. And so with the development of the Knights of Labor, the I.W.W., the American Federation of Labor, independent unions and the C.I.O., working women helped to write glorious chapters in labor history.

Labor history is full of heroines who distinguished themselves second to no force in U.S. history in general, and the labor movement in particular. Although women are supposed to be "softer than men," they, in addition to doing all the laborious detail work of organizing, added a new dimension of militancy to the whole movement. There are a whole number of situations and women leaders who emerged that verify this fact. For the purposes of this summarized version a few incidents and personalities are cited.

First of all, the class backgrounds of the women who composed the women's suffrage movement and the labor movement are of importance. The struggle for the suffrage movement and allied struggles were led primarily by women of middle-class backgrounds. The working-class struggles were led primarily by working women of immigrant backgrounds. They brought from Europe much of the experience of the European working class, which had come upon the stage of history earlier than the American working class. It was the Irish, the Jewish and later the Italians and Black women who played outstanding roles, adding much fire and vigor to the house of labor.

Take the case of Mother Mary Jones who was called by Clarence Darrow "the Wendell Phillips of the labor movement." She came from Ireland and worked as a teacher and dressmaker. Her husband and four children all died in an epidemic. Later she became an organizer for the Knights of Labor and for fifty years she was in the thick of many struggles of miners. Sinclair says: "She was shot at, mobbed, beaten, and jailed, an old woman, armed only with a hair pin. When Deputies with rifles beat back striking men she led forward armies of women, brandishing mops and brooms against the bayonets. With them she chased away scabs and strike breakers, and organized the miners."[8] Her effectiveness and influence among working class women was great. Once when she was arrested, she organized, from jail, her women supporters to bring their babies into the courtoom where for five days they sang patriotic songs while the babies howled until she and others were released.

One of the most powerful factors in developing militancy and the organization of labor in general has been the role played by women in the garment industry. Composed mainly of Jewish immigrant workers, they were the main driving force behind the development of the International Ladies Garment Workers Union and the Fur and Leather Workers (which is now merged with the Amalgamated Meat Cutters and Butcherworkers of America). Both of these unions have played a significant role in the development of the labor movement as a whole.

In the textile industry, the base of the garment industry, most of the workers were women. Throughout the history of this industry, they waged long hard strikes to introduce some of the most elementary rights. A great, outstanding strike of enormous significance was waged in the textile mills in Lawrence, Massachusetts in 1912. One of the most effective leaders in the strike was Elizabeth Gurley Flynn, who at that time was only twenty-one years old. She later joined the Communist Party and became its national chairperson. Boyer and Morais in *Labor's Untold Story* tell of that strike. "If there was any trickery or any violence or any fraud that was not used by the employers to smash the Lawrence strike it has never been discovered in all the lexicon of reaction."[9]

The strike broke out in response to speedup in the mills and a cut in pay. "It was a new kind of strike. There had never been any mass picketing in any New England town."[10] The power of ten thousand people on the picket lines each day evoked the fear and wrath of the power structure. Twenty-two companies of militia were sent out to crush the strike. The employers also brought in over fifty thugs who assaulted people on the streets, planted dynamite near the strike headquarters, and shot at women strikers. In the face of such violence it was like a miracle for the workers to keep their hopes alive. But this is where Elizabeth Gurley Flynn came in. It was she who inspired the workers to keep on struggling. Mary Heaton Vorse describes the effect she had on them:

When Elizabeth Gurley Flynn spoke, the excitement of the strikers became a visible thing. She stood up there, young, with her Irish blue eyes, her face magnolia white, and her cloud of black hair, the very picture of a youthful revolutionary girl leader. . . . It was as though a spurt of flame had gone through the audience, something stirring and powerful, a feeling which has made the liberation of people possible.[11]

Throughout the pre-New-Deal period, where labor reforms took a leap upward, women through militant struggles such as Lawrence, wrested many concessions from the industrial overlords. However, most of the concessions were won on the state level, although a breakthrough was also made at the federal level. The Supreme Court throughout the latter part of the nineteenth century had been the bulwark protecting the interest of big business. The pressures of the times, and not the least the women themselves, in 1908 forced the court to reverse a lower court decision on the ten-hour day for women. This was the case of *Mueler* v *Oregon*. By 1917 thirty-nine states passed laws regulating women's work hours. Equal pay laws were won for women in a few western states and by the turn of the century roughly half of the states had factory inspection laws.[12] The victories won on these fronts facilitated better conditions for all workers.

BLACK women also made outstanding contributions to the cause of labor. But it must be borne in mind that Black women did not come into the factory system in significant numbers until World War I, and even more so during World War II. Even today, of two million Black women in the work force, over a million still do domestic work. But notwithstanding these facts, with the coming of the C.I.O., in a number of situations Black women led the way. Especially was this true in the South in the tobacco industry.

On May 6, 1937, 400 Black women, stemmers employed in the I.U. Vaughen Company of Richmond, Virginia, walked out in protest against wages amounting to three dollars a week and terrible working conditions. This was the first strike in the city of Richmond in thirty years. However when the workers sought aid from the A.F. of L. they were turned down on the grounds that Black tobacco workers were unorganized. The women turned to the Southern Negro Youth Congress to help in organizing an independent union. Christopher Austin and James Jackson (presently National Education Director of the Communist Party) went to their assistance. After a year and a half of struggle the workers were organized, and contracts negotiated with about $500,000 in wage increases. Later these independent locals joined the C.I.O. Philip Foner documents the significance of this struggle in his book *Organized Labor and the Black Worker* and describes how: "The successes of the tobacco unions . . . stirred other ranks in Richmond."[13]

Another pioneering effort by Black women took place at R. J. Reynolds Tobacco Company in Winston Salem, North Carolina. On June 17, 1943, a Black worker died after dizzy spells. A foreman had refused to let him see a doctor and the workers went out on strike. This strike occurred during the war years when great pressures were being exerted for workers not to strike. There were threats of government intervention, but it did not take place and the Reynolds management caved in and gave the union recognition. A payment of $1,250,000 for retroactive pay was one of the concessions made, and wages began to go up. Foner says that Louis Burnham, a leader of the Southern Negro Youth Congress characterized Winston Salem as "legendary." Among the outstanding leaders of the union was

Miranda Smith. Like Elizabeth Gurley Flynn, in an earlier period, she became a legend in her time. Thus, it can be said that Black women, who provided many of the sparks, had a profound effect on organizing many workers in the South.

WOMEN have had a powerful effect on American democracy. Yet to this day they play an insignificant role in the power bases of the nation. Their continued oppressed status, notwithstanding some significant victories, is another case in point that democracy in a capitalist system is inherently limited. The women's suffrage fighters waged a long and determined struggle for the right to vote. But they did so with illusions about what would be obtainable by the vote alone. No one understood the limitations better than Mother Ella Bloor, a famous socialist and later Communist leader. Sinclair defined her position:

Ella Bloor's priority was better working conditions, while that of the suffragists was the vote. They did not understand each other's point of view. In one strike Ella Bloor had seen seventy-three children suffocated to death in a crush probably caused by deputies or scabs. She could not forget such episodes, and she could not explain them to the suffragists. "For many of the secure middle class ladies, the suffrage movement was a fad, was a mere feminist fad. I tried to make them see the really vital importance of suffrage for the working women, as a weapon against economic inequality. And I tried to make them see that the vote alone was not important."[14]

Subsequent events have proven Mother Bloor correct. Women got the vote, but the female sex still remains at the rock bottom of the society.

Today Black and white women in industry are becoming organized into movements to pressure the house of labor to combat the overlords of industry and government to deal with the special problems of women workers; problems of equal pay for equal work, the right to work in all industries, ending racism, and the need for child care facilities are of major importance. No doubt, the women's movement for equality will in our time play as significant a role in meeting the problems of today as it did in the ending of slavery, in winning the right to vote, and in the victories achieved by the labor movement in the past.

PART IV

THE LABOR MOVEMENT

13 • LABOR BEFORE THE NEW DEAL

THE ROLE played by the American working class has been pivotal in U.S. history. Labor has been one of the most decisive forces generating social progress for all the American people. The contributions of the work force to the technological advancement of agriculture and industry are also an untold story.

But more importantly, what labor has done to establish better living conditions, and advancements toward popular democracy is least understood in our country. Indeed, the American working class is the most misunderstood and underestimated class in the international working class. Its political status in reference to the working class in the major capitalist countries has always been on a lower level. At a time when American workers were powerless in almost every respect, European workers had forced their way into the machinery of government. They not only had built powerful trade unions, but also powerful political parties. In the late 1920s William Z. Foster pointed this out when in reference to Europe he wrote: "There organized labor is a great political power, and one which must be reckoned with on all vital issues. In Germany the workers parties control 42 percent of the members of the Reichstag, in

Austria 38 percent, Czechoslovakia 36 percent, Belgium 35 percent, Denmark 34 percent, Italy and Bulgaria, Norway, Holland and Switzerland 22 percent."[1]

William Gompers, at one time head of the American Federation of Labor, visited Europe and had this to say: "We in the United States are two decades behind many European countries in the protection of life, health and limb of the workers . . . We are behind England ten years, we are behind Germany 20 years."[2]

Since those observations were made, under the leadership of the working class in the Soviet Union and other countries, one third of the world passed out of the orbit of capitalism. The socialist societies have become a major factor in destroying the stranglehold of world imperialism in Asia, Africa and Latin America. When U.S. workers are viewed from this contrast, then conclusions can be and are drawn that our working class is still one of the most backward forces in today's world. On the surface of things this would appear to be a true assessment of the situation. But when this problem is viewed from an internal historical perspective, then an entirely different conclusion can be drawn.

The American working class has had to wage its struggles under a set of conditions different from that of any other working class. In the first place capitalism, due to a combination of historical reasons, reached its highest form of development in the United States. Unfettered by feudal restraints and fixed class relations, it was possible for some people to rise out of the lower classes and become extremely rich. While this was not true for the class as a whole, there were enough exceptions to create illusions about the system as being the best possible of worlds.

It was in this context that most immigrants came to the United States. Therefore it was much easier here than in Europe to foster illusions in capitalism. Capitalism in the name of "rugged individualism" instills the deepest selfishness in people. The morals of the society are based upon "Do unto others before they get a chance to do unto you." In this framework it was easier to divide the ranks of the workers in many respects. Throughout U.S. labor history the ruling class has endeavored, with some degree of success, to divide the ranks of the workers. Foreign-born workers were pitted against the native born, white against Black and peoples of color, and creed against creed. As already pointed out, here in the United States chauvinism and racism reached its highest and most destructive form of development. Thus, the working class has had to struggle in circumstances of ideological problems that have been major obstacles in forging unity of the class and class consciousness.

In addition to these obstacles, the workers have had to struggle against the most greedy and ruthless class of capitalists the world has ever known, a class without any morals or scruples whatsoever. It is a class that makes no concessions until forced by struggle and/or circumstances to do so. Of all the capitalist classes in the world, it is the most die-hard. Throughout capital and labor history in this country, the monied classes have used the most terroristic methods to prevent the mildest forms of reforms within the system. Violence has been the name of the game, against the indentured servants, Native Americans, the small farmers, Blacks, Mexicans and Asians, women and finally against the men and women in the working class. Many are the struggles waged by the workers for a few more pennies an hour, for a shorter work day, against unsafe and hazardous working conditions only to be met with the "iron heel" of U.S. capital. Even after the Declaration of Independence, the adoption of the Constitution, and all the proclamations of democracy (the hidden forms of class dictatorship within government), the shops, factories, mills, mines and workshops represented the more open forms of class rule. Within them, the workers were almost like chattel slaves. They were completely at the mercy of the employer. They "had no rights" that a boss "was bound to respect." They not only had no legal rights, but whenever they went into struggle to achieve them, in many cases the entire apparatus of government, including the military on a state and federal level, were used against them.

These have been some of the main causes for a lower level of class consciousness in the United States in contrast to most European workers. Yet in the face of such difficulties, the American workers have waged some of the most militant struggles in world labor history. By such struggles, a new dimension has been added to American democracy. The labor movement in its history, taken in its entirety, has stood in the forefront of the extension of democracy. Especially has this been true since the Reconstruction period. But even of the gains made, some of which relate to previous periods, and are far reaching, they nevertheless provide additional evidence that reforms within the system are of a limited character and cannot ameliorate the situation or make fundamental changes to provide for a real people's democracy.

EARLY in the century, around the 1830s, struggles for reforms began to develop. This was the period of the birth and growth of the movements to end slavery. Slave rebellions began to surface and the Abolitionist movement was born. It was also a period when labor began to flex its muscles. Although it had not yet become an organized force along trade union lines, the workers through various forms of organization entered the arena of struggle.

At the beginning of the nineteenth century, factory workers had to go to work at 4 A.M. and work until dark. Fourteen hours a day were not uncommon. Wages were miserably low. A first class mechanic often received 50¢ per day, while women workers were forced to toil in textile mills from dawn to dusk for $1.50 a week.

It was against these intolerable working conditions that the workers began to struggle. The main issue around which struggles began to focus was a change from a fourteen-hour day to a ten-hour day. This struggle began about 1825 and went on for many years. Gustavus Myers says:

The politicians denounced the movement; the cultured classes frowned upon it: the newspapers alternately ridiculed and abused it; the officials prepared to take summary action to put it down. As for the capitalists—the shipping merchants, the boot and shoe manufacturers, the iron masters and others— they not only denied the right of the workers to organize, while insisting that they themselves were entitled to combine, but they inveighed against the ten-hour demand as "unreasonable conditions which the folly and caprice of a few journeymen mechanics may dictate."[3]

By 1840 the workers became so powerful in some crafts that some employers were forced to concede to the demand for a ten-hour day on the grounds that this might contribute to the efficiency of the workers and provide greater profits within the shorter work period.

The movement had the effect of forcing President Van Buren to introduce the ten-hour day in all government work. The struggles during this early period had a profound effect on many aspects of social life as they related to all lower-class strata. The workers carried on their banners a whole number of issues and problems that the people in general confronted. Simons, in his book, *Social Forces in American History,* produces resolutions and platforms of labor parties which he declared were new declarations of independence.

Perhaps the most outstanding contribution that labor made in this period was the establishment of free public education. At a later period during Reconstruction, in the South, the ex-slaves were the major force to bring about free public education. This combination of labor and the ex-slaves was the major force behind the winning of education for children of the poor. Until the Soviet Union came into existence, the achievement of this goal went farther in the United States than in any other country.

The labor movement was able to achieve this because, according to Simons: "The one dominant feature of every section of this labor movement was the almost fanatical insistence upon the paramount importance of education. In political platforms, in resolutions of public meetings, and in the labor press the statement is repeated over and over, that the fundamental demand of Labor is for an adequate system of education."[4]

The battle for democratic reforms has come in waves throughout U.S. history and the people's movements have had their ups and downs. The upsurge in 1830 and 1840 receded before the Civil War. It was revitalized during the Civil War and Reconstruction periods, but after the Reconstruction period there was a lull in struggle. As the nation came toward the end of the nineteenth century and the beginning of the twentieth, a democratic upsurge took place that embraced almost all sectors of the American people. The period was characterized especially by greater struggles of an offensive nature by farmers, the working class, and disillusioned intellectuals. The first phase of the struggle has been labeled the Populist period, the latter, the "Progressive Era."

Both followed one of the most disgraceful periods in the nation's history, a period that Mark Twain called "The Gilded Age." This was the time that followed the Civil War, a time when the Northern capitalist class brought into its hands industry, commerce, state power, press, schools—every institution of society.

Lippincott says:

The decade following the close of the Civil War marks the beginning of one of the greatest industrial eras of all times. Even the most enthusiastic word painters of former times failed to foresee the magnitude of coming economic achievements. With their limited vision it was not possible to forecast the rapid growth of population, the opening of many raw resources, the appearance of hundreds of new industries, the unusual development of business enterprise, and the great increase of wealth. Nor was it possible to appreciate the significance of the powerful economic forces . . . beneath these changes.[5]

In a period when all opposition had been defeated, a period when the possibility of achieving wealth was perhaps greater than any other time in history, the robber barons, later the corporate giants, became insane from greed and power. They needed all the money they could get to build their vast financial empires. While the government was one of their major supports to take over the nation's resources and to subsidize their expansion, the surplus value from low wages and poor working conditions became their main source of capital. This called for an intensification of exploitation of every conceivable source of labor, including women and children.

Thus in this period, more than ever, the open face of class dictatorship had to be shown and enforced. While in most cases the government was securely in the hands of the industrialists and bankers, the U.S. Supreme Court was the power standing behind the throne of big business, exercising its dictatorial power to keep the labor movement in line.

Acheson states that: "It was the courts which retarded the growth of the labor organizations more than anything else. This they did by issuing injunctions to prevent strikes and by interpreting the Fourteenth Amendment and the Sherman Anti-Trust Act to mean that labor had no right to strike and that states could not pass laws regulating hours or wages."[6]

The combination of court-issued injunctions plus the usage of military forces were the main weapons used to thwart workers' strikes and their efforts to organize. In this connection, a whole number of advances made by labor in the lower levels of government were struck down when they reached the Supreme Court.

ONE OF the clearest cases of how the court was used to defend the property of the rich, uphold injunctions and prevent strikes was in the case against Eugene V. Debs, an outstanding socialist labor leader. It came in connection with a strike in 1893. Eugene V. Debs had organized about 150,000 workers into the American Railway Union, affecting 23 railways lines within 27 states. Violent fighting broke out and President Grover Cleveland claimed that the mails had been intercepted and he sent in federal troops. He also got an injunction from a Federal Circuit Court. Debs was arrested and charged with violating the injunction. The Supreme Court sustained the arrest. Debs was also arrested on the charge that he had violated the Sherman Anti-trust Act, that he had conspired to restrain trade.

The high Court rendered numerous decisions of this nature to aid and facilitate the robber barons and the corporate thugs to paralyze every effort of labor to break through fortresses of American capitalism. Decisions were handed down by the Court affecting all kinds of problems confronting the American working class. For example: *Lockner* v. *New York* in 1905 was a case where a law had been passed in New York which limited the bakers to a ten-hour day. The Supreme Court threw it out. In the case of *Adkins* v. *Children's Hospital,* 1923, the Court threw out a law which set up minimum wages for women. The Court in the case of *Hammer* v. *Dagenhart,* threw out a federal act in 1918 which was passed to curtail the exploitation of child labor.

These cases are but a few that were used to enforce class dictatorship in the factories and workshops.

In addition to the courts, the employers used many illegal tactics to keep the workers under control in order to extract greater profits from the industries. Among these were spies sent in to labor organizations, provocateurs whose job was to provoke violence and then blame it on the workers, and private detective agencies such as the Pinkertons. This whole period to the beginning of this century stank from such filthy methods. A whole number of cases could be catalogued to back up these assertions. But there are a few examples in labor history that stand out and are of historic significance.

Among these were the struggles waged by the working class in this period for the eight-hour day. During the period of 1886–1900 this struggle occupied the center of all strike struggles. It was after the militant struggles and the frame-ups during the Haymarket struggles at the International Harvester plants in Chicago in 1886, that the employers through their control of the courts began to use the injunction. (The first such case of an injunction that was issued was in 1888 in Massachusetts against a spinning company.) After 1886, when the leaders of the Haymarket strike were framed-up and hanged, the movement for the eight-hour day took on a new impetus and became worldwide. May 1 became a symbol—a working-class holiday dedicated to struggle which is today observed worldwide.

In 1888 the combined forces and influences of the employing and speculative classes had effectively swayed the unorganized working people into submission. Obnoxious rules were forced on the workers and they were compelled to sign ironclad contracts giving up their right to organize for self-protection. Labor was humiliated, browbeaten, and scourged. But the spirit was not broken.

It was in these dark days that the proclamation was sent over the world that the eight-hour day would be enforced May 1, 1890. From that moment a change took place. Hope was instilled into the minds and hearts of the workers to supplant despair. To the rallying cry of eight hours the working people again stood erect and staunch in their manhood. The tide had changed. This appeal was answered with enthusiasm.[7]

The American Federation of Labor, at its convention in 1888, laid plans to make May 1, 1890 the day for a general strike to achieve the eight-hour day. This decision was met by a widespread response all over the country and in foreign lands. In this regard, the American working class gave leadership to the working class of the world.

However, the general strike did not take place. Strike actions were limited by labor leaders, who began to fear the militancy of the workers. This was especially true of Samuel Gompers and other leaders who were oriented mainly to a policy of conciliation with big business. However, during the entire period, strikes took place increasingly.

It has been estimated that between 1881 and 1905 more than 35,000 strikes took place. There were mass walkouts in the railroad industry from coast to coast. The strikes in the railroad industry, together with a strike in the steel industry, the Homestead strike on the outskirts of Pittsburgh, were among the bitterest fought battles between capital and labor. In the Homestead strike, the Governor sent the militia in and broke the strike. Clark Spence points out that:

Of the more than 35,000 strikes between 1881 and 1905, a few stand out as being particularly significant. Especially bitter were the mass walkouts on numerous railroads throughout the country in 1877, with rioting in Chicago, St. Paul, Omaha, and San Francisco, and in Pittsburgh, where troops clashed with the strikers and a mob fired the roundhouse and burned 104 locomotives and more than 500 coaches and box cars. Another particularly bitter strike came in the summer of 1882 on the New York Central System, where freight handlers demanded an increase in pay from seventeen to twenty cents an hour, only to be defeated by strikebreakers brought in by the railroad[8]

Despite the betrayals of labor leaders and the intensification of terroristic methods, the workers broke through in many areas and laid the basis for some major reforms which began early in the twentieth century. This process began in what is called the "Progressive Era," the period between 1901 and 1917, during the administrations of President Theodore Roosevelt and after him, Presidents Taft and Wilson.

The refusal of workers to accept intolerable work conditions, the high cost of strikes, and the moral atmosphere created by the corporate giants' vicious attacks on labor which began to undermind confidence in the system, laid the basis for some ruling class forces to think in terms of concessions to the working class.

The new situation was portrayed by Elihu Root in his presidential address before the New York Bar Association in 1912. He stated:

The relations between the employer and the employed, between the owners of aggregated capital and the units of organized labor, between the small producer, the small trader, the consumer, and the great transporting and manufacturing and distributing agencies, all present new questions for the solution of which the old reliance upon the free action of individual wills appears quite inadequate. And in many directions the intervention of that organized control which we call government seems necessary to produce the same result of justice and right conduct which obtained through the attrition of individuals before the new condition arose.[9]

What Root was calling for was an end to the period of laissez-faire capitalism and for a controlled capitalism. It was a call for the regulation of commerce, transportation and finance.

But there were many capitalist forces who continued to argue and fight for the laissez-faire creed. It was likened to a tree which should be allowed to grow as high as it can, even if the tree overshadowed and sucked the life out of all bushes and plants in its radius.

However, despite the vicious opposition of forces who expressed this creed, a process of change began during the period of the so-called Progressive Era.

Some progress was made during the "Progressive Era," mainly on the legislative front. In 1916 Congress enacted a law which made the eight-hour day standard for all interstate railroad workers. A department of labor was set up on a separate basis in 1913. On two occasions Congress attempted to prohibit child labor. It tried to do so in 1916 under a law to regulate commerce and in 1919 under a law dealing with taxation. In both instances the Supreme Court declared them unconstitutional.

Clark C. Spence in *The Sinews of American Capitalism* shows some of the achievements as well as limitations in that period:

In general, prior to World War I social legislation affecting labor came through state action rather than federal, and was based on the police powers of the Constitution giving the right to protect the morals, health, safety, and welfare of the people. Still, conservative courts often nullified such legislation as violating the due process clause of the Fourteenth Amendment, although in time the courts would assume a more liberal position. . . . In some areas considerable success was achieved; in others very little. State laws setting minimum age limits for workers were enacted by every state except one by 1914, but many were wholly ineffective. A few states prior to 1900 had limited the hours women might work to sixty per week, and the movement spread rapidly in the next few years.[10]

The fact that the New Deal had to be enacted in the middle of the 1930s is in itself evidence that much of the reform sentiment, as far as conditions for the working class was concerned, turned out to be rhetoric. All through this period, the employers met the efforts of labor to organize with the most repressive methods.

ONE OF the most scandalous developments was what happened when the Industrial Workers of the World, (I.W.W.), attempted to organize workers on an industrial union basis. Up to that point in labor history, the labor movement consisted mainly of skilled workers organized along craft lines. The craft unions were organized amidst a reign of terror. But what happened in this connection, was mild compared to what happened when the workers in the mass production industries attempted to organize into industrial unions. There were many reasons for the difference but the central one was that if the workers were organized along industrial lines, their capacity to paralyze the whole economy would be enhanced. Such organization would place labor in a position to compete with the corporations in the entire power structure of the country.

Another factor of importance was the sanctioning of concessions to a small strata of workers in the craft unions; thus, dividing the skilled workers from the unskilled. And since the unskilled labor force was composed in large part of immigrant workers from Eastern Europe, as well as Asians, Mexicans and Blacks, the ability of the ruling class to use chauvinism and racism was made easier.

During the "Progressive Era," the I.W.W. organization began to emerge as a potent labor force. Its chief concern was to organize the working class along industrial lines. It was also the most militant force in the labor movement at that time. It was led by uncompromising dedicated labor leaders who opposed the class collaborationist policies expressed by the officialdom of the A.F. of L. which was organized almost exclusively along craft lines. As the I.W.W. proceeded to organize, a new dimension was added to the measures to suppress labor.

Between 1912 and 1914 a whole series of free speech struggles erupted. They took place from coast to coast, but they began on the West Coast around the lumber industry. In a number of instances the I.W.W. was banned from the usage of the streets to speak to workers. But the workers mobilized their forces and compelled the authorities to remove their bans against free speech.

These I.W.W. successes so frightened the employers that they decided that new tactics were needed to prevent the Wobblies (I.W.W. members) from moving on from victory to victory. The M.& M. (Merchants' and Manufacturers' Association) in various West Coast cities and towns organized a counter free-speech movement to smash the I.W.W.'s right to free speech as the first step in their determined drive to destroy the I.W.W. itself. The M. & M. strategy was to organize small armies of vigilantes or deputies to invade the jails, drive the Wobblies out of town, and, by the most brutal terror, keep them out. "Harrison Gray Otis, whose *Los Angeles Times* was an official spokesman for the M. & M., summed up this savage strategy: 'During the visit of the Industrial Workers of the World they will be accorded a night and day guard of honor, composed of citizens armed with rifles. The Coroner will be in attendance of his office every day' "[11]

In spite of "armed terror," the Wobblies persisted in speaking on the streets. They were arrested and turned over to the citizen police to escort them to jail. . . . The *Industrial Worker* condemned the conspiracy of "the gang of sluggers in Aberdeen to club our members to death." But it advised against meeting terror with terror: "We must be prepared to meet these new tactics and we must not meet them with axe handles because we have the queer faculty of knowing that there is no such thing as *equality before the law*."[12]

It is reported that in one struggle about 1500 men were deputized in Portland to prevent the arrival of I.W.W. members into the town. But the Wobblies came on, about 250 left St. Louis and travelled all the way to the West Coast. They were met by the civilian police with unprecedented violence as they took the platform to speak.

Similar struggles had to be waged all over the country. In most cases the struggle was won. Those victories were of historic significance in maintaining and defending the First Amendment. The I.W.W., as was the case of the labor movement as a whole, and as has been the case of other victims of injustice—the slaves, women suffragettes, etc.—in the defense of their own specific problems, advanced the battle for democracy for all the American people.

Courtenay Lemon writing in *Pearson's Magazine* took note of this fact. He wrote:

Whether they agree or disagree with its methods and aims, all lovers of liberty everywhere owe a debt to this organization for its defense of free speech. Absolutely irreconcilable, absolutely fearless, and unsuppressibly persistent, it has kept alight the first of freedom, like some outcast vestal of human liberty. That the defense of traditional rights to which this government is supposed to be dedicated should devolve upon an organization so often denounced as "unpatriotic" and "un-American," is but the usual, the unfailing irony of history.[13]

The violence employed by the corporations against the workers between 1910 and 1915 became so sharp that the U.S. Commission on Industrial Relations was forced to make a study of the problem. The fact that such a commission and study came into existence was of some importance.

The commission was authorized by Congress and appointed by President Wilson. It examined several strike situations. Among them was the New York City Garment Workers strike, Paterson Silk strike, the Los Angeles bombing case, the Bethlehem Steel strike and the situation around the Ludlow Massacre in Colorado.

The findings of the commission represented a powerful anti-monopoly trend in the country; so powerful that even a congressional commission was compelled to verbalize the concrete status of things. In respect to the disparity between the rich and the poor it reported:

The ownership of wealth in the U.S. has become concentrated to a degree which is difficult to grasp. The "Rich," 2 per cent of the people, own 35 per cent of the wealth. The "Middle Class," 33 per cent of the people, own 35 per cent of the wealth. The "Poor," 65 per cent of the people, own 5 per cent of the wealth. The actual concentration, however, has been carried much further than these figures indicate. The largest private fortune in the U.S., estimated at one billion dollars, is equivalent to the aggregate wealth of 2,500,000 of those who are classed as "poor," who are shown . . . to own on the average about $400 each.[14]

Continuing the report on the concentration of wealth, the commission said:

Incapable of being spent in any legitimate manner, these fortunes are burdens, which can only be squandered, hoarded, put in so-called "benefactions" which for the most part constitute a menace to the State, or put back into the industrial machine to pile up ever-increasing mountains of gold. We have, according to income tax returns, forty-four families with an income of $1,000,000 annually or more, whose members perform little or no useful service, but whose aggregate incomes, totalling at the very least fifty million a year, are equivalent to the earnings of 100,000 wage earners at the average rate of $500.[15]

The commission's exposures were so clear that the whole world could see it. Thus, an added impetus was given to the reform movement, curbing some of the worst features of the open capitalist dictatorship in the factories and workshops. But the reforms of the "Progressive Era" were shortlived, labor still had tremendous ground to plow, not to speak of reaping a harvest.

AMERICA'S entrance into World War I unleased a new wave of labor suppression. As the war developed, a hysteria was created against many prominent labor leaders, like Eugene Victor Debs who opposed the war. The opposition to the war was branded as treasonable and some of the most terroristic actions were carried out against workers who stood for peace. In addition to terror, the workers were forced to forego many of the barest necessities during the war years. They were forced to do so while the nation's millionaires grew richer and richer. The war ended in 1918. In 1919 a wave of strike struggles swept the nation. Conditions by this time had deteriorated to such an extent that from 1914 to 1919 milk had jumped from nine to fifteen cents a quart, eggs from thirty-seven to sixty-two cents a dozen, butter from thirty-two to sixty-one cents a pound, and sirloin steak from twenty-seven to forty-two cents a pound. Those were the kinds of conditions that led to a strike wave in which over four million workers participated. The strike wave took place at a time when the whole world was seething and in turmoil.

It was a period of wars and revolutions. It was the period of the Great Russian Revolution which ushered in revolutionary upsurges all over the world. The full meaning and the impact of the Russian Revolution was not lost upon the Wall Street bankers and monopolies. They sensed the beginning of the end of their system and they went to work to defeat the strikes with everything within their power. Their main strategy on the propaganda front was to separate the middle class from the working class by appeals to their sense of patriotism and the alleged despotism of Bolshevism. Every strike struggle was given this twist.

Frederick Lewis Allen points out how these methods were employed:

Innumerable... gentlemen now discovered they could defeat whatever they wanted to defeat by tarring it conspicuously with the Bolshevist brush. Big-navy men, believers in compulsory military service, drys, anti-cigarette campaigners, anti-evolution Fundamentalists, defenders of the moral order, book censors, Jew-haters, Negro-haters, landlords, manufacturers, utility executives, upholders of every sort of cause, good, bad and indifferent, all wrapped themselves in Old Glory and the mantle of the Founding Fathers, and allied their opponents with Lenin. The open shop, for example, became the "American plan." . . . A cloud of suspicion hung in the air, and intolerance became an American virtue.[16]

Racial divisions were also used to divide the workers. During the war years, manpower shortages in the industries led to a massive migration of Blacks from the plantations of the South to the North. These workers who had no previous background in labor organizations were taken advantage of by the employers. Racial frictions were deliberately fostered which eventually led to race riots in several cities in the country.

This was especially true in the meat packing industry in Chicago. At that time, the Chicago labor movement possessed one of the most advanced and progressive labor leaderships in the country. William Z. Foster, together with several other progressives, entered the Chicago labor movement and helped to transform it into a viable labor force.

Two major organizational drives started from their initiatives. A drive was launched to organize the steel industry. This campaign led to the great steel strike in 1919 of over three hundred thousand workers. It was the most massive strike in a major industry of that time. The campaign was conducted under the aegis of the A.F. of L.

But the A.F. of L. leadership threw all kinds of obstacles into Foster's way as he attempted to organize one of the main arteries of the economy. Under these conditions the steel strike was defeated. Nonetheless, the strike was a harbinger of things to come.

On July 25, 1917, William Z. Foster, Jack Johnstone and John Fitzpatrick launched a campaign to organize the meat-packing industry in Chicago. The campaign was quite successful. In several months 35,000 to 40,000 workers were organized, about 20,000 were Black workers. But it wasn't long before the council lost much of its effectiveness. In 1919 a race riot was stirred up by the packers which had a devastating effect on Black - white unity.

This factor coupled with the craft mentality and class collaboration outlook of some of the forces in the leadership brought about the demise of the union. Thus, both the initiatives in steel and the meat-packing industries failed to achieve their objectives. But there can be no doubt that this background contributed to the successful drives by the C.I.O. at a later date.

AFTER the great upsurge in strikes in 1919, most of which were defeated, the trade union movement suffered a sharp decline. Red-baiting was a major factor. The A.F. of L. declined in membership from 4,000,000 in 1920 to under 3,000,000 a few years later.

The early post-World War I years were also characterized by a depression and inflation. This situation also made it more difficult for labor to take the offensive. But the main problem from 1921 to the outbreak of the crisis of 1929 was ideological. The United States, during this period, enjoyed a high degree of prosperity. Although relatively, the workers received little more than previously, illusions were created and a tremendous propaganda campaign was conducted on how every American worker was going to become a capitalist. In Europe the capitalist class rode out of the postwar storms by making concessions to the working class in the form of unemployment insurance, social security, certain health measures, etc. These reforms were made in order to take the sparks out of working-class militancy and disillusionment in capitalism. To some extent they succeeded in Europe. However, in the United States a different path was chosen. Here the workers were advised to buy stocks in the corporations. Every American worker was to become a capitalist.

Most of the leaders of the American Federation of Labor bought this bill of goods. Typical of the mentality of such leaders is contained in a speech by H. V. Boswell, president of the Brotherhood of Locomotive Engineers, to the Bank of New York. He exclaimed:

Who wants to be a bolshevik when he can be a capitalist instead? We have shown how to mix oil and water; how to reconcile capital and labor. Instead of standing on a corner soapbox, screaming with rage because the capitalists own real estate, bank accounts, and automobiles, the engineer has tuned in and become a capitalist himself. Now it stands to reason, doesn't it, that such men won't start any movement to destroy property or ruin big business? Why, only last spring we bought a substantial interest in the Empire Trust Company of New York City. If you could have seen Schwab, Heckscher, and the locomotive engineers seated around the directors' table, you'd have recognized the whole scene as an entirely new turn in what used to be called the "fight" between capital and labor.[17]

During this period many A.F. of L. unions organized banks and tried to worm their way into the system. The *Daily Worker* of May 25, 1925, reports a meeting called to celebrate the second anniversary of the founding of a labor bank:

The gathering might have been a meeting of the manufacturers' or bankers' association, judging from those who took part in the celebration. The speakers in addition to William Green, were James A. Drain, commander of the American Legion, Senator James J. Walker and the Rt. Rev. A. S. Lloyd, Bishop of New York. The invited guests present included Dwight Morrow, partner of J. P. Morgan, Owen D. Young, head of the General Electric Company, Lewis E. Pierson, chairman of the board of the Irving Bank, Columbia Trust Co., Benjamin Strong, governor of the federal reserve bank, Senator Copeland, Nicholas Murray Butler, president of Columbia University, Hugh Frayne, representative of the A.F. of L. in New York, Bernard Gimbel, millionaire department store owner, J. I. Straus, and Rear Admiral C. P. Plunkett.[18]

President Coolidge sent a message to the gathering stating: "The bank is a strong piece of evidence that the people of this country own the property of the country. America is neither owned by nor controlled by a small group of rich men."[19]

This whole period represents one of the lowest points in the history of organized labor. Corruption of labor leaders was at an all time high. Bimba says:

Probably in no other country is the corruption of the labor leaders so shameful and so open as in the United States. It will suffice to mention only a few outstanding cases. John Mitchell amassed enormous wealth as president of the United Mine Workers. Frank Farrington of the Illinois miners was secretly an agent of the Peabody Coal Company, and when exposed openly became its paid official. The Brindell case in the building trades disclosed a corruption involving millions of dollars. The leaders of the New Jersey State Federation of Labor themselves admitted at the convention held in Camden, N.J., in 1927, that they accepted over $100,000 from the open shop manufacturers and employers.[20]

Such was the situation when the nation entered the economic crises of 1929.

14 • LABOR AND THE NEW DEAL

THE DECADE of the 1930s brought profound changes in the whole of U.S. society. Against this background, the labor movement experienced an explosive growth and made its greatest contribution in the defense and the advancement of democracy.

The 1920s began against the backdrop of great illusions in the viability of the American system of capitalism. Though U.S. capitalism was a part of the world capitalist system, it was considered by many to be a unique form of capitalism. A form in which not only would the big capitalists share in the prosperity, but the lowly masses as well. Henry Ford, one of the biggest moguls in the land, went so far as to make a prediction that every American worker was going to become a capitalist. Spence, in *Sinews of American Capitalism,* says:

> From all sides in the 1920s, Americans were being assured of the triumph of prosperity and the eradication of want. Herbert Hoover accepted the nomination of the Republican Party in 1928 optimistically predicting that "we shall soon, with the help of God, be in sight of the day when poverty will be banished from this nation." John Raskob, vice-president of General Motors and chairman of the Democratic National Committee, outlined a simple investment plan whereby a man could invest $15 a month and accumulate $80,000 over twenty years. "In my opinion," he said early in 1929, "the wealth of the country is bound to increase at a very rapid rate.... I am firm in my belief that anyone not only can be rich, but ought to be rich."[1]

U.S. capitalism had experienced a unique growth. It developed on the most favorable grounds. Not held back by the old feudal order, under no legal or moral restraints, in possession of tremendous natural resources, fed by a huge supply of cheap labor, including its former slaves, and geographically isolated from European wars, conditions were created for a massive expansion of the system. These factors made it possible for the United States, in less than a hundred

186

and fifty years, to become the most powerful capitalist nation in the world, a process accelerated by World War I. At war's end, the United States possessed the industrial capacity to feed a devastated planet. It also possessed some of the major markets in the world. Thus, U.S. capitalism entered the decade of the 1920s on a wave of unprecedented prosperity.

During the same period, many European nations were forced by revolutionary events to make concessions to its working class— through the enactment of social legislation which eased the conditions of the workers and provided for their greater participation in the power structure.

The United States at that point was not compelled to make any major shifts in the economy. Still it was bound by the laws governing capitalist development. There was, and is, no such thing as "American exceptionalism." Moreover, the very character of the wave of prosperity became an enabling act for the intensification of all the general laws of capitalism.

So in spite of certain unique features, in October 1929 a crash on the stock market took place, which was the inevitable outcome of the contradictory forces at work, even at the height of the prosperity wave. Moreover, it was a shocking experience for almost the entire nation. The dream of a new povertyless age was shattered.

Sid Lens documents the effect of the crash, especially on how it affected the lower stratas of the society:

Millions of families watched their life savings disappear. In 1931 alone, 17,000 retail stores closed their doors. Many Goliaths of the business world went under—Van Sweringen, Insull, Krueger, the United States Bank, to name a few—and with them they pulled under hundreds of thousands of small investors and members of the middle class. Through it all the most glaring symbol of the era's social sickness was the increasing army of the unemployed. By March 1933 the number of jobless workers was at least thirteen million, and with just about the same number working only part time. By 1934 there were two and a half million workers who had not been employed for two years or more, and six million who had not received a pay check for at least a year.[2]

These were the circumstances that sank the slogan, "My God! How the money rolls in" and replaced it with "Brother, can you spare a dime?" Even as the crisis grew, most bourgeois economists were still under illusions about the special nature of American capitalism and they predicted an early return to normalcy. Herbert Hoover, then president, also suffered from such illusions. He had a deep-seated faith in laissez faire capitalism which made him unwilling to see the necessity for a shift toward relief and social reform. Hoover was convinced that a government dole would weaken the system rather than strengthen it. Later he saw the necessity for government aid, but this took the form of priming the pump from the top. The Reconstruction Finance Corporation was formed to give aid to the corporations. Fiorello La Guardia, at that time a congressman and later the mayor of New York City, correctly labelled it as a "millionaires dole." The Reconstruction Finance Corporation was capitalized $500 million and authorized to borrow three times that much. It was permitted to lend to banks, insurance companies, and building and loan associations

Herbert Hoover came out with this program under the slogan that "Prosperity is just around the corner." But the depression did not go away. It was like some natural physical catastrophe. It continued year after year, 1929, 1930, 1931, 1932, 1933, getting worse and worse, deeper and deeper, stripping millions of jobs and shelter, forcing millions to the homeless road. The depth to which the crisis sunk was without parallel in American history.

Of all the forces in the country, the Communist Party of the United States was the most prepared to meet the outbreak of the crisis. It had cleaned the decks in its own ranks in 1928 when it ousted from its leadership Jay Lovestone, who had raised the theory of American exceptionalism. It was his view that while a worldwide crisis was inevitable, U.S. capitalism would be able to by-pass the approaching storms. Based on the clear understanding that the United States would go into crisis, the organization was prepared to give leadership to the oppressed masses. The first nationwide protest around the problems related to unemployment was held on March 6, 1930. It was called by the Trade Union Unity League and the Communist Party. It is estimated that around the country over 1,250,000 people participated. There were over a hundred thousand in New York and Detroit, and 50,000 in Chicago.

In New York where 110,000 people assembled, there began a wave of terror that characterized this whole period. The police acted insanely. Hundreds of unarmed people were beaten to the ground with clubs. Others were trampled by the charge of mounted police.

Unemployed councils were organized in all parts of the country and one of their main tasks was to prevent evictions. Eviction orders were issued against nearly 100,000 families in the two and a half years beginning in January 1930. In Chicago, 3,611 families, including 26,515 children, were evicted. But the unemployed councils moved 77,000 of these families back into their homes.

In addition to unemployed workers going on the offensive against the terrible conditions, almost all segments of the population took the path of organization and militant struggle, especially the masses of poor farmers. Between 1929 and 1933, it is estimated that over a million farmers lost their property through foreclosure, and evictions became widespread in the countryside. The struggle against evictions, and strikes to withhold farm produce from a market which was being bought at prices where farmers would bear the brunt of declining prices, were the main areas of battle. In 1932, in one farm community after another, organizations came into existence. Among them was the Farmers Holiday Association in Iowa. The most effective struggles were the resistance to evictions. Sometimes the farmers and their neighbors would band together to stop an eviction completely.

In the deep South, for the first time since the Reconstruction period, Black sharecroppers went into struggle. In 1932 a sharecroppers union was formed and in a short period it boasted of a membership of over five thousand. The president of the union was lynched, and terror typical of the South since the Reconstruction period was employed. But the sharecroppers did not give. They found underground methods of work and continued the struggle.

All across the country, Blacks were the backbone of the unemployed councils. They constituted about half of a hunger march to Washington in 1932 in which this writer and Henry Winston, National Chairman, CPUSA, participated in the leadership. Around the struggles of the unemployed, Black and white unity was established at the grass roots level in a way that had not been witnessed since the almost forgotten days of the Black freedom movement and the Abolitionists. In this connection once again the Communist Party, notwithstanding all kinds of lies and misrepresentation, played the key role.

The unity that was forged among the unemployed played a key role in what followed with the birth of the C.I.O. The upsurges during those stirring days played a decisive role in the birth of the

New Deal. All over the country, confidence in the system hung in the balance.

The administration of Franklin Delano Roosevelt went through two phases. Historians commonly call them the first and second New Deals. The unemployed workers, farmers and Blacks were the spark plugs igniting the first phase of his program. The labor movement was the most potent force in the second phase, and it was labor which was the driving force which put all the major reforms of the period into effect.

The first phase of the struggle, which introduced governmental intervention into the economy, was not as far reaching as in the latter period, that is, the period between 1935 and World War II. All through both periods a new British economist, Lord Keynes, appeared on the scene and called for governmental intervention in the economy as the central factor of the new times. He called for all kinds of regulations and restrictions that had heretofore been banned by the U.S. Supreme Court as unconstitutional and against laissez faire capitalism.

Keynes placed his major emphasis on purchasing power as the main lever to overcome the crisis. The relationship of Keynes and Roosevelt was not too close in the immediate period following World War I and during the first phase of the New Deal. This was true even though Roosevelt, upon coming into office, launched a spending program in order to stimulate the economy.

What marked the differences between the two phases of the New Deal? Arthur Schlesinger Jr., a leading New Dealer says:

> The early New Deal had accepted the concentration of economic power as the central irreversible trend of the American economy and proposed the concentration of political power as the answer. The effort of 1933 had been to reshape American institutions according to the philosophy of an organic economy and a co-ordinated society. The new effort was to restore a competitive society within a framework of strict social ground rules on the foundation of basic economic standards—accompanied, as time went on, by a readiness to use the fiscal pulmotor to keep the economy lively and expansive.[3]

The second period was to witness an accelerated process of open state-controlled capitalism. It was not fascist in style but was based on making some substantial changes in the role of government and the toiling masses. The central purpose was to save capitalism, even from some of the main capitalist forces, many of whom at that point were already embracing fascism as the solution to the problem. Roosevelt explained this contradiction in one of his election speeches during the 1936 campaign when he pointed out that when he came to office, Washington was like a drowning man who, when rescued, berated his savior for not having brought his silk hat out of the water too.

The second phase of the New Deal was in large part a response to the struggles waged by labor organizations and to the opposition to changes that Roosevelt had gotten from powerful business interest.

Upon coming to office, one of the first actions of the Roosevelt administration was the passage of the National Industrial Recovery Act which included a section popularly known as Section 7 (A). The law contained a number of sections offensive to labor, but as a whole it became a stimulus for workers to enter into the unions since some clauses protected the rights of workers to organize free from oppressive reprisals by the bosses. It also made it illegal for an employer to require membership in a company union "as a condition of employment." Although this provision was in the law, it was used in many cases to promote company unions, instead of dissolving them.

If President Roosevelt had any hopes for curbing the militancy of the workers, they were soon dashed to atoms. The inadequacies of Section 7 (A) were quickly revealed, especially the lack of authority to enforce decisions. The employers defied the government and the workers were compelled to resort to militant strike actions to get results.

In 1934 the Liberty League was formed to defend the open shop and as a counterforce to the New Deal. Its members controlled investments in business enterprises to the tune of thirty-seven billion dollars. Later a secret organization known as the Special Conference Committee was set up. It included some of the biggest corporations in the country, such giants as General Motors, Standard Oil of New Jersey, General Electric, Goodyear, Westinghouse, A.T.T., DuPont, U.S. Rubber, Bethlehem, International Harvester, and U.S. Steel.

These forces organized a new version of the vigilantes which were organized in the West against the I.W.W. earlier in the century. An organization came into existence in Detroit known as the Black Legion, which was a Northern version of the Ku Klux Klan. It is estimated that about a thousand people were involved. Their main activity was to employ terroristic measures against auto workers who were active in setting up union organization. They kidnapped workers, flogged them, and killed at least ten. The governor of Pennsylvania made an open charge that the organization was being financed by the DuPonts, General Motors and the Liberty League. Largely due to terrorism, progress was minute in auto, steel and other basic industries. However, progress was made in many other industries and the labor movement began to grow. John L. Lewis enrolled hundreds of thousands of miners who had drifted away. The needle trades unions also grew. It is estimated that about a million new workers came into the house of labor. In the face of increasing attacks by big business and inadequate protection from government, the workers began to rely on their own strength more and more.

The general strike in San Francisco marked one of the high points of labor solidarity. It had a profound affect on the whole working class. The situation began in San Francisco in 1933. The rank-and-file longshoremen, under the leadership of Harry Bridges, frightened the shipping magnates to such an extent that they refused to negotiate with the people that the workers had chosen. Moreover, they proceeded to discharge four rank-and-file leaders of the union. After the employers, over a period of months. refused to negotiate or recognize the union, about 12,000 longshoremen went out on strike. The strike spread from San Francisco to Seattle, Tacoma, Portland, San Pedro, San Diego and many other Pacific Coast ports. The Marine Workers Industrial Union also walked off, and by May 1934, thirty-five thousand workers were on strike. Once again the shippers resorted to red-baiting as their main ideological weapon and police terror as its physical means. Mass picketing was the only weapon the strikers possessed, so the employers decided to thwart the picketing by using police terror. On July 4, 1934, thousands of pickets gathered on the piers. Police control cars moved in and launched a vicious attack on the strikers, who resisted the assault.

After a one day truce, the fighting continued, this time with the police firing guns even more promiscuosly than on the previous day. The employers thought they had won, but the workers did not give up so easily. And what followed was one of the greatest displays of working-class solidarity in U.S. labor history. Various union locals began issuing calls for a general strike. A painters local issued a call, and was followed by a machinist local. At a workers' funeral, over thirty-five thousand workers walked behind the coffins. After the funeral, many other locals and labor councils began calling for a general strike.

Mike Quinn described the general strike: "The paralysis was effective beyond all expectation. To all intents and purposes industry was at a complete standstill. The great factories were empty and deserted. No streetcars were running. Virtually all stores were closed. The giant apparatus of commerce was a lifeless, helpless hulk."[4]

Despite the terror, despite sabotage by conservative union officials, the workers made substantial gains. On July 30 the 35,000 maritime workers went back to work. Longshoremen gained, as a result of the strike, the six-hour day, a thirty-hour week, and time and a half for overtime. Wages were raised to ninety-five cents an hour, $1.40 for overtime. They also won the basis for the union hiring hall.

The seamen returned under conditions which granted recognition to the International Seamen's Union. It won recognition, but other things were limited because the union was controlled by a reactionary clique who was subservient to the shipping interests. In contrast, Harry Bridges, the rank-and-file leader, was elected president of the San Francisco local of the International Longshoremen's Association and later elected to the presidency of the entire West Coast District. There can be no doubt that the San Francisco general strike was one of the catalyst agents for what took place in 1934 with the passage of the Wagner Labor Relations Act.

ANOTHER major force which laid the basis for the birth of the C.I.O. was the Trade Union Unity League (T.U.U.L.). Very few historians have properly defined the role it played in the advancement of the labor movement. Its contribution to what took place with the birth of the C.I.O. can be likened to the agricultural process. The league, its leadership and membership, plowed up the ground and planted the seeds. Later on, the cultivation came and the plants took on a quick growth.

The Trade Union Unity League was organized in Cleveland on August 3, 1929. It was a reorganization of the Trade Union Educational League, (T.U.E.L.) which was mainly a force working inside the conservative-led unions. The Trade Union Unity League took as its main task the organization of the unorganized into industrial unions, independent of the A.F. of L. At the same time, it conducted activities in the conservative-led unions to change their class collaboration policies. It worked to unify the unemployed and the employed. Perhaps its greatest organizational accomplishment was the building of the Unemployed Councils, although during the period between 1929 and 1935 it also organized and led numerous strike struggles. Its major contribution was in the areas of class ideology, class unity and industrial unionism. In this respect it carried forward the best traditions of the I.W.W. of a previous period.

At the heart of the league's program was the clarity it contained for industrial unionism. In its statement of purpose it proclaimed:

The class struggle unions are industrial in structure. They organize all sections of the working class—Negroes, women, youth, skilled, unskilled, native, foreign. The great consolidation of the forces of capitalism makes industrial unionism imperative for a fighting labor movement. Craft unionism, born in the early stages of capitalism, is worthless in these days of monopoly capitalist organization. In trustified industries, where 90 per cent of the workers can learn their "trades" in a week, organization by craft is criminal betrayal of the workers. Even in those industries which are more competitive in character, such as textile, needle, mining, etc., the great banks exert the controlling force, and make necessary an all-inclusive, militant, industrial unionism. Only by great mass movements, drawing in all the workers, and capable of paralyzing whole industries and groups of industries, can the workers make headway against the powerful employers, who are aided by the state and their . . . labor leader allies. The A.F. of L. craft system of one or more "trades" striking while the rest remain at work is a crime against the working class. It must be utterly wiped out.[5]

Writing in the organ of the Trade Union Unity League, *The Labor Herald,* Jay Fox showed the advantage of industrial unionism as against the crafts:

With the advent of departmentalized industrial unionism will come many advantages. One will be the end of the dual union scourge. Once industrial unionism is established all the workers, regardless of their other differences, will gravitate to the powerful organizations. Likewise great financial economies will be made. The amount of money and time wasted through the duplication of offices, officials, journals, conventions, etc., in our craft unions is appalling. Let us consider the metal industry as an example. In that great industrial division there are 24 International Unions, maintaining 24 expensive headquarters, with 24 high-salaried presidents, and 24 high-salaried secretaries to adorn them. They publish 24 costly journals, and have 24 international executive boards that keep the industry going 24 ways and getting nowhere. They have 24 sets of organizers and their combined work totals less than 10% of the total workers in the industry. They hold 24 separate conventions, each one of which costs the workers large sums of money. They have thousands of duplicate sets of local officers, business agents, etc., at a tremendous cost. When these 24 unions are amalgamated all this wasteful duplication will be abolished by the introduction of an efficient system of modern management. There will be but one headquarters, one set of officers, one journal, and one convention. Where chaos and wastefulness now exist, then there will be order and economy. By combining their plants the masters of industry cut out such foolish wastefulness many years ago. It is high time that Labor did the same.[6]

In contrast to the racist policies pursued by most A.F. of L. leaders and unions, the stand taken by the league pointed the way to class unity and unity between Black and white. Its position was stated as follows:

The TUUL conducts an aggressive struggle in defense of the Negro workers. These are the most oppressed, exploited and persecuted section of the entire working class. The advancement of the workers generally is inseparably bound up with the advancement of the Negroes. Every blow struck at the Negroes by the bosses is a blow at the whole working class. The TUUL has one of its most fundamental program demands the fight for full racial, political and social equality and the right of national self-determination for Negroes. It makes relentless war against lynching, Jim-Crowism, and discrimination of all kinds against Negroes. It roots out the race prejudice of chauvinism of white workers against Negroes. The TUUL demands the fullest participation and leadership of Negro workers in all the organizations and movements of the working class.... The TUUL organizes Negroes into the new industrial unions with the white workers on the basis of the fullest equality. In the old unions, it combats all discriminatory practices aimed against Negroes. It demands the admission of Negroes into these unions and, where this admittance cannot be accomplished, and where there are no revolutionary unions, it organizes separate unions for Negroes. The TUUL Negro Department connects up the fight of the Negro workers in this country with the world-wide struggle of the Negro race through the International Negro Labor Bureau of the RILU [Red International of Labor Unions]. The TUUL endorses and supports the general work of the American Negro Labor Congress.[7]

The League also took a position on women workers that was far ahead of the time. It stated:

With the simplification and mechanization of the industrial process, women are being brought into the industries in huge and increasing numbers. They are subjected to the fiercest speed-up and compelled to work for wages 25 per cent to 40 per cent lower than male workers at similar occupations. They are an important factor in the military mobilization plans of American imperialism. The trade union leaders have altogether failed to defend the interests of the women workers, barring them from the unions and discriminating against them in industry as they have done against the youth, the Negroes and the foreign-born.

The TUUL works to unite the women workers for a joint struggle with the workers generally. It maps out programs of demands for them, embodying equal pay for equal work, general raising of women workers' wages, establishment of a 7-hour day and 5-day week, with a 6-hour day for harmful and strenuous occupations and a full month holiday annually with full pay; for the elimination of night work and overtime and work in harmful occupations; protection during child-birth periods; installment of proper sanitary regulations; protection by social insurance against unemployment, old age, sickness, etc. To further these programs the TUUL has a National Women's Department, establishes women's commissions in the unions, and develops periodic trade union conferences for women workers. The winning of the women workers for the class struggle is a major objective of the TUUL.[8]

These programatized statements were later enhanced by the upsurge that took place in the labor movement.

The foregoing developments should suffice to show that the groundwork for the birth of the C.I.O. had been plowed up before it came into existence, and therefore is an integral part of what developed later. Most historians ignore this background because Communists were the pivotal forces sparking these developments.

Based on the aforementioned factors and developments, a clash took place in the A.F. of L. on organizing the unorganized in the mass production industries along industrial union lines. This clash was also accelerated by the new organizing possibilities. Senator Robert F. Wagner introduced the National Labor Relations bill into Congress and it was passed and became the law of the land in July 1935. The act forbade company unions, it recognized the right of workers to collectively bargain and created a three-man board with power to guarantee the right. It was a big advancement over the inadequacies of Section 7 (A). Thus, the debate on industrial unionism that took place between John L. Lewis and several other union leaders and the old guard conservatives around William Green was facilitated by the recognition now of tremendous organizational possibilities in the trustified industries. At the 1935 A.F. of L. convention the clash took on a physical form with John L. Lewis punching Bill Hutchinson of the Carpenter's Union on the nose. Lewis and those who were behind him left the convention and set up a new organization. The new committee met on November 10, 1935, in Washington. Present at the meeting were: Lewis, Charles P. Howard of the International Typographical Union, Sidney Hillman of the Amalgamated Clothing Workers, Thomas McMahon of the Textile Workers, Thomas Brown of the Mine, Mill and Smelter Workers, Harvey Fremming of the Oil Field and Refinery Workers, David Dubinsky of the International Ladies Garment Workers Union, and Max Zaribsky of the Hat, Cap and Millinery Workers.

These men represented about a million organized workers—one-third of the membership of the old A.F. of L. Moreover, it is of some significance that they represented, in the main, industrial unions, and therefore came to the new tasks with some background and experience.

If there is any evidence to back up Victor Hugo's expression, "There is nothing more powerful than an idea whose time has come," then what followed the birth of the C.I.O. should suffice. Almost overnight event after event occurred and the labor movement found itself engaged in a most massive organizational drive. The working class had been ready for organization for some time but could not see the possibility of victory. However, with a legal weapon now in their hands and a powerful organized force entering the arena of battle, the workers felt that the huge and powerful corporations could be beaten.

Thus, the years 1936–1938 became the years of a historic turning point in labor history. Strikes became nationwide. There was hardly a category of workers that did not in one way or another enter into struggle. White-collar workers, many of whom in the past had looked with contempt on the unskilled labor force, now identified themselves as workers.

While strikes were taking place in many industries, most of them were accelerated by the sit-down strike in the auto industry at plants in Cleveland, Ohio, Atlanta, Ga., Anderson, Ind., and Kansas City. But the one that became the spark which ignited the whole country was the sit-down strike in Flint, Michigan. The sit-ins led to strikes and organization in virtually all the mass production industries. When steel became organized it was one of labor's greatest achievements.

THE GROWTH of the C.I.O. in two years was miraculous. It started out with 1,000,000 members. According to a report by John L. Lewis, in a radio broadcast on September 4, 1937, the C.I.O. had an enrollment of 3,718,000 members. It had 32 affiliates, national and international unions. There were 600,000 coal miners organized, 400,000 auto workers, 375,000 steel workers, 300,000 textile workers, 250,000 garment workers, 200,000 electrical workers, and 100,000 packing workers. The successful C.I.O. campaigns spurred the A.F. of L. on to an organizing drive. By 1940, the A.F. of L. had 4,247,433 members; the C.I.O. 3,810,318; independent unions some 2,000,000 more. In less than four years the labor movement grew from 3,000,000 to 10,000,000.

The accomplishments of the C.I.O. in every area of a worker's life, compared to all previous periods, almost baffles the imagination. In regards to wages and hours, the C.I.O. estimated that by 1937 it had added an additional billion dollars to the workers wages and had cut the work hours by 2,000,000 a week. Nearly a million workers won agreements for a 35 or 36 hour week. A six-hour day was won in several industries, including some in the glass and rubber industries. Provisions were written into contracts providing for overtime pay at the rate of time and a half or double time, covering 1,500,000 workers. The holidays, which workers previously could take but were not paid for, were changed in most contracts. They were now able to take four holidays a year with pay. Contracts were also negotiated providing measures for safety and health. In contracts covering 1,350,000 workers, specific provisions were made for job security by clauses which forbade summary dismissals and managerial abuses.

With the labor movement now embracing over 10 million members, labor's political clout became tremendous. A whole number of substantial gains were made on the legislative front, at both the federal and state levels.

At the federal level one of the most significant bills passed, after a three year struggle, was the Fair Labor Standards Act of 1938. The law provided for many things including a minimum wage. At the state level similar progress was made. Twenty-eight states ratified the child labor amendment. Nineteen states passed anti-injunction laws. Twenty-three states passed minimum wage laws and four set up state departments of labor.

S. Uminsky, who categorized the achievements of labor in the 1930s, points out that in respect to labor legislation, New York State was the most outstanding in the nation. He quotes a message delivered by Governor Lehman to the New York legislature on January 5, 1938, in which the governor cited some of the gains:

Indeed, much has been done in the last five legislative sessions to guarantee to labor its fundamental rights. We have enacted the Unemployment Insurance Law, the Minimum Wage Law and the Social Security Law. We have outlawed yellow-dog contracts, defined the conditions under which labor injunctions may be issued, and included all occupational diseases under the coverage of the Workmen's Compensation Law. These and many other measures have materially added to the well-being of wage-earners. Moreover, they have more equally balanced the position of the employee with that of the employer.[9]

During this period labor entered into political action in a new way. Backed up by a combined membership of 10,000,000 members the C.I.O. and the A.F. of L. became more power conscious at the ballot box. The old method of merely endorsing candidates at conferences was replaced by vigorous organizational activities in both the shops and precinct levels. The most outstanding contribution at the grass-roots level was made by Labor's Non Partisan League which was formed by the C.I.O. Through the League, labor not only took steps to organize the participation of its own members in electoral contests, but it also became a vital force in mobilizing all categories for political action along progressive lines. Its members canvassed the precincts, ringing door bells from house to house as most political parties do. In many states labor became the balance of power in electoral contests. The most outstanding example of political action at that time was the formation of the American Labor Party (A.L.P.) in New York State. The tactics employed by the A.L.P. were suitable to the times. Indeed, if they had been followed by the labor movement throughout the country, a new dimension would have been added to the politics of the country.

One of the big problems of the period was how labor could conduct independent political activity, build up its own party form of organization, run its own candidates, and yet by so doing not defeat more progressive type candidates within the two old parties. The American Labor Party provided an answer. It placed its own party on the ballot. It ran its own candidates for office where it made no difference at all which candidate would win, Republican or Democrat. In so doing it was able to reflect in each election how labor stood as an independent force without at the same time jeopardizing the election of more progressive candidates of the old parties.

An example of this approach and its positve value was the campaign to re-elect Fiorello LaGuardia as mayor of New York in 1937. The mayor, although a Republican, had an excellent labor record both as a congressman and as mayor of New York City. The reactionaries in both parties went hog wild to defeat him. Early in the campaign the A.L.P. placed him on their slate for mayor while it ran Labor candidates for other offices. The party polled 482,489 votes under its own emblem. The A.L.P. vote was the deciding factor in the election of LaGuardia. At the City Council level the A.L.P. nominated eight candidates and five were elected, including Michael Quill, leader of the Transport Workers Union. Four American Labor candidates for the state legislature were elected and others it supported, running on other tickets, were also elected. The significance of the role played by the A.L.P. is highlighted by a commentary in the *New York Times* the day after the election:

A new party, the American Labor Party, holds the balance of power in New York City and State elections, it was clearly indicated by the results of the voting here yesterday . . . Both major parties are certain to make overtures to it in the coming year, with the important 1938 Gubernatorial election at stake. The Labor Party was organized last year to support Roosevelt and Lehman, and it polled 238,000 votes in the city. Political leaders doubted its ability to repeat that performance, but . . . yesterday it polled an indicated vote of over 400,000.[10]

There were some labor forces who viewed the A.L.P. as a mirror through which all Americans eventually could be seen marching. There were others who were still too steeped in the past to take such bold initiatives. But even some of those who were bold enough to form the party in New York were timid in facing the national scene. An example of hesitancy was the position taken by Charney Vladeck, an A.L.P. leader, after he had been elected. Speculating over the party's future, Vladeck emphasized his belief that the outcome of the New York experiment would have national repercussions. In journeys to other cities after the election, he found widespread interest in the New York party. But the party's impact upon the future, in his judgment, was not exclusively dependent upon its local accomplishments.

The future of the Labor Party idea may depend upon what the old parties decide to do. There are great stirrings in the minds of the American people. If neither of the old parties insists upon progressive, socially minded legislation, upon faithfulness to the principles of the New Deal, a great realignment may occur. But it is too early to say whether that will be necessary.[11]

These remarks show that even Vladeck still had illusions in the two party system as a vehicle for labor's political action.

Alex Rose, state executive secretary of the American Labor Party at that time, took a more optimistic view, although later he backtracked. In a welcome address given to Herbert Morrison of the British Labor Party, Rose declared: "In a very short time there is going to be a national labor party which would be able to elect its own President on a straight party ticket."[12]

Notwithstanding the progress made in general, the most tragic thing that occurred was the continued illusions held by labor leadership, including many in the C.I.O. and the A.F. of L., in the old parties and the failure to build, based on the A.L.P. example, a labor party in all the states and eventually a national party. If this problem had been approached with the same zeal and vigor and clarity and sincerity as had been done in organizing on the industrial level labor would have emerged from this period with assets that could have led to different results than those which followed World War II. But in spite of this weakness, labor's influence in the political arena was still decisive around some of the main burning issues of the day.

THE QUESTION can be put: Why was labor, with the birth of the C.I.O., able to achieve so much for the working class and the American people? No doubt, the objective situation was an important factor. But objective conditons do not always lead to positive social change. History demands as a prerequisite for all great changes in society a proper correlation of objective conditions and subjective factors, particularly leadership. The kind of leadership given can be of decisive importance. Generally speaking the times, the problems of the times, throw up leaders, "who seize the times." But this is not a mechanical process. Leaders can also come forward who derail the moment off course, or fail to take full advantage of what is possible. In the days of the birth of the C.I.O. the time was ripe and leadership was forthcoming from many levels, especially the rank and file. Aside from leadership there were three main reasons

for the explosive growth of the labor movement and the achievements it made to advance democracy to a new level. They were : first,
a high degree of class unity. Unity of native and foreign born, and
above all unity of Black and white; second, the unity of the working
class with other class forces and social strata who followed labor
initiatives and converged their power against all the citadels of
reaction; and thirdly, the refusal of the working class at that time to
fall victim to anti-Communist propaganda. The key element behind
the victories of the time was the achievement of unity between labor
and the Black people. American history as a whole has confirmed
how profound Karl Marx was when he wrote: "Labor cannot
emancipate itself in a white skin where in the black it is branded."[13]
U.S. history has also confirmed that there cannot be progress for all
the U.S. people when progressive Black and white forces are divided.

The C.I.O. at birth grasped this lesson. It could not have
organized the mass production industries without forging such
unity. It was the recognition of this vital necessity that brought great
victories. Labor had taken a long time to arrive at this conclusion.
But the problem of establishing Black and white equality in the full
sense of the word wasn't fully understood then or today. It is still one
of labor's unsolved problems. But relative to the period that gave
birth to the C.I.O., enough understanding was mustered in order to
react in a way that pulled these forces together.

SOME of the most shameful pages in U.S. history were written by the
A.F. of L. leadership under Samuel Gompers and William Green.
They perpetuated divisions in the ranks of labor along craft and
color lines throughout its history. They were the conveyors of racist
ideology in the ranks of the white workers. They cultivated and
appealed to the lowest manifestations of human selfishness. Thus for
decades the working class stood before the most powerful aggregate
of capital in the world—divided. The rich ruling class made
concessions to the most skilled workers in order to keep the unskilled
workers unorganized. And since Black workers in the main were
unskilled, they were at the bottom of the society. Moreover, most of
the craft unions operated in a way to perpetuate this situation. Most
of them banned Blacks from membership.

Against a background of exclusion and hostility by labor, the
Black community almost as a whole became alienated from the labor

movement. In periods previous to the C.I.O., Black workers were brought off the plantation of the South not only to meet pressing labor shortages, but also to break strikes. But with the emergence of the C.I.O. a new day dawned. The C.I.O. adopted strong statements of policy at its conventions. And its propaganda organs constantly argued for class unity along racial lines. Among these were:

> Resolved, that the CIO reaffirms the position which it has consistently maintained from the beginning in opposition to any and all forms of discrimination between one worker and another based upon considerations of race, creed, color, or nationality . . . and that the CIO condemns the policies of many employers of discriminating in their hiring and other employment conditions against Negroes. (Adopted at the 1941 Convention of the CIO.)
>
> Negro workers, join the CIO union in your industry. The CIO welcomes you. It gives you strength to win justice and fair play. The CIO unites you with fellow workers of all races and all creeds in the common struggle for freedom, for democracy, for a better life. (From *The CIO and the Negro Worker—Together for Victory,* C.I.O. publication no. 62.)[4]

Also in this regard Sumner Rosen says: "Most people who remember the CIO would probably describe its position on race in language similar to these quotations. The CIO is remembered for its militancy on the burning questions of its era and the question of racial discrimination was one key to the politics of that period."[15]

These programatized and ideological pronouncements were firmly rooted in the developments within the unemployed movement and the Trade Union Unity League. An impartial survey will show that the cadre that came from these sources, Communist and non-Communist left forces, were the yeast that caused the bread to rise. The unions they built and led went further in building class unity of Black and white than all others.

Most outstanding is the role played by Blacks in the meat-packing industry. The Chicago area, which during those days was one of the main centers of the industry, was largely organized by Black and white Communists with Blacks in the leading role. Even together the Amalgamated Meat Cutters and Butcher Workmen of North America, which represents a merger of a left-led union, a C.I.O. union and an A.F. of L. union has established Blacks in leadership on a broader basis than any multi-racial union in the country.

The position of the C.I.O. on the Black question evoked favorable response from even the most conservative elements in the Black community. Many of such forces had formerly supported the employers. The most potent organizing force that worked to draw the leadership of the Black community behind the C.I.O. effort was the National Negro Congress in which Black Communists like James W. Ford, Benjamin Davis, William L. Patterson and Henry Winston shared leadership with John P. Davies and A. Phillip Randolph. Any objective historian will find that the role played by the Communist Party in establishing bi-racial cooperation in the labor movement is one of the brightest spots in U.S. history. Yet there are some labor commentators who seek to play that role down and in so doing betray their own racist attitudes. For example, Sumner Rosen writing about the C.I.O. era and in regards to Communist efforts to place Blacks in more prominent positions of leadership had this to say:

Where the Communists were in control, Negroes who received support for leadership positions were generally men who would respond to Party influence. Where Communists did not control, they often sought to elevate to a principle the election of Negroes to leadership positions, making of this question an issue on which to build support among the Negro workers. The most celebrated instance was the concerted campaign to put a Negro on the Executive Board of the UAW, an effort which, though it failed, worked as a chronically divisive factor in the immediate prewar years of that union's life.[16]

Rosen's thesis of the Black question not being a principled question is the main problem for most Americans today. Yes, Communists did prod the union to accept the Black question as a principled question. But this racist minded so-called radical, (basically a lukewarm liberal), criticizes the Communist effort. Whatever mistakes Communists made on the Black question had been of a tactical nature, and not a matter of principle. During the war years a survey of C.I.O. unions will show that the unions in which some Communist Party members led or shared in leadership made the most progress in building Black and white relations on the basis of Black equality in leadership.

In addition to class unity which cut across craft, racial and religious lines, the C.I.O. in the decade of the thirties was the key force which forced an alliance which embraced the great majority of the American people. The coalition it led embraced labor, farmers, minority groups, middle-class reformers, cultural and intellectual forces. It was formidable and became decisive in preventing fascistlike forces from taking the United States down the path followed in Nazi Germany.

The lessons from this are clear. Organized labor is the most potent, the most powerful social force for progress in American life. Its achievements in the face of great odds have been monumental. The role it has played has fluctuated from time to time. More than often the rank and file have been victims of traitorous leadership. The post-world war years represented set backs from the days of the birth of the C.I.O. But if the nation is to make greater progress in today's conditions, if we are to reverse fascist-like trends, if we are to live in a world of peace, if we are to survive as a nation, then a revival under new conditions of the labor movement in the spirit and examples of the C.I.O. at its birth is a basic requirement.

SUMMARY

THIS SUMMARIZED version of how U.S. history developed along class, racial and sexual lines should suffice to show how hypocritical the capitalist class, its politicians and ideologues are when they parade around the world proclaiming that they stand for "Human Rights," champions of the "free world." Our national tradition is one of the most distorted affairs in all the annals of humankind.

Historians, at different stages of our development, have varied in their interpretation of our background. Some have exposed the rotten deeds perpetuated in the name of civilization and progress. But most, while admitting the negative features in our history, still present our system of government as the best possible of all worlds. Every time the ruling circles are compelled to make concessions of a democratic character they hail them as proof of the viability of the system. Very few historians point out that, after great struggles by the people, when concessions are made, in most cases they are limited and of a temporary character.

The best example of this fact is what has happened in the 400 year struggle Black people have waged for equality. The Civil War ended slavery, but a new form of slavery was founded. Concessions which were made after the Civil War were wiped out at the close of the Reconstruction period. During these Cold War years, the ruling class in the pursuance of its foreign policy objectives and in response to struggles waged by the popular masses, made concessions to Blacks mainly in the area of the social aspect of discrimination. But at no time were any major concessions made on the economic front to the broad mass of Black people. In fact the economic status of Blacks has recently severely deteriorated. And the U.S. Supreme Court, which yesterday laid the legal foundation to end the system of jim crow, now comes forward and renders a decision upholding the system of seniority in industry even if racial or sexual discrimination is involved.

President Carter speaks loud and clear about "human rights" in the Soviet Union and he is applauded by all the racist bigots in the country. But the President does nothing to challenge the Court's decision which adds a new dimension to the violation of human rights of minority groups and women.

Our whole history provides proof that reforms may be possible in our democratic structure but that they are inherently limited. And in circumstances when the masses seek solutions outside of the system of capitalism, the open dictatorial face of the capitalist class is more and more revealed. In these Cold War years we have witnessed two periods where the country has been driven along the lines of a fascist police state. The period known as McCarthyism and the revelations made in the Watergate situation show that an open dictatorship of the capitalist class can happen here too if the people are not vigilant. It is in this context that we have examined the negative features in our American heritage.

Many profound lessons can be learned from this history. If we fail to do so we will be deprived of much knowledge on how to meet the present crisis the nation confronts. Our country since birth has faced several crucial periods. But the problems we confront today have no precedent in history. The future of the nation and of all humanity is at stake.

The crises of today are many. We face the choice of escalating cold war policies or moving decisively in the direction of detente, of peace. We face the necessity of readjusting our nation's foreign policy toward equality with all the former and presently exploited peoples in Asia, Africa and Latin America, for an end to imperialism. On the home front we face a growing political crisis reflected in all institutions and out of which there has evolved an unprecedented moral crisis. And all of these problems are greatly aggravated by the growth of crisis features in the economy.

The economy, after thirty years of relative prosperity, shows signs pointing to an economic catastrophe. In addition, the main capitalist powers in varying degrees are also in the throes of severe economic difficulties, while, in contrast, the socialist sector of the world is increasingly growing stronger. In fact, unless radical changes take place, by all odds the Soviet Union will surpass the United States in every respect in the next ten or fifteen years.

Capitalism has always been pregnant with conditions that erupted periodically into cyclical crises. But as time passed the crises went deeper and deeper and the means to overcome them became more difficult. Eventually a point was reached where major wars or fascism became the means; reforms alone were unable to do the job. This was demonstrated by the economic crisis in the 1930s. The reforms under the New Deal of President Roosevelt did not solve the crisis feature in the society. Some relief was given which took us from the lowest point of the crisis, but a full "solution" was not found until World War II broke out. When the war started there were still nine million workers unemployed.

After World War II our country had not experienced a major economic crisis until 1974. We have had several recessions, but not a full-blown crisis. However, the factors that made this possible have eroded and we now confront ongoing major economic difficulties. For over thirty years the war economy was the main factor stimulating the economy. But recent events have shown how futile these measures have become. In the post-World War II years the nation has fought two big wars in Korea and Vietnam. Yet as war production went forward we witnessed a growth in poverty for a large segment of our people, a crisis in social services, and the deterioration of most major cities. Finally inflation and unemployment have become major chronic problems.

It is evident from the foregoing that the conduct of local wars or a war economy will not suffice to meet the problems of today. It should also be evident that while World War II did "solve" the problem, it cost the world over fifty-five million casualties. And at this time, such a war could not solve anything because it would result in nuclear disaster that would destroy a few billion people, if not the entire world. The situation therefore requires some radical changes within the system, and finally a change in systems.

IF WAR and a war economy cannot solve the problems of today, then what is an approach that can provide some substantial relief until such a time when a more fundamental solution can be achieved? It is this author's view that a full solution to the problem of periodic economic crises cannot be obtained within the framework of the capitalist system. While there are laws within capitalism which generate crises from time to time, it does not follow that some of the most harmful features of a crisis cannot be alleviated within the system, or that a full-blown crisis cannot be averted for longer periods of time. Such possibilities exist. But to accomplish this goal will require making some of the most radical changes that have ever been undertaken in this country. Several major reforms are required.

First and foremost is a complete change in foreign policy: To establish a firm and durable peace. Given this approach, appropriations for military purposes can be substantially reduced and upward of 50 to 60 billions of dollars a year can be used to provide jobs, create a more rational health system, remove slums and ghettoes, and cure the ailments of our sick cities. Such a program could begin now. Both the Soviet Union and the United States have already achieved the capacity to destroy each other. If we discard our cold war mentality it will have a profound effect on the whole world. In an atmosphere of peace between the capitalist and socialist worlds, trading possibilities would open up that could ease considerably the present trends toward a major catastrophic crisis.

Our foreign policy in relation to third world countries must also undergo drastic changes. The imperialist features in our relations with them must go completely. Gone are the days when we as a nation, as well as others, can go the the underdeveloped countries and extract wealth from them on a superexploitative basis. Given an approach of equal economic and political relations with such countries, and if we are prepared to make major capital investment in these countries that will benefit their industrial and cultural development, then means will exist for a gigantic stimulus to the U.S. economy.

In respect to domestic policies, far reaching changes also must be made. We must bring into existence a government that will curb the power of the giant corporations who have established a monopoly over the wealth and resources in the land. A government that will execute a program to reduce the work week from forty hours to thirty hours with no reduction in pay. Such a program would put a few million people back to work immediately. Within the context of the government pouring funds into the economy to meet the needs of the people, special considerations will have to be made for those stratas of the population who are on the lowest level in the economy.

Categories such as Black youth, Spanish speaking, Native Americans, Asians, as well as poor whites and women workers must be given top priority in the expenditure of funds by the government.

Finally some sectors of private enterprises must be nationalized. This is especially necessary for all the related industries that deal with the source of energy and transportation. The present gas and oil crisis has been used to increase corporate profits while the people have been forced to suffer. The government has poured billions of dollars into the railroad and airline industries to make them more profitable. This approach must be changed. Whenever an industry fails to meet certain standards of operation they must be nationalized without hesitation.

These are some of the main options that are open to meet the problems of today. But even with such far reaching changes, the problem of crises in capitalist economy will not be permanently solved. Nevertheless they would be important as way stations to a complete change, away from capitalism and toward socialism.

IT IS in this context that this examination of U.S. history will be useful. At every stage of history when changes in the status quo are required, certain social forces, and individuals, emerge who "seize the time" and make the changes. U.S. history has been no exception. The survey in this book shows which forces worked to force through changes and which opposed them. Our history reveals that the monied classes, regardless of which category, were not the forces who led the fight for changes, but that it was the common people of all categories.

Our history also reveals that no reliance can be placed on the liberal bourgeoisie. This assessment does not rule out the possibility that such forces at a given time may not initiate a struggle or be forced by circumstances to join the struggle. But it shows that reliance on such forces to go all the way with the struggle can prove fatal.

An examination of the time and deeds of the foremost liberal presidents in U.S. history proves this point. Jefferson, Lincoln, Wilson and Roosevelt are acclaimed as the most liberal and greatest presidents in our history. And there can be no doubt that these men did achieve greatness and aided democratic advances. But in each case it was the people who propelled them forward. And, also in each situation there also came a point when certain things were done under these presidents that were of an extreme reactionary character.

Jefferson, in his time, led the struggle against the mercantile capitalist interest. He was the author of the Declaration of Independence which proclaimed certain inalienable rights of all men. He took a stand against slavery. But when he became president he did much to advance the capitalist system in some of its most sordid deeds, i.e., the removal of the Indians westward and compromises with slavery which gave much power to slaveholders.

Woodrow Wilson also provides a great lesson for the contradictory character of the liberal community. Under his administration in World War I the rich got richer. And what was done in regards to civil liberties was worse than the Alien and Sedition Laws under the administration of John Adams.

Civil liberties also eroded under F.D.R. What he did in putting big business in a position to profit from World War II while the people suffered all kinds of deprivations, what was done to scuttle the New Deal and to curtail civil liberties, shows that liberalism is no defense against capitalist dictatorship, in wither its hidden or open forms. The Smith Act, under which Communists were persecuted immediately following World War II, was enacted during the Roosevelt regime. This act laid the basis for the growth of fascistlike trends in these cold war years.

The foregoing should clearly show that at a moment of crisis and as the fascist danger is escalated, liberals, whether of good intentions or not, have not been and are not the major forces to prevent a fascist takeover of the government. Experience in Nazi German shows that such forces helped pave the way for Hitler to come to power.

One of the main lessons to be drawn from this narrative of U.S. history is that the common people, those who have no material stake in persecuting other people at home or abroad, are the major forces to promote world peace, to take drastic measures in the economy to protect the nation from money-hungry pirates, to meet the fascist danger in a decisive manner, and to bring high moral standards to the country.

At every stage in the battle for democracy it has been such forces. In the battle for the Bill of Rights and the excessive exploitation during the Industrial Revolution, it was the farmers. In the battle to end slavery it was the slaves, the freedmen, the Abolitionists, women and Marxists in the first place. This was true even when northern industrialists had a direct stake in the ending of slavery.

In more recent times, during the New Deal era, it was radicals, Communists, the unemployed, Black people, the poor farmers, the working class that took the lead and forced through the reforms of that period. It was labor that led the way to prevent the United States from a fascist takeover.

In our time these are still the forces who constitute the yeast that can make the bread of progress rise to new heights. These are the forces that must be relied upon to prevent our nation from traveling pathways leading to disaster. Today the main forces which must be united are: the labor movement, Black Americans, other oppressed minorities, Native American Indians, Spanish speaking and Asian peoples. At this stage of the struggle and based on this alliance, unity on specific measures must be sought with the middle class, the professional community, liberals of goodwill, and in some cases sectors of big business. Only a coalition such as this possesses the power to turn the country around. The building of such a coalition will not be simple or easy. For those classes who run the system and have much to lose, work overtime to prevent the unity of these diverse forces. Throughout U.S. history this has been the case.

IN THIS connection the weapons have been of a material and ideological character. As we have noted, at certain points terror is always employed. But bribery and corruption have been the main weapons. Usually when these vices are used, they come mainly in the form of corruption of personalities in government. But such practices occur in almost all institutions and organizations within the capitalist society. As previously indicated, capitalism in the sphere of ideology generates selfishness in the name of hard work, thrift and brain power, that has no hesitation to exploit and to mislead.

Children are indoctrinated with this view on life from the cradle upward. And so, much of this poison seeps into the ranks of common people and becomes a stumbling block to unity. Each category of the people are trained to seek solutions to their problems at the expense of others. All through history, the ruling circles have adopted measures which provided some minor concessions to some categories among the people to prevent them from finding common cause with others. This has been the background for conflicts between farmers and labor, between the foreign and native born, and along racial lines of Black and white, although in this connection the concessions go to whites not to Blacks.

Alongside all these divisive measures the working class has been divided along the lines of skilled and unskilled workers. In all areas of peoples organizations especially those that could play an important role in making a significant challenge to the status quo, the ruling circles appeal to selfish instincts instead, and provide some material concessions to keep such forces under "safe leadership." And in this respect they have been quite successful especially in the house of labor, and to some extent among Blacks and minority groups. Other divisive ideologies have been male supremacy, national and racial chauvinism and in modern times, anti-communism.

Although the monied class, the corporate interest, has had these weapons at their disposal throughout our entire history, there have been periods where the people found the means to break through such barriers and gain some major victories. Perhaps the most important victories in the battle for democracy were the ending of chattel slavery, the reforms of the New Deal era, the civil rights movement during the period of Dr. Martin Luther King, Jr., as well as the peace movement during the Vietnam War.

The battle to end slavery contains one of the most important lessons for all Americans today, especially for whites. The tragic losses which occurred during the Civil War as outlined by Charles and Mary Beard could have been avoided if the forces involved had understood that, in their own material interest, slavery had to be eliminated. But the best among the Founding Fathers viewed ending slavery as a secondary problem.

From the founding of the nation through two years of the Civil War, the northern industrialists compromised with the South on the question of the ending of slavery. Even after the Civil War broke out, it took two years for President Lincoln to learn that compromises on the ending of slavery could and would lead the nation to ruin. And to this day most progressive whites have not grasped this fundamental lesson. Priorities are often given by some of the most advanced whites to other questions which can and do lead many to compromises on matters involving racial minorities. Appeasement of racism in the society can in the long run become the most disastrous course we can follow. The Civil War is a prime example.

Racism in the labor movement until the New Deal period was one of the main weapons used by the companies to prevent union organizations in the basic industries, and as a consequence a lower standard of living for all workers. In fact, in the post World War I years, Blacks were brought en masse to the North to break strikes and prevent unionization. During this same period anti-communism was brought into sharper focus and was used to break strikes and justify terroristic measures which were applied by company police and the police power of government.

It was only in the period when both these divisive ideologies were rejected, that the labor movement made substantial progress. Many of the present-day reforms in relations between employers and employees could not have been established without the firmest unity of the class, Black and white in the first place, but also native and foreign born, skilled and unskilled, women, Communist and non-Communist. Without this unity the workers would still labor and sweat long hours at starvation wages and have no rights at all, not to speak of certain social benefits.

Thus, the main lesson of this historical treatment is that it will take a united people, a people who in the main have no stake in the exploitation of others, a people that will not allow material, terroristic or ideological weapons to divide their ranks.

With this historical experience in proper focus, "we shall overcome."

REFERENCE NOTES

1. EUROPEAN BACKGROUND

1. Littlefield, Henry W. *History of Europe, 1500-1848*. Barnes and Noble Co., New York, 1939, pp. 1-2.
2. Fiennes, Gerard. *Sea Power and Freedom*. G.P. Putnam's & Sons, New York and London, 1918, p. 5.
3. Hammond, J. L. and Hammond, Barbara. *The Rise of Modern Industry*. Harcourt, Brace Company, New York, 1926, pp. 22-23.
4. Marx, Karl. *Communist Manifesto*. International Publishers, New York, 1948, p. 11.
5. Hammonds. Loc. cit., p. 216.
6. For an excellent presentation of this whole development, see R. H. Tawney, *Religion and Capitalism*. New Library, Inc., NY, NY, 1954.
7. Hammonds. Loc. Cit., p. 91.
8. As cited by Karl Marx in *Capital*, Vol. I. International Publishers, New York, 1967, p. 760.
9. See Anthony Bimba, *History of the American Working Class*, International Publishers, New York, 1927, p. 11.
10. Ibid., p. 16.
11. Ibid., p. 17.

2. THE STRUGGLE FOR A DEMOCRATIC CONSTITUTION

1. James Adams, *The March of Democracy*, Scribners and Sons, New York and London, 1932, pp. 139-140.
2. Cited by Samuel Eliot Morison, *The Growth of the American Republic*, Oxford University Press, New York, 1950, pp. 274-275
3. Ibid. p. 275.
4. Ibid., p. 276.
5. Ibid. p. 276.
6. Donald Childsey, *The Birth of the Constitution*, Crown Publishers, New York, 1964, p. 66.
7. Esmond Wright, *Fabric of Freedom*, Hill and Wang, New York, 1800, p. 147.
8. Cited by Morison, loc. cit., p. 297.
9. Samuel Eliot Morison, *Oxford History of the American People*, Oxford University Press, 1965, p. 274.
10. Ibid., p. 274.
11. Wright, loc. cit., p. 146.

12. Morison, loc. cit., p. 281.
13. Ibid. p. 281.
14. John Locke, in *The Liberal Tradition in European Thought*, edited by David Ledorsky, J. P. Putnam and Sons, New York, 1970, p. 84.
15. J. William Fulbright, *The Crippled Giant*, Random House, New York, 1972, pp. 230-231.
16. Morison, loc. cit., p. 272.
17. David G. Loth, *Public Plunder*, Greenwood Press, Westport, 1938, p. 74.
18. Irving Brent, *The Bill of Rights: Its Origin and Meaning*, Bobbs Merill, Co., Inc., New York, 1965, p. 137.

3. CONCENTRATION OF WEALTH

1. Ferdinand Lundberg, *The Rich and The Super Rich*, Banton Books, New York, 1968, p. 1.
2. Gustavus Myers, *The History of the Supreme Court*, Charles H. Kerr & Co., 1925, p. 22.
3. Ibid., p. 165.
4. Cited by Anna Rochester, *The Populist Movement in the United States*, International Publishers, New York, 1943, p. 7.
5. Patricia Acheson, *The Supreme Court*, Dodd, Mead and Co., New York, 1961, p. 144.
6. William Z. Foster, *Outline History of the Americas*, International Publishers, New York, 1951, pp. 232-233.
7. Ibid., p. 233.
8. Myers, loc. cit., pp. 496-497.
9. Acheson, loc. cit., p. 149.
10. Ibid., p. 154.
11. Victor Perlo, *American Imperialism*, International Publishers, New York, 1951, p. 16.
12. *Political Affairs*, June 1971, p. 30.
13. Epstein, Edwin M., *The Corporation and American Politics*, Prentice-Hall Inc., Englewood Cliffs, N.J., 1969, p. 2.
14. Roosevelt, Franklin D., *Address Commonwealth Club*, San Francisco, September 23, 1932.
15. Rochester, Anna, *Rulers of America*, International Publishers, New York, 1936, p. 128.
16. Dolenberg, Richard, *War and Society*, J. B. Lippincott Co., New York, 1972, p. 12.
17. Cited by Fred J. Cook, *The Warfare State*, Macmillan Co., New York, 1962, p. 87.

4. DESTRUCTION OF NATIVE AMERICANS

1. Cited by Karl Marx, *Capital*, Vol. I, International Publishers, New York, 1967, pp. 751-752.
2. Frederick Engels, *The Origin of the Family, Private Property and the State*, International Publishers, New York, 1942, p. 161.
3. As cited in Engels, loc. cit., pp. 162-163.
4. Will Durant, *Our Oriental Heritage*, Simon and Schuster, New York, 1954, p. 52.
5. James Wharton, *Learning from the Indians*, Running Press, Philadelphia, 1968, p. 15.

6. Wilbur Jacobs, *Dispossessing the American Indian,* Scribner, New York, 1972, p. 27.
7. Peter Farb, *Man's Rise to Civilization,* E. P. Dutton & Co., New York, 1968, p. 247.
8. Marx, loc. cit., p. 753.
9. Farb, loc. cit., p. 65
10. Alexis De Tocqueville, *Democracy in America,* Random House, New York, 1945, pp. 352-353.
11. Farb, loc. cit., p. 65.
12. William Meyer, *Native Americans,* International Publishers, New York, 1971, p. 32.

5. NOT A BACKWARD RACE

1. A. M. Simons, *Social Forces in American History,* Macmillan, New York, 1911, p. 29.
2. Alexis De Tocqueville, *Democracy in America,* Random House, New York, 1945, p. 355.
3. Will Durant, *Our Oriental Heritage,* Simon and Schuster, New York, 1954, p. 5.
4. Samuel Eliot Morison, *Oxford History of the American People,* Oxford University Press, New York, 1957, p. 15.
5. Ibid., p. 4.
6. William H. Prescott, *The Conquest of Mexico and the Conquest of Peru,* Random House, New York, 1923, p. 33.
7. Ibid., p. 34.
8. Ibid., p. 27.
9. Morison, loc. cit., pp. 5-7.
10. Wilbur R. Jacobs, *Dispossessing the American Indian,* Scribner, New York, 1972, p. 163.
11. Ibid., p. 9.
12. Ibid., p. 160.
13. Cited in ibid., p. 33.
14. Engels, *The Origin of the Family, Private Property and the State,* International Publishers, New York, 1942, p. 86.
15. George Pierre, *The American Indian's Crisis,* Naylor Co., 1971, Printed in the U.S., pp. 4-5.

6. CAPITALISM AND THE SLAVE TRADE

1. Zoe Marsh and G.W. Kingsnorth, *A History of East Africa,* Cambridge University Press, New York, 1972.
2. Frank Tannenbaum, *The Slave and the Citizen,* Alfred A. Knopf, New York, 1947, p. 15.
3. Milton Meltzer, *Slavery Two,* Henry Regnery, Chicago, 1972, p. 43.
4. Karl Marx, *Capital,* Vol. 1, International Publishers, New York, 1967, p. 751.
5. Meltzer, loc. cit., p. 39.
6. Dr. W. E. B. Du Bois, *The World and Africa,* International Publishers, New York, 1946, pp. 16, 163.
7. Ibid., p. 163.
8. John W. Williams and Charles F. Harris, *Armisted,* Random House, New York, 1972, p. 7.
9. John W. Blassingame, *The Slave Community,* Oxford University Press, New York, 1972, p. 7.

7. SLAVERY: ITS WORST FORM

1. David Walker, *One Continual Cry*, ed. by Herbert Aptheker, Humanities Press, Atlantic Highlands, N.J., 1965, p. 63.
2. Ibid., p. 75.
3. Meltzer, loc. cit., p. 141.
4. Ibid., p. 148.
5. Kenneth W. Stampp, *The Peculiar Institution*, Vintage Books, New York, 1956, p. 21.
6. Ulrich B. Philips, "The Economic Cost of Slave Holding in the Cotton Belt," *Political Science Quarterly*, XX, June 1905, p. 257.
7. John Hope Franklin, *From Slavery to Freedom*, Random House, New York, 1947, p. 172.
8. Stanley M. Elkins, *Slavery*, University of Chicago Press, 1969, p. 63.
9. Gilberto Freyre, *The Master and the Slaves*, Alfred A. Knopf, New York, 1956, p. 270.
10. Elkins, loc. cit., p. 82.
11. See Clark D. Moore and Ann Dunbar, *Africa Yesterday and Today*, Praeger, 1969 for full background.
12. Freyre, loc. cit., p. 13.

8. THE BATTLE TO END SLAVERY

1. Charles Beard and Mary Beard, *The Rise of American Civilization*, Vol. II, Macmillan Co., New York, 1927, pp. 98-99.
2. Lerone Bennett, Jr., *Before the Mayflower, A History of Black America*, Johnson Publishing Co., Inc., Chicago, 1969, p. 49.
3. Ibid., p. 49.
4. Ibid., p. 49.
5. Herbert Aptheker, *And Why Not Every Man?*, International Publishers, New York, 1970, p. 18.
6. Cited by Merton L. Dillon, *The Abolitionist*, Northern Illinois University Press, Dekalb, 1974, p. 5.
7. Aptheker, loc. cit., p. 147.
8. From the "Notes of Virginia" as quoted in *The Complete Jefferson*, arranged by Saul K. Padoner, Dual Sloan and Pearce, Inc., New York, 1943, pp. 661-662.
9. De Tocqueville, loc. cit., p. 373.
10. Leon F. Litwack, *North of Slavery: The Negro in the Free States*, University of Chicago Press, 1961, p. 11.
11. William Z. Foster, *The Negro People in American History*, International Publishers, New York, 1973, p. 47.
12. Benjamin Quarles, *The Negro in the Making of America*, Collier Books, New York, 1971, p. 54.
13. *Letters and Speeches of Wendell Phillips*, Walker, Wise and Co., Boston, 1964, p. 491.
14. W. E. B. Du Bois, *The Suppression of the African Slave Trade to the United States of America*, Schocken Books, New York, 1969, p. 64.
15. Quarles, loc. cit., p. 75.
16. Litwack, loc. cit., p. 214.
17. Quoted in *Political Affairs*, New York, June 1971, p. 25.
18. Dillon, loc. cit., p. 146.
19. Ibid., p. 218.
20. Ibid., p. 242.

21. Henry Winston, *Strategy for a Black Agenda,* International Publishers, New York, 1973, p. 281.
22. Dillon, loc. cit., p. 226.
23. Ibid., p. 226.
24. Foster, loc. cit., p. 128.
25. Cited by Dillon, loc. cit., p. 212.
26. J. A. Rogers, *The Civil War Centennial—100 Years Later, 1861-1961,* New York, 1961.
27. Max Lerner, *America As a Civilization,* Simon & Schuster, New York, 1957, p. 17.
28. Cited by Dillon, loc. cit., p. 264.
29. John R. Lynch, *The Facts of Reconstruction,* Neale Publishing Co., New York, 1914, p. 291.

9. RACISM AND THE EXPANSION WESTWARD

1. Morison, *Growth of the American Republic,* op. cit., p. 581.
2. Cited by Patricia Bell Blawis, *Tijerina and the Land Grants,* International Publishers, N.Y., p. 11.
3. Carey McWilliams, *North of Mexico,* Greenwood Press, Westport, 1969, p. 103.
4. Ibid., p. 106.
5. Morison, op. cit., p. 583.
6. Blawis, op. cit., p. 26.
7. Ibid., pp. 26-27.
8. U.S. Senate Hearings Committee on Appropriations, farm labor programs, 78th Congress, first session, Part IV, Washington D.C., 1943.
9. Article 15 of Public Law 78, 1951.
10. U.S. House of Representatives Hearings Committee on agriculture farm labor, H.R. 2955 2nd Congress 1st session, 1951, p. 78.
11. William Z. Foster, *Outline History of the Americas,* International Publishers, New York, 1951, p. 315.
12. Ibid., p. 315.
13. Protection of Americans Abroad, Official bulletin of the Ministry of Foreign Affairs, Mexico City, Vol. LXV, July 1933.
14. Ibid., Mexico City El National July 9th 1933: Daniels to the State Department July 10th 1933.
15. Karl G. Yoneda, "A Brief History of U.S. Asian Labor," *Political Affairs,* New York, September, 1976, pp. 5, 6, 7.
16. Ibid., pp. 7-8.
17. Ibid., pp. 12-13.

10. BACKGROUND OF SEXUAL OPPRESSION

1. John Locke, *Second Treatise of Government,* Great Books Foundation, Chicago, 1947, p. 48.
2. Jean Jacques Rousseau, *L'Emile on a Treatise on Education,* edited by W. H. Payne, New York, 1906, p. 263.
3. John Stuart Mill, *On The Subjection of Women,* Fawcett World, New York, 1971, p. 170.
4. Cited in *Sexual Politics,* Kate Millet, Avon, New York, 1973, pp. 93-94.
5. Cited by Eleanor Flexner, *Century of Struggle,* Harvard University Press, Forge Village, Massachusetts, 1959, p. 22.
6. Andrew Sinclair, *The Better Half,* Harper and Row, New York, 1970, p. 24.

7. *Feminism,* ed. Miriam Schneir, Random House, New York, 1971, p. 4.
8. Ibid., p. 85.
9. Bimba, loc. cit., p. 68.

11. WOMEN: SLAVERY AND SUFFRAGE

1. Schneir, loc. cit., see Introduction.
2. Ibid., Introduction.
3. Cited in Flexner, loc. cit., xii.
4. Sinclair, loc. cit., p. xii.
5. Cited in Millet, loc. cit., p. 80.
6. Ibid., p. 80.
7. T. U. Smith, *American Philosophy of Equality,* University of Chicago Press, 1927, p. 85.
8. Schneir, loc. cit., p. 86.
9. Ibid., p. 87.
10. Flexner, loc. cit., p. 91.
11. Ibid., p. 91.
12. Ibid., p. 43.
13. Ibid., p. 109.
14. Ibid., p. 109.
15. Ibid., p. 111.
16. Sinclair, loc. cit., pp. 182-183.
17. Karl Marx, *Capital,* Vol. I, International Publishers, New York, 1967, p. 287.
18. Catt and Shuler, *Women Suffrage and Politics,* Charles Scribner and Sons, New York, 1923, p. 40.
19. Flexner, loc. cit., p. 145.
20. Catt and Shuler, loc. cit., p. 125.
21. Ibid., p. 126.
22. Ibid., pp. 107-108.

12. WOMEN AND THE LABOR MOVEMENT

1. Cited by Flexner, loc. cit., p. 51.
2. Senate report, Women in Industry, as cited by Schneir, loc. cit., p. 259.
3. Ibid., p. 259.
4. Cited by Flexner, loc. cit., p. 53.
5. Ibid., p. 53.
6. Kirsten Amundson, *The Silenced Majority, Women and American Democracy,* Prentice Hall Inc., Englewood Cliffs, N.J., 1971, p. 59.
7. Ibid., p. 56.
8. Sinclair, loc. cit., p. 308.
9. Richard O. Boyer and Herbert M. Morais, *Labor's Untold Story,* Cameron Associates, New York, 1955, p. 175.
10. Ibid., p. 175.
11. Ibid., p. 175.
12. See Clark C. Spence, *Sinews of American Capitalism,* Hill and Wang, New York, 1964, p. 219.
13. Phillip S. Foner, *Organized Labor and the Black Worker,* Praeger Publishers, New York, 1974, p. 224.
14. Sinclair, loc. cit., p. 312.

13. LABOR BEFORE THE NEW DEAL

1. *Trade Union Unity League,* Chicago, Ill., 1929, p. 54.
2. Ibid., p. 54.
3. Gustavus Myers, *History of the Great American Fortunes,* Random House, New York, 1907, p. 244.
4. Simons, loc. cit., pp. 181-182.
5. As cited by Bimba, loc. cit., p. 137.
6. Acheson, loc. cit., pp. 169-170.
7. Bimba, loc. cit., p. 210-211.
8. Spence, loc. cit., p. 216.
9. Cited Morison, *Growth of the American Republic,* pp. 811-812.
10. Spence, loc. cit., p. 218.
11. Philip S. Foner, *History of the Labor Movement in the United States,* Vol. 4, p. 191.
12. Ibid., p. 192.
13. Boyer and Morais, loc. cit., p. 213.
14. Ibid., p. 185.
15. Ibid., p. 185.
16. Ibid., p. 204.
17. Cited in Bimba, loc. cit., p. 347.
18. Ibid., p. 347.
19. Ibid., p. 348.
20. Ibid., p. 338.

14. LABOR AND THE NEW DEAL

1. Spence, loc. cit., p. 264.
2. Sidney Lens, *The Labor Wars,* Doubleday, Garden City, New York, 1973, p. 240.
3. Arthur M. Schlesinger, Jr., *The Age of Roosevelt,* Houghton Mifflin Co., Boston, 1957, p. 385.
4. Boyer and Morais, loc. cit., p. 287.
5. *The Trade Union Unity League,* Chicago, Ill., New York, October 1929, p. 19.
6. Jay Fox, *Amalgamation, Labor Herald Library,* no. 5., Chicago, 1929, p. 35.
7. *Trade Union Unity League,* loc. cit., p. 25.
8. Ibid., p. 27.
9. S. Uminsky, *Progress of Labor in the United States,* House of Fields, New York, 1939, p. 175.
10. *New York Times,* November 8, 1937.
11. Uminsky, loc. cit., p. 207.
12. Ibid., p. 207.
13. Karl Marx, *Capital,* Vol. I, International Publishers, 1967, p. 287.
14. From *The C.I.O. and the Negro Worker—Together for Victory,* C.I.O. Publication no. 62.
15. As cited by Julius Jacobson, *The Negro and the American Labor Movement,* Doubleday & Co., Inc., Garden City, New York, 1968, p. 188.
16. Ibid., p. 188.

INDEX

ABOUT THE AUTHOR

Claude M. Lightfoot was born in Arkansas in 1910 and has lived most of his life in Chicago. He has been active in the Black liberation movement since the 1920s and has led many struggles of Black workers. He headed the Chicago-area campaigns to free the Scottsboro Boys and Angelo Herndon. He has a long history of providing leadership to the struggle for Black representation. In 1931 he joined the Communist Party and has been a member of its Central Committee since 1950. In the 1930s and 1940s he was active in anti-fascist activities and worked with leaders of the German anti-fascist movement. He was a delegate to the 7th World Congress of the Communist International in 1935. In the 1950s he was prosecuted under the Smith Act, but his conviction was later reversed by the Supreme Court. His first book, *Ghetto Rebellion to Black Liberation,* was published in 1968. He has visited and studied extensively the two German states and their differing approaches to racism; his second book, *Racism and Human Survival,* published in 1972, is based on those visits. In 1973 he received the Georgi Dimitrov award from the Bulgarian government and was also awarded an honorary Doctor of Philosophy degree by the University of Rostock in the German Democratic Republic.